THE
PALESTINIANS:
NEW DIRECTIONS

Edited by
Michael C. Hudson

Center for Contemporary Arab Studies
Georgetown University
Washington, DC

Published by Center for Contemporary Arab Studies,
Georgetown University, Washington, DC

Library of Congress Cataloging-in-Publication Data

The Palestinians.

   1. West Bank—History—Palestinian Uprising,
1987-   . 2. Gaza Strip—History—Palestinian
Uprising, 1987-   . 3. Jewish-Arab relations—
Public opinion. I. Hudson, Michael C.
DS110.W47P34 1990   956.95'3044   90-1807
ISBN 0-932568-18-1
ISBN 0-932568-19-X (pbk.)

CONTENTS

Acknowledgements

Introduction........................ *Michael C. Hudson*   vii

Part 1: The Resistance to Israeli Occupation

1. The Politics of the Intifada.............. *Ziad Abu Amr*   3
2. Revolt of the Petite Bourgeoisie: Urban
   Merchants and the Palestinian Uprising .... *Salim Tamari*   24
3. Mass Mobilization and the Uprising:
   The Labor Movement .... *Joost Hiltermann*   44
4. The Evolution of the Political Role
   of the Palestinian Women's
   Movement in the Uprising .... *Islah Abdul Jawwad*   63
5. The Politics of Cultural
   Revival.................... *Hanan Mikhail Ashrawi*   77

Part 2: The Intifada and the World

6. The Palestinian Challenge to
   US Policy...................... *Michael C. Hudson*   87
7. The Soviet Union, the *Intifada* and
   Changes in PLO Policy .... *Igor P. Belyayev* 119
8. Reflections on Recent Changes
   in the Conflict .... *Yehoshafat Harkabi* 127
9. The Meaning of the *Intifada*
   for Jordan .... *As'ad Abdul-Rahman & Riad al-Khouri* 138

Part 3: Imagining the Palestinian State

10. A Look Ahead: The Future State
    of Palestine .... *Hisham Sharabi* 155
11. A Two-State Solution: Security, Stability
    and the Superpowers .... *Valerie Yorke* 165
12. The Economic Viability of a
    Palestinian State...................... *George Abed* 199
13. The Shape of Things to Come: Policy
    and Politics in the Palestinian State .... *Laurie Brand* 227

Appendix: Selected Statistics on
   the Palestinian Population . . . . . . *compiled by Samer Khalidi* 259
Contributors 262
Index 264

ACKNOWLEDGEMENTS

It is a pleasure to acknowledge the assistance of many friends and colleagues, in addition to the contributors of papers, who have made this volume possible. The project has been a collective effort. It began in Aqaba, Jordan in June 1988 at a Center for Contemporary Arab Studies faculty and staff retreat. The Center's Executive Committee decided to devote the 1989 Annual Symposium to the subject "The Palestinians: New Directions." Members of the Executive Committee are Halim Barakat, Michael Hudson, Ibrahim Ibrahim, Ibrahim Oweiss, John Ruedy, Hisham Sharabi, Barbara Stowasser, Seth Tillman, and Judith Tucker. A symposium steering committee was created consisting of Michael C. Hudson and Seth Tillman, co-chairs, Halim Barakat, Ibrahim Ibrahim, Hisham Sharabi, and Judith Tucker. The Center's Public Affairs Officer, Anne-Marie Chaaraoui, was the symposium manager and organized the logistics of the conference. Mary McDavid, Assistant Director of the Center, helped in many ways, particularly in fund-raising. Dr. Michael Simpson, the Center's Director of Publications, played a crucial role in helping select and organize the papers for publication, editing the papers, and bringing the volume to speedy completion. Samer Khalidi, a research intern at the Center in the summer of 1989, prepared the statistical appendix and helped in many other ways.

We are grateful to Dean Peter F. Krogh of the School of Foreign Service, Georgetown University, for permission to include Dr. Ziad Abu-Amr's paper, which was prepared for a symposium on "Palestinians Under Occupation," sponsored by the School of Foreign Service on March 3, 1989.

Michael C. Hudson
Center for Contemporary Arab Studies
April 1990

INTRODUCTION

Michael C. Hudson

The conflict over Palestine has been generating tragedy ever since the First World War over 70 years ago. It has erupted in violence with a regularity that has almost become monotonous. Neither wars—those of 1948, 1956, 1967, 1969-70, 1973 and 1982—nor diplomacy—such as the landmark Camp David Accords—have put it to rest; and even two decades of ever-deepening Israeli occupation of the West Bank, East Jerusalem, and the Gaza Strip could not induce the Palestinians and the other Arabs to give up and accept total defeat. Those who lived it, and even those who have studied it, have largely resigned themselves to a seemingly endless cycle of violence and tension, but one that poses ever greater risks as the capacities for destruction and bloodshed increase.

The Palestinian uprising, or *intifada,* began in December 1987. Was it designed to be yet another bloody milestone on a road with no end? Or was it in fact something quite different? Did it possibly have the potential of altering the unstable status quo in some way, perhaps by challenging Israel's superior strength in a way that previous conventional wars had not done, perhaps by creating a climate propitious for a serious diplomatic process toward a just peace, perhaps by generating new confidence and flexibility on the part of the Palestine Liberation Organization, perhaps by inducing a sense of urgency on the part of the United States and other major powers toward giving it a higher priority on their international agendas?

Certainly the *intifada* was a new phenomenon: never since the establishment of the State of Israel in 1948 had there been a sustained popular uprising among the Palestinians. It was also unexpected: neither Israelis, foreign governments, nor even, one suspects, most ordinary Palestinians had any inkling that it was coming; and even after it had been going for several weeks few believed that it could continue for months and even years.

New Middle East Realities

The biggest change in the Arab-Israeli conflict is the political transformation of the Palestinians. The *intifada* is not the only new reality on the Middle Eastern scene, however. The polarization and rightward drift in Israeli politics is another, and one that now poses obstacles to a negotiated solution, as does the prospect of a massive inflow of Soviet Jews. There are also changes elsewhere in the Middle Eastern environment that affect the Palestinian-Israeli conflict. These include domestic political trends in the neighboring Arab countries; the impact of the oil boom and recession; Islamic revivalism; and pressures for economic and political liberalization. The regional strategic balance is also shifting as new military technologies are introduced and various other regional conflicts, such as the Iraq-Iran war, go into a period of remission. On the international level, the dramatic reorientation of Soviet politics, foreign and domestic, under President Mikhail Gorbachev, and the upheavals in eastern Europe affect the strategic position of Israel, the PLO, and the Arab states. Now there are possibilities for US-Soviet cooperation in the Arab-Israel arena that were scarcely thinkable during President Reagan's first term.

The recent political transformation of the Palestinians as players in the tragic Arab-Israeli "game" is two-fold. Not only has the *intifada* challenged Israel's occupation of the West Bank, East Jerusalem and Gaza, it also has stimulated the PLO to make compromises that could revive the prospects for a just and peaceful diplomatic solution to the conflict. The *intifada* has breathed astonishing new life into a cause whose dynamism had flagged under the weight of Israeli hegemony and growing world indifference. The PLO leadership admits the fact openly. Nabil Sha'th, a key advisor to Chairman Arafat, stated it clearly at a 1989 conference of Israelis, Palestinians, and Americans: "This [PLO (two-state)] peace plan could not have been offered had it not been for the *intifada* in the occupied territories. The *intifada* is the mother of the peace plan, and it will prove to be the mother of peace in our part of the world."[1] The fortunes of the PLO had been in steady decline since its expulsion from Beirut in 1982 and northern Lebanon in 1983. Even during its period of hegemony in southern Lebanon and west Beirut from the mid-1970s until 1982 it was making little progress toward recovering Palestine. It had been unable to organize active opposition in the occupied territories; its cross-border guerrilla forays were largely counter-productive, fueling the image of Palestinians as terrorists; a series of terrorist outrages in Europe (primarily the work of Palestinian dissidents, especially the Abu Nidal group) sapped its international legitimacy; and its regional and international diplomacy was stalled. The setback in Lebanon only deepened the factionalism afflicting the Palestinian community: the PFLP and other groups supported by Syria challenged the leadership of Fatah and Yasser Arafat. So enervated was the movement that the Arab summit in Amman in November 1987 relegated the Palestinian problem, for the first time, to a secondary level. This downgrading was one of the precipitating causes of the *intifada* which broke out only a month later. Whether the PLO actually initiated the *intifada* is unlikely, but it immediately mobilized considerable resources—financial, diplomatic, and logistical —to help it survive Israel's brutal efforts to suppress it. That the Israelis took seriously the PLO's role was demonstrated by the assassination of Khalil al-Wazir (Abu Jihad)—the PLO official responsible for liaison with the *intifada*—in Tunis in April 1988. The *intifada* had given the PLO a new function in the now-revived Palestinian struggle against Israel. The *intifada* was also a tonic for the PLO as an organization and movement. Having wooed back the militants by adopting a tough line at the Palestine National Council meeting in Algiers in May 1987, Arafat and his colleagues now were galvanized to move the Palestinians toward the diplomatic mainstream and thus to re-engage the United States. In June 1988 Arafat's senior advisor, Bassam Abu Sharif, circulated a statement at the Arab summit conference in Algiers which signalled the Chairman's readiness to accept UN resolutions 242 and 338, one of the American prerequisites for recognizing the PLO. In August in Geneva, meeting with UN Secretary General Javier Perez de Cuellar, Arafat invoked the 1947 UN resolution 181 that called for the partitioning of Palestine into two states—another sign of PLO readiness to recognize Israel's right to exist. In September in Strasbourg, addressing socialist members of the European parliament, he spoke again of an international conference within the framework of UN Resolution 242, at which both Israel and the PLO would be represented. And in November in Algiers he convened an historic meeting of the PNC which formally accepted UN Resolution 242 and declared an independent State of Palestine. As we have seen, it took just a few more weeks of fine-tuning to win American agreement to open an official dialogue with the PLO. And, as Nabil Sha'th remarked, none of this could have happened without the *intifada*.

The *intifada*'s effects on Israel—once it became clear that it could not be immediately crushed—were considerable. A year and a half into the *intifada* Israeli officials calculated that it was costing Israel two percent of its gross national product—about $750 million, plus some $300 million in lost export earnings to the occupied territories.[2] Israeli sources stated that the military cost of the uprising was a half million dollars a day. Increased military expenditures, increased tours of duty for soldiers, losses due to the diminished availability of cheap Arab labor, and a serious falloff in tourism all were adding serious strains to an economy already afflicted by recession. As the regular donor of some $3 billion in economic and military assistance annually, the United States government was understandably concerned about a situation that was soaking up the equivalent of perhaps a third of that huge contribution.

The *intifada* also generated new tensions within the Israeli body politic which contributed both to paralysis and rigidity on the part of the Israeli government on the Palestinian issue. To be sure, the uprising prompted some serious soul-searching on the political left, in the academic community, and—most interestingly—among some military officers. The Peace Now movement could mobilize thousands of Israelis to demonstrate in support of Palestinian rights. Moral concerns certainly motivated many of these Israelis, but some academic experts and officers had also reached the conclusion that the *intifada* could not be put down by military means alone: a political solution was necessary.[3]

But the predominant trend was rightward. A poll conducted in March 1988, some three months into the uprising, revealed a marked increase in popularity for the ultra-right nationalist parties, Kach (led by Rabbi Meir Kahane) and Tehiya.[4] For a country that had hoped to celebrate its fortieth anniversary (in 1988) with confidence and pride, the national mood—owing mainly to the *intifada*—was confused and angry. This was brought out by the national election results in November, which saw a continuing erosion of the Labor Party, with its more flexible position on a Palestinian settlement, and an increase in the small, rightwing religious and ultra-nationalist parties, known for their unyielding stand on the occupied territories. Under pressure from the American Jewish community and the secular mainstream in Israel, Yitzhak Shamir eventually outmaneuvered the religious parties and formed a coalition with Labor. Like the previous so-called "National Unity government," this one spoke with two voices: Shimon Peres, the Labor foreign minister, committed to "land for peace," and Yitzhak Shamir, the prime minister, committed to Greater Israel.

But Shamir found himself increasingly outflanked from the right, by the militant and influential Jewish settler movement and by a long-time political rival, Ariel Sharon.

In December 1988, when the US opened its official dialogue with the PLO, Shamir also came under pressure to respond to the PLO's diplomatic offensive. Israeli leaders were aware of the negative image they were generating in the US and worldwide as a result of extensive media coverage of their brutality against Palestinian teenagers, women, and even small children armed only with stones. It would have been impolitic for the Prime Minister to make his official visit to Washington in April 1989 without some kind of diplomatic initiative in hand. So Shamir arrived with a proposal for elections in the territories, and it instantly met with the Bush Administration's approval. On May 14, 1989, the Israeli government formalized this proposal into a "peace initiative" calling for "free and democratic elections among the Palestinian Arab inhabitants of Judea, Samaria and the Gaza district . . ." to select representatives "to conduct negotiations for a transitional period of self-rule." After this testing period, "at a later stage, negotiations will be conducted for a permanent solution, during which all the proposed options for an agreed settlement will be examined, and peace between Israel and Jordan will be achieved."[5] Although tightly hedged with conditions (notably, that Israel would not conduct negotiations with the PLO or accept the establishment of an "additional" Palestinian state in the area between Israel and Jordan), the proposal was eagerly seized upon by American officials as the proper vehicle to restart the paralyzed "peace process." By maintaining the dialogue with the PLO, on the one hand, and supporting Shamir's election plan, on the other, the Bush Administration hoped to exert leverage on both parties to move forward toward a negotiated solution. As the *intifada* entered its third year with few signs of an end to it, many ordinary Israelis, resigned to living with it indefinitely, reportedly were increasingly supportive of the government's hard line. Accommodation, in the prevailing hawkish discourse of Israeli politics, seemed "unrealistic." At the same time, dovish elements in the Labor Party and on the left did not appear to be able to put forward persuasive non-confrontational alternatives.[6] The increasing rightward polarization in Israeli politics, indicated by growing settler vigilantism[7] and the growing challenge of Sharon, seemed to augur poorly for the success of Washington's strategy, particularly since Shamir did not appear to have the makings of a General De Gaulle. In March 1990,

Shamir's "national unity" government collapsed, further paralyzing the Israeli political scene.

Just as we see a radical new situation involving the two antagonists, we also observe important new trends on the regional and international levels. In the Arab world the stability of domestic social and political structures is tested by economic upheavals, Islamic revivalism, and growing demands for liberalization: the authoritarian Arab state, as we have known it since the middle-1950s is experiencing pressures that may affect its regional and international behavior. The regional order is also being affected by the introduction of new military technologies and capabilities. At the same time there has been a slackening of several of the other conflicts in the region.

The roller-coaster of the oil boom and bust over the past two decades has tested the social and political stability of most regimes in the region, rich and poor alike. If the windfall of the 1970s initially was thought to cement a new conservative order across the Arab world, anchored in Saudi Arabia, the results actually were mixed. The distortions, corruption, and inflated expectations that accompanied the development explosion dampened the enthusiasm of those who had envisioned the "Arab century." Those who had hoped for a broadening of political participation found that existing regimes were unreceptive to such ideas. Then, when oil prices collapsed, the reverberations of the new austerity created tensions, not so much in the oil-exporting countries themselves, but among their neighbors which had become dependent on the spillover of oil wealth: Egypt, Sudan, Tunisia, Jordan, Syria, the Palestinians, and of course Lebanon. Even the wealthier states like Kuwait, the United Arab Emirates and Algeria experienced difficulties, while Iraq's rulers paradoxically were insulated by the solidarity generated by the war emergency from the discontents produced by the war itself. Regional stability will not be unaffected by the difficult economic and social conditions in countries such as Jordan and Egypt, where sparks from the Palestinian-Israeli struggle might ignite larger fires. The rise of Islamic radical movements is another development with implications for regional stability and the future of the Palestinian uprising. Relatively secular governments throughout the area feel threatened. Both the United States and the Soviet Union, for different reasons, are alarmed by the trend. To be sure, the US has had some experience in using Islamic movements for its own purposes, as in Afghanistan; but it cannot be comfortable watching Islamic radicals threaten pro-American regimes in countries such as Egypt and Jordan. And with the rise of ethnic-religious communalism in the Soviet Union, Moscow must be apprehensive about the effects on 50 million Soviet Muslims even more than the challenge to its Middle Eastern clients.

While some analysts believe that Islamic radicalism is in decline, owing to the weakening influence of the Islamic revolution in Iran, others observe that its force derives essentially from indigenous social conditions and values. The convergence of Islamic as well as Arab nationalist hostility against Israel could only heighten the chances of new conflict. Within the occupied territories, the rise of the Islamic movement Hamas signals a more militant attitude than that of the nationalist and secular leadership of the *intifada*.

Another important trend is the emergence of economic and even political liberalization in several countries. The tendency toward curbing the public sector and encouraging private and foreign investment is widespread, evident in the state-socialist economies of Egypt, Syria, Algeria, and Iraq, as well as in the conservative monarchies. Political liberalization is more limited, with Egypt the best example, and yet there are signs of a modest opening in Tunisia, Algeria, North Yemen and South Yemen. While most of the monarchies remain highly authoritarian, there are stirrings of liberalization, notably in Jordan. If the liberalization trend means a more significant role for public opinion in the political process, what might this portend for the internal stability and foreign policy orientation of Middle Eastern governments? Could liberalization get out of hand, threaten the position of authoritarian rulers and generate pressures for war? Or might liberalization strengthen "the moderates"?

Foremost among the changing strategic realities in the region is the spread of new military technologies, including a nuclear weapons capability.[8] In the long and costly Iraq-Iran war, both antagonists developed missile and chemical warfare capabilities quite new to the region. Syria was said to be acquiring a chemical warfare capability and new, longer-range ground-to-ground missiles which stimulated the Israelis to strengthen their own superior missile systems, along with their known nuclear arsenal and anti-chemical warfare measures. Saudi Arabia purchased a long-range missile from China, to the dismay of Israel and the United States. Libya was accused of trying to build a chemical warfare factory. In the endless Lebanese civil war, the destructive capacity of weapons available to the Maronite Christians and the Syrian forces supporting the Lebanese Muslims was substantially increased in the spring of 1989, when Iraq began supplying the Christian forces with longer-range, heavier guns and missiles.[9] And in the *intifada* warfare, Israel has employed a variety of new weapons to combat the stones of the Palestinians: rubber and plastic-coated bullets and more powerful tear gas. Thus the arms race, qualitative as well as quantitative, rolls along; few would argue that it is enhancing regional stability.

On the regional strategic level, the challenge to stability posed by the Iranian revolution has eased with Iran's failure to win the war with Iraq. It had been a two-fold challenge: ideological, through the medium of Islamic radicalism, and militarily, through the war against Iraq. The declaration of a cease-fire in 1988 diminished the military threat, but a peace treaty remained elusive. Iran continued to promote Islamic radicalism, however, particularly in Lebanon, where Iran-backed Hizballah sought to gain influence in the south facing Israel. Elsewhere, developments were mostly positive. In North Africa, the long, intermittent war over the former Spanish Sahara territories appeared to be winding down as Algeria and Morocco moved to mute their rivalry for hegemony in the region. Libya has reduced its involvement in neighboring countries, notably Chad. The Soviet Union withdrew its forces from Afghanistan, a move which did not end the war there but diminished its regional significance. Within the Arab world, there is more general consensus than in previous years which had been characterized by ideological sparring between conservative and radical blocs. Syria is the only major Arab country still standing somewhat outside the Arab consensus on the Arab world's two major conflicts: Palestine and Lebanon. But even Syria restored diplomatic relations with Egypt in 1990, accepted the Taif plan for Lebanon, and maintained a high-level dialogue with the United States. Thus, regional conditions are more favorable than they usually had been in the past for a diplomatic solution. It was the impasse between Israel and the PLO that presented the main obstacle to what American officials referred to as the peace process.

Finally, in the international arena, the trend of overarching significance has been the Soviet Union's dramatic shift in policy orientations, foreign and domestic, under President Mikhail Gorbachev. As Gorbachev concentrates Soviet energies on burgeoning domestic issues, social and economic, he appears to be curtailing the country's overseas involvements and ambitions, from Africa to Afghanistan. At the same time, the collapse of Soviet and communist hegemony over the countries of eastern Europe further erodes superpower rivalry and diminishes the importance of the Middle East as a field of competition. In the Middle East, Soviet initiatives to re-establish normal diplomatic relations with Israel are in harmony with American wishes. A new and complicating factor is the dramatic increase in the number of

Soviet Jews emigrating to Israel, the result of a relaxation of Soviet policy and a tightening of American immigration procedures. For President Bush, the possibility of a degree of cooperation with what his predecessor had called the "evil empire" on the Arab-Israeli question has become a reality. For some Israeli officials and analysts, however, the warming of US-Soviet relations and the strategic weakening of the Soviet Union and the Soviet bloc were seen as eroding Israel's importance to the US as a "strategic" asset.[10]

Certainly, the changing realities of the region have varied implications for regional order and for the Arab-Israeli problem. Some no doubt are conducive to stability. But on balance, the socio-economic upheavals, the new ideological trends, and the proliferation of new military technologies generate new pressures on Israel, the PLO, and the Arab states. The prospect of continued stagnation or even bloody deterioration in the Palestinian-Israeli conflict could only exacerbate tensions in the volatile area. Inasmuch as the Palestinian-Israeli conflict is an added burden on Middle East regimes, especially Arab governments friendly to the United States, an objective assessment of the American interest would indicate the desirability of vigorous and evenhanded US diplomacy on this issue.

The Plan of This Book

In 1988 the Georgetown University Center for Contemporary Arab Studies undertook a project to investigate the Palestinian *intifada* and its consequences for the region and the world. The Center devoted its annual symposium in May 1989 to the *intifada* and commissioned a series of papers by internationally respected specialists from the Palestinian community, Arab countries, Israel, Europe, the Soviet Union, and the United States to analyze the various facets of the problem. Although there is a voluminous literature on the Arab-Israeli conflict, much of it is narrowly descriptive or polemical and there is still a serious absence of work on the Palestinians—certainly in comparison to what has been devoted to Israelis, the Jews, and Zionism. Moreover, there has not been enough attention given to the work of Palestinian intellectuals. The Center sought, therefore, to organize a set of complementary research papers and essays that would analyze matters more deeply and emphasize the Palestinians as a primary element in the equation, focusing on the *intifada* and its consequences. To that end, we enlisted a sizeable proportion of

Palestinian participants. The present volume consists of eleven of the papers presented at the CCAS symposium, revised and updated for publication, plus two additional papers (Abu-Amr and Hudson).

One of the most extraordinary aspects of the *intifada* is the extent to which the whole range of Palestinian society has been involved. Part I of the book consists of papers designed to document and explain this involvement. Ziad Abu-Amr maps the political landscape of the *intifada* and shows how diverse ideological groupings have cooperated, and how the structural gap between the Palestinians under occupation and the external leadership vested in the PLO has been bridged. Joost Hiltermann and Islah Abdul Jawad discuss the participation of groupings often excluded from political activity in Arab society—the working classes and women—and Salim Tamari charts the behavior of another element, the merchant class, whose values and interests would not normally incline them toward radical action. What emerges is a picture of a society rent by discontinuities, severely repressed over a long period of time, disillusioned by its traditional leadership, and frustrated by the paralysis of international efforts at a just settlement, and that therefore mobilizes almost spontaneously for collective action. Hanan Mikhail-Ashrawi's paper examines the emerging political culture of the *intifada* and helps explain the movement's solidarity. We hope that these papers provide a fuller picture of the social dynamics of the *intifada* than is conveyed by the news media's limited focus on confrontation incidents and youthful stone-throwers.

Like a stone thrown into a pond, the *intifada* has created ripples throughout the region and the world. Part II explores some of these consequences. Michael Hudson's chapter suggests that the Palestinians have launched a double challenge to US policy through the *intifada* and the PLO's explicit acceptance of a two-state solution, and he attempts to document how Washington is responding. His paper emphasizes the domestic political context of US policy Middle East policymaking as of March 1990, and suggests that some positive structural changes may be taking place. President Bush's pointed reference to East Jerusalem as occupied territory was seen by some observers as a sign of new American evenhandedness.

A Soviet perspective on the *intifada* and the subsequent change in the PLO's position is presented by political commentator Igor Belyayev, who also provides a survey of Soviet involvement across the entire area through Afghanistan, and makes some comments about American policy. Yehoshafat Harkabi, drawing on his long experience in Israeli government and academic circles, offers reflections on the *intifada* in the context of regional and international conditions and warns of the negative consequences of overreaching both for Palestinian Arabs and Israeli Jews. The paper by As'ad Abdul Rahman and Riad al-Khouri discusses its implications for the Arab world—especially Jordan—and reveals both "positive" and "negative" features.

It is of course too early to ascertain whether the Palestinians will succeed in altering a regional and international constellation of power and interests that so far has offered them more moral than practical support. But there can be little doubt that it has created significant tremors at both levels.

The final section of the book looks to the future. On the assumption that a consensus on a two-state solution is growing among Palestinians, Israelis, and the regional and international actors, we felt that it is time for all concerned to begin thinking carefully about the practical problems associated with such an outcome. "Imagining the Palestinian State" consists of four essays that represent such creative thinking. Hisham Sharabi, one of the most prominent Palestinian intellectuals, soberly assesses the historical obstacles to such an outcome but goes on to assert that the Palestinians have both the possibility and capabilities to create a genuinely democratic state and a society free of the "neo-patriarchy" he observes in other Arab countries. Valerie Yorke addresses in considerable detail the fundamental question of security—the *sine qua non* of a durable two-state arrangement. She argues that the conventional wisdom of the Palestinian state presenting an unacceptable danger to Israel is incorrect, and she describes a number of procedures and arrangements to back her position. In his statistically based analysis of economic conditions, George Abed identifies three major development problems in a post-settlement era: demography, resource constraints, and economic structure. Arguing that an economically viable state is possible, he proposes that the Palestinian economy "leapfrog current technology and prepare for the 21st century almost immediately." Finally, the politics of a future Palestinian state are projected by Laurie Brand with a review of current thinking in the PLO leadership about the future constitution, and an analysis of class structure, civil society, and the predictable "loads" on the new political system. She foresees a difficult initial period but holds out some hope that the experience of the *intifada* might allow the Palestinian state to escape the prevailing pattern of authoritarianism in the region.

It surely is no exaggeration to suggest that a broad international consensus now exists favoring a two-state solution to the historic problem of Palestine. Its juridical bases can be traced to UN General Assembly Resolution 181, the famous partition plan of 1947, and its principles certainly are compatible with UN Security Council Resolutions 242 and 338 (of 1967 and 1973, respectively) and the Camp David Accords of 1978. The Arab states are on record, through the 1982 Fez Plan, as accepting all the existing states plus a Palestinian state. The Palestine Liberation Organization in 1988 made its acceptance of Israel, alongside a Palestinian state, so explicit that the United States government agreed to open an official dialogue with it. The State of Israel is committed through its acceptance of Resolutions 242 and 338 to the principle of trading land for peace, even though the powerful Likud bloc and other right-wing elements have sought to renege on that commitment and are unmistakably, intensely hostile to an independent Palestinian state in the territories occupied in 1967.

Through the *intifada* the Palestinians have dramatically reasserted their insistence on achieving their political right to self-determination and freedom. Through their painful, courageous—and indeed magnanimous—decision to accept a two-state solution, they have made their best effort to move the Palestine conflict toward a just, compromise solution through a process of diplomatic negotiation rather than armed violence. The window of opportunity is open. But it will not stay open indefinitely without steady progress in the negotiating process. We hope that the papers in this book will shed some light on the complexities of the Palestinian and regional situation and lead to a better understanding of the importance—and the fragility—of the opportunity at hand.

Notes

1. Speech before the "Road to Peace Conference," New York, March 1989; cited in *Israeli-Palestinian Digest,* July 1989, p. 2.

2. According to Deputy Finance Minister Yossi Beilin, quoted in the *Washington Post,* July 24, 1989.

3. See, e.g., *The West Bank and Gaza: Israel's Options for Peace,* a report from the Jaffee Center for Strategic Studies (JCSS) of Tel Aviv University, 1989. See also the excerpts from "an independent JCSS study group offshoot of research" for the above-mentioned report, entitled "Israel, The West Bank And Gaza: Toward A Solution," published in *Israeli-Palestinian Digest,* July 1989. Some 150 retired officers formed a "Council for Peace and Security," arguing that Israel should end its occupation and reach a political compromise with the Palestinians in order to achieve real security. See Joel Brinkley, "Ex-Israeli Officers Ask Deal on Peace," *The New York Times,* May 31, 1988.

4. Robert I. Friedman, "No Land, No Peace for Palestinians," *The Nation,* April 23,

1989, p. 562, citing Israeli pollster Hannoch Smith's survey results.

5. Consulate General of Israel in New York, *News Letter,* May 18, 1989, "A Peace Initiative by the Government of Israel."

6. See, e.g., the comments of Israeli public opinion pollster Hannoch Smith in the *Christian Science Monitor,* June 22, 1989: "They're patiently supporting the government position" (on dealing with the uprising), "but not confident it will save them from an outcome they fear" (establishment of a Palestinian state). A similar analysis was presented by Israeli journalist Hirsh Goodman at a conference at the Center for Strategic and International Studies, Washington, December 7, 1989.

7. See, e.g., Joshua Brilliant, "New Militancy Among Settlers," *Jerusalem Post,* May 19, 1989.

8. See Leonard Spector, *Going Nuclear* [A Carnegie Endowment Book] (Cambridge, Mass.: Ballinger, 1987), Ch. 4, "The Middle East."

9. For a description of the missile capabilities of Israel, Syria, Iraq, Iran, Saudi Arabia, Libya, Egypt, and South Yemen, see "Ballistic Missiles in the Third World," *New York Times,* July 3, 1988; and David B. Ottaway, "Middle East Weapons Proliferate," *Washington Post,* December 10, 1988.

10. For examples of this concern see Glenn Frankel, "Anxious Israel Fears Disaffection of US in Shifting International Climate," *Washington Post,* December 19, 1989.

PART 1: THE RESISTANCE TO ISRAELI OCCUPATION

1 THE POLITICS OF THE INTIFADA

Ziad Abu-Amr

A radical shift has taken place in Palestinian attitudes and political thinking, dictated by a number of important factors. First, the Palestinian national question has entered a new phase because the Palestinian national identity and Palestinian nation building have become institutionalized. Second, the *intifada,* which came as the culmination of a national struggle which has been going on for decades, has served as a catalyst in bringing Palestinian political thinking to maturity. There is a strong desire among the Palestinians in the occupied territories for a settlement and a compromise. Their pragmatic reading of the situation says that Israel is there to stay, but that Palestinians must have their equal rights.

A third factor contributing to the shift in the Palestinians' political stance has been King Hussein's disengagement from the West Bank, which came as a direct challenge to the Palestinians to assume control of their own destinies.

A fourth and very significant factor is that a new international situation exists characterized by superpower detente and the peaceful resolution of regional conflicts.

This international development is particularly important because the Palestinians are now taking positions based on the premise that the Soviet Union under Gorbachev will not accommodate, or even tolerate, radical Palestinian demands. They also realize that no political settlement in the region is feasible without the active involvement of the United States. Palestinians now believe that any political settlement of the conflict is bound to be American-shaped and sponsored. This realization emanates from the following assumptions: first, vigorous American involvement is an indispensable prerequisite for moving the local actors toward positions upon which a permanent settlement can be based; second, no party other than the US government can exert effective pressure on Israel; third, the Soviet Union is preoccupied with its own internal affairs and its commitment to detente, as the way it handled the question of Afghanistan demonstrates.

The Palestinians understand that the Soviet Union is not going to accommodate radical positions. There are, of course, those among the Palestinians who wish to see a more active involvement by the

Soviet Union in the political settlement process. This Soviet involvement is bound, from the Palestinian point of view, to safeguard
Palestinian rights and at least improve the Palestinians' negotiating
position. There are also Palestinians who do not object to the US
playing the godfather role, as long as Palestinian demands are met.
Yasser Arafat has alluded to the Palestinian desire and preference for
an active American role, and, in his speech to the UN in Geneva in
1988, even made reference to the fact that the Palestinians requested
an American mandate over Palestine in 1919, through the King-
Crane Commission.

The Nineteenth Session of the PNC

The nineteenth session of the Palestine National Council (PNC) in
Algiers (November 12-15, 1988) was convened against the background
mentioned above. The resolutions of the PNC formalized the new
political stands, including the Declaration of Independence and the
acceptance of UN resolutions 242 and 338. Of equal importance was
Arafat's speech to the UN General Assembly meeting in Geneva on
December 13, 1988, and his subsequent press conference on December
14, in which he unequivocally recognized Israel's right to exist,
renounced terrorism, and reiterated the PLO's acceptance of 242 and
338. The PNC resolutions, Arafat's speech and press conference, and
the subsequent talks between the PLO and the US, marked a formal
and historic shift in Palestinian positions.

The acceptance by the PLO of UN resolutions 242 and 338 meant
the following:

1. For the first time, the Palestinians conceded what they considered
to be their historic right to the whole area of Palestine. They were
now willing to settle for part of that territory. For the first time also,
the Palestinians conceded Israel's right to exist. A number of
pronouncements made by PLO leaders came to emphasize these
concessions, as reflected by a statement made by Salah Khalaf,
second-in-command of Fatah, in which he said: "In the past we
believed that this land [Palestine] is for us alone and we did not
believe in the idea of peaceful coexistence between our two states.
There is room in Palestine for the two peoples in two states."[1]

2. The acceptance of UN resolution 242 also meant the abandonment of the Palestinian military option, generally known as armed
struggle. Resolution 242 calls for the "termination of all claims or

states of belligerency," and for the resolution of conflicts by peaceful means. The positions declared by the PLO outside the occupied territories have been matched by the leadership of the uprising inside the occupied territories. The final statement of the nineteenth PNC in Algiers stated: "The State of Palestine herewith declares that it believes in the settlement of regional and international disputes by peaceful means in accordance with the United Nations Charter and resolutions, without prejudice to its natural right to defend its territorial integrity and independence. It therefore rejects the threat or use of force, violence and terrorism against its territorial integrity and political independence, as it also rejects their use against the territorial integrity of other states.[2]

Inside the occupied territories, the Unified National Command of the Uprising applauded the PNC statement. One of its leaflets (No. 29) referred to "the stone and the olive branch," and not "the gun and the olive branch."[3]

Even the radical Popular Front for the Liberation of Palestine (PFLP) has now become willing to give primacy to political struggle. In an interview with a Lebanese newspaper, George Habbash stated: "The mechanism to actualize the declaration of statehood is the winning of the recognition of the state by the largest number of states in the world . . . The mechanism is political and diplomatic activity undertaken by the PLO and the Arab states which recognized the state," as well as by the friends of the Palestinian people in the world. According to Habbash, "the uprising should continue, escalate, dig roots, and expand to the areas of 1948. After that, the uprising should interact with the Palestinians and the Arabs outside the occupied territories in order to offset the balance of power in a way to force the Zionist enemy to concede our right to establish our state." Only at the very end of his analysis did Habbash talk about the need "to establish alliances with the Lebanese national resistance movement and the opening of all Arab fronts for the Palestinian gun."[4] This position has been reiterated on more than one occasion. In an interview late in 1989 on the second anniversary of the *intifada,* Habbash stressed the need to reopen Arab borders to armed struggle, but opposed turning the *intifada* into an armed resistance movement.

Before the uprising, armed struggle had been reduced to an empty slogan. At most, it was applied as a matter of tokenism and applied rarely. If it is occasionally resorted to in the future, it will be as a token. The uprising bailed the PLO out of an already faltering armed struggle. For this reason, ironically, it could be said that the uprising has also been some kind of blessing for Israel politically and in terms of security.

3. The acceptance of Resolutions 242 and 338 meant that the various PLO factions, and the PLO itself, have in effect disregarded the PLO charter and their respective political programs and ideological doctrines. These programs and doctrines have become outdated or even obsolete, and as such require revision. To provide only a few examples, the PLO charter treats "armed struggle" as a strategy, not a tactic, for the liberation of Palestine. The Fatah political program speaks of "the total liberation of Palestine." The programs of the leftist factions refer to the "tripartite enemy" comprising imperialism, Zionism and Arab reactionary regimes. Since the PNC and its resolutions, the United States, the leader of world imperialism, has openly been courted by the PLO, and the opening of a dialogue with it celebrated. Israel has been recognized and peace and coexistence with it have become a strategic goal. As for Jordan, long considered a bastion of Arab reaction, it is being considered as the partner in a Jordanian-Palestinian confederation.

There has been a cessation of attacks and negative remarks against Arab leaders or governments, which until recently were subject to labels such as reactionary, repressive, conspiratorial, among others. The final statement of the nineteenth PNC affirmed instead: "The Council expresses its great confidence that the leaders of the Arab nation will remain, as we have known them, a bulwark of support for Palestine and its people."[5]

The resolutions of the nineteenth PNC enjoyed the support of the majority of the Palestinians. Differences over the details should not obscure the widespread agreement on the strategy. It is still too early to assess the overall consequences of the PNC resolutions, Arafat's speech to the UN in Geneva on December 13, 1988 and his subsequent press conference on December 14, 1988, and the talks that have followed with the United States. Much will depend on how well the PLO leadership conducts itself and on how much it can deliver to the Palestinian people. Among the principal concerns are:

1. *Unity Within the PLO.* Unity among the four major PLO factions may suffer eventually, since this unity cannot be an end in itself. So far, differences have been contained. The PFLP objection to the PNC resolution considering UN resolutions 242 and 338 the basis for a political settlement did not cause a split or withdrawal from the PLO. In a statement issued on November 16, 1988, just after the nineteenth session of the PNC, the PFLP explained that while it was a party to

the Declaration of Independence, and to the final statement of the PNC, it objected to the articles concerning the recognition of UN resolution 242 and did not consider them binding. Both the PFLP and the DFLP issued statements saying that Arafat's utterances in the Geneva press conference reflected his personal position and did not reflect the positions of the PLO as stated in the PNC resolutions. A statement issued jointly by the PFLP and the Democratic Front for the Liberation of Palestine (DFLP) stated that Arafat's Geneva statements "contradicted the resolutions adopted by the Palestine National Council . . . and do not commit the PLO to anything and they do not represent official policy."[6] Another statement issued by the politburo of the PFLP, which was circulated in the occupied territories, included the following: "The policy of free concessions adopted by some influential circles in the PLO leadership, especially after the press conference of the head of the Executive Committee of the PLO in which he regretfully complied to American conditions, especially Israel's right to exist, raises numerous fears, since many revolutions were killed politically, after the failure of the enemy to kill them through repression, terrorism, and force."

These opposition pronouncements, which were not backed by any action, might have been meant to maintain the positions of the leftist PFLP and DFLP *vis-à-vis* Fatah. They were probably meant for Palestinian public consumption and in deference to other Palestinian opposition groups outside the framework of the PLO, and to Syria itself where a major portion of these two factions are situated.

During the first year of US-PLO talks, similar criticisms were leveled from the left against Arafat's flexibility on the issue of whether or not the PLO should openly participate in the Israeli-Egyptian-Palestinian talks on elections in the occupied territories that were proposed by the United States. These criticisms were not, however, accompanied by actions of the kind that might split the PLO.

Splits may occur, however, over more critical issues. A confederation with Jordan along the lines of the ill-fated Amman Accord of 1985 is bound to create a split. The Accord talked about Palestinian self-determination within the framework of a confederation with Jordan and did not make any explicit mention of an independent Palestinian state or of the PLO. The opposition of the PFLP and that of the DFLP is mitigated by the dependence of the latter two factions on Arafat and his Fatah organization for financial and political support. The two groups need the money to run their institutions. They also need political protection in some host Arab countries, which Arafat is the only person capable of providing. Fatah also controls most logistical facilities, services, and institutions inside and outside the occupied territories.

If the political process initiated by the PLO stumbles, internal differentiation and polarization within each PLO faction is likely to occur or be exacerbated, especially if the uprising goes on. The uprising will require creative moves and results to match its impact. Before and after the PNC session and Arafat's UN speech in Geneva, leaflets carrying the name of Fatah were distributed in the occupied territories denouncing the PLO moves. It cannot, however, be determined how representative these voices are within the Fatah following. Disagreement within the DFLP has also been reported.

2. *Pro-Syrian Groups.* The PNC resolutions, Arafat's speech and press conference, and the opening of talks with the US, were bound to generate strong opposition among the Palestinian groups which are currently not participating in the PLO Executive Committee and are residing in Syria. Outside the occupied territories, that opposition is vocal. Inside the occupied territories, these groups have an extremely marginal following. Leaflets carrying the name of the Popular Front for the Liberation of Palestine-General Command of Ahmad Jibril were distributed attacking the resolutions of the PNC and accusing Arafat of treason. But because they have no important support within the occupied territories, and cannot back words with deeds, the Palestinian opposition groups in Syria do not enjoy credibility.

It seems that the opposition groups are waiting for the current political process to falter on its own, or for a controversial agreement to create new opportunities for them to mobilize opposition to Arafat.

3. *The "Interior" and the "Exterior."* In the West Bank and Gaza the PNC resolutions generated reactions which varied from the expression of strong support to an attitude of skepticism. Support came from the majority, as reflected in the leaflets published by the Unified National Command of the Uprising and other expressions of public sentiment. Reservations and skepticism came from different sources. Some (the Islamic movement) explicitly opposed the resolutions, and others (e.g., supporters of the PFLP) expressed reservations on some of the PNC resolutions, especially the acceptance of UN resolutions 242 and 338. There were also those who viewed the resolutions as giving too many concessions to Israel without reciprocity. Yet, except for the reactions of the Islamic movement, these responses came in a context of national unity where the PLO

was considered the only legitimate political framework. The status of the PLO was thus enhanced. It has continued to stand for Palestinian national identity and to be the vehicle for the realization of national objectives and the national unity of the Palestinian people everywhere.

Although there is no real Palestinian division between the "interior" and the "exterior," the reactions and attitudes of the "interior" can be crucial. The "interior" today, under the conditions of the uprising, can give a mandate to the PLO leadership in exile. It can strengthen the PLO position against Palestinian and Arab opposition (especially the pro-Syrian Palestinian groups and Syria itself). The interior can also exercise a certain degree of restrictive influence over the PLO leadership. It can hold this leadership accountable. Only if it delivers results can the PLO leadership escape the criticism and accountability of the interior.

4. *The Islamic Movement.* The opposition of the Islamic movement in the occupied territories to the PNC resolutions and subsequent stances of the PLO during its talks with the US was not unexpected. It emanated from the opposition of the Islamic movement to the idea of achieving a political settlement of the conflict, as well as to the political program of the PLO. While all the PLO groups, and the nationalist camp in general, agree on the principle of establishing a Palestinian state and on an international conference as the vehicle for reaching a negotiated settlement, the Islamic movement rejects the proposed Palestinian state and the international conference and calls for the establishment of an Islamic state in the entire area of Palestine. In an appeal sent to the PNC's nineteenth session in Algiers, the Islamic camp stated:

> The Islamic Resistance Movement (Hamas) has committed itself to the comprehensive *jihad* (holy war) until the liberation of the whole of Palestine . . . We condemn all the attitudes calling for ending the *jihad* and struggle, and for establishing peace with the murderers, and the attitudes which call for the acceptance of the Jewish entity on any part of our land . . . Our people offered sacrifices to protect the pride and dignity of the nation and to destroy the cancerous Jewish entity, which tries to spread its hegemony over our area. We believe that Palestine belongs to the Muslim generations until the Day of Judgment.[7]

The Islamic movement is also ambiguous about accepting the PLO as the only representative of the Palestinian people, since the movement will not accept a leadership that is not Islamic. The ideological differences between the nationalist and religious camps are irreconcilable, and the religious camp may try to impede or abort any future political settlement. Islamic religious opposition is not, however, entirely ideologically-based, and it is possible that the religious leadership may be trying to assert itself in order to secure a share of power in case a political settlement is reached.

During the uprising, the attitude of the religious camp has clearly become more aggressive. In addition to its own political agenda, which is different from that of the nationalist camp, the religious camp has issued its own leaflets and frequently designated different days from those designated by the Unified National Command for comprehensive strikes. A struggle for the leadership of the uprising has become more visible recently.

It should be stated that the religious camp cannot, for the foreseeable future, be a substitute for the nationalist camp (the PLO) and what it stands for. The Islamic movement in the West Bank and Gaza Strip can neither sustain the uprising without the participation of the PLO factions, nor can it impede a future political settlement that is acceptable to the nationalist camp. A majority of the Palestinians in the occupied territories still view the PLO as the embodiment of the Palestinian national identity, and treat it as the organization which defined and consolidated Palestinian national goals. In contrast to the PLO's nationalist record of more than two decades, the Islamic movement played no noteworthy role in any form of resistance to the Israeli occupation for 21 years. While the movement theoretically calls for the establishment of an Islamic state in the whole area of Palestine, this ideological position has never been matched by any practical program. This kind of major discrepancy undermines the credibility of the Islamic movement among the Palestinian people, since its demands are perceived not to be realistic and are not backed up by action. It is also clear that the Islamic movement (the Muslim Brotherhood in particular) cannot afford to alienate Arab countries such as Saudi Arabia and Jordan, whose political and material support is critical for the survival and strength of the religious camp. These countries, however, are not advocating the liberation of all of Palestine and the establishment of an Islamic state in it. After all, Saudi Arabia devised the Fahd Plan which implicitly recognized Israel, and King Hussein advocates the principle of "land for peace."

The Islamic movement could become a menace and a serious threat to the PLO inside the occupied territories with the establishment of an alliance between the Islamic movement in the West Bank and

Gaza, the pro-Syrian Palestinian groups, and the Islamic groups in Lebanon. It is, however, doubtful that the religious movement in the West Bank and Gaza would trade Saudi Arabia and Jordan, its traditional allies and patrons, for an alliance championed by Syria, the archenemy of the Muslim Brotherhood everywhere.

Nevertheless, the uprising has produced a new breed of activists within the Muslim Brotherhood who are discontented with the politics of the traditional leadership, and who are susceptible to the new ideas of militant Islamic groups, such as the Islamic Jihad in the occupied territories. The latter has already established links with Iran, the Islamic groups in Lebanon and some opposition PLO groups based in Syria.

Recent social changes in the politics of the occupied territories might also favor the Islamic movement. The locus of politics has shifted to the villages, refugee camps and popular urban quarters, where Islam is a strong social force. The lower social strata, who are now playing the key role in the resistance, are a group more likely to favor the Islamic movement than are the educated middle-class activists who have traditionally articulated nationalist demands.

The Islamic movement could eventually become a serious contender for power if, on one hand, the PLO failed to deliver results, and on the other, the Islamic movement produced a dynamic and popular leadership with the flexibility to incorporate nationalist demands in its programs, and the ability to demonstrate practical achievements in an effective resistance to Israeli occupation.

5. *The Syrian Role.* Syria is interested in a political settlement, since a resolution of the conflict would lessen its domestic economic and political burden, but it is only interested in a settlement which takes its concerns and interests into account. Syria can claim that if the Palestinians are happy with a certain settlement, Syria will not be more Palestinian than the Palestinians, and will not object to a settlement accepted by the Palestinians, provided that Syrian land is returned to Syria. If Syria is excluded, no lasting political settlement of the Palestinian-Arab-Israeli conflict is in sight. Syria has many cards which could impede a settlement, and it would be rash if US policymakers forgot the fate of the May 1983 American-sponsored agreement in Lebanon, which Syria opposed.

6. *Prospects for a Settlement.* In spite of their euphoria at the political and diplomatic developments of the late 1980s, the Palestinians in the occupied territories believe that the realization of a political settlement will still be a very complicated process. While the US decision to talk to the PLO provided a glimpse of hope, a year after

the PLO-US dialogue was opened, there seemed to be no chance of a major breakthrough toward achieving the major Palestinian objectives, or of a wish by the US or Israel to bring one about. In the eyes of the Palestinians, the US still remained Israel's closest ally and protector. The disappointment felt by many Palestinians was expressed in remarks by leaders such as Salah Khalaf early in 1990 to the effect that the Palestinian-American dialogue had reached a dead end.[8] Given the difficulties of even negotiating Palestinian representation in prospective talks about elections in the occupied territories, it will be hard to reach a formula for overall peace that can win the acceptance of all the parties involved in the conflict. The Palestinians point out that Israel has never advanced any plan for a peaceful settlement that takes into account the fundamental Palestinian aspirations. The autonomy plan envisaged in the Camp David Accords sidestepped the issue of Palestinian sovereignty and statehood. In talk about a settlement, Israel limits the problem to the "residents of Judea and Samaria and the Gaza area," while the Palestinians talk about a national question and about the Palestinians inside and outside the West Bank and Gaza.

The Palestinians know from bitter experience that Israel's primary concern today is to put an end to the uprising. While Israel's hope of bringing the situation in the occupied territories to what it used to be prior to the uprising is no longer attainable, Israel will try to abort Palestinian gains by proposing plans that cannot meet Palestinian demands, such as the revival of the Camp David Autonomy Plan or the conducting of municipal elections in a way that would allow Israeli control of the occupied territories to continue.

To counter the peaceful Palestinian political offensive, Israel advanced its own political initiative—Shamir's highly restricted proposal for elections. In so doing, Israel sought to present itself as the party most interested in reaching a peaceful settlement to the conflict. Israel is also trying to minimize the international attention given to the Palestinian political offensive. But Israel's basic attitude toward the PLO has not changed. It dismissed the resolutions of the nineteenth PNC, and Arafat's speech in Geneva and subsequent press conference, as tactical moves of a "terroristic PLO which has not changed in essence." By intensifying its harsh measures against the uprising, and by continuing to raid Palestinian targets in Lebanon, Israel hopes to provoke the PLO leadership into committing acts which would discredit the PLO internationally. If the PLO does not react to these attacks, it risks being embarrassed before its own constituency. By raiding the bases of Palestinian opposition groups in Lebanon, Israel also tries to widen the gap between these groups on one hand, and Arafat and the PLO factions allied to him, on the other, in the hope of increasing divisions within the Palestinian community.

The Intifada

In its early stage Palestinians viewed the uprising in two different ways. One approach was to treat it as a catalytic event that was bound to activate the stagnant political situation in the area. A Palestinian political initiative, according to this view, should be undertaken to capitalize on the uprising. The other interpreted the uprising as a turning point in the Palestinian struggle, an initiative for national independence that should not stop before it achieves an end to the Israeli occupation.

The uprising did indeed stir up the situation. The *intifada* led to the convening of the nineteenth PNC, the declaration of statehood, the significant resolutions undertaken in the PNC, the international interest in finding a solution to the Palestinian problem, and the opening of an official dialogue between the US and the PLO, among other things. The Palestinians would now like to see the uprising continue both as a catalyst and, at the same time, as a mechanism to end the Israeli occupation. Evidence on the ground indicates that the uprising, having put down roots in Palestinian society, has seriously challenged the acceptability of the occupation.

Despite the heavy toll the uprising is taking on them, the Palestinians in the occupied territories have made a personal as well as a collective investment in it. Every Palestinian has, in one way or the other, paid a price. Few would want to see their suffering wasted without the cherished salvation, the end to Israeli occupation. The need to continue the uprising enjoys Palestinian consensus as a means for a political settlement. Even traditional figures, such as Elias Freij, Mayor of Bethlehem, talk only about a truce for a period of time and not an end to the uprising.

For the PLO leadership in exile, the uprising was one of the most welcome developments in Palestinian history. It extricated the leadership from a crisis that had become almost chronic. The need of the PLO leadership for the uprising to continue became even greater following the nineteenth PNC resolutions in Algiers, in which the PLO accepted resolution 242. In practice, this meant the abandonment of armed struggle, or the Palestinian military option. After the abandonment of armed struggle, the PLO needed some kind of leverage to back its political and diplomatic struggle. The uprising is the only such mechanism.

That the PLO leadership understands the importance of the uprising is indicated by its repeated calls for the uprising to continue, and to be escalated. The concern was illustrated clearly by Arafat himself. In response to the idea of a truce for one year between the Israelis and the Palestinians (proposed by Bethlehem mayor Elias Freij), Arafat was reported to have said that any leader who proposed an end to the *intifada* exposed himself to the bullets of his own people.[9] It was also reported that Arafat said: "Whoever thinks of stopping the *intifada* before it achieves its goals, I will give him bullets in the chest."[10] Coming from Arafat at a time he was trying to strengthen a moderate image for the PLO, these statements only indicate the seriousness with which the PLO viewed the need for the uprising to continue. And in the occupied territories, a leaflet issued by the Unified Command of the Uprising rejected the call for a truce and mentioned Freij by name, "Freij and his like." The call for a truce, the leaflet stated, is a "desperate attempt to weaken the flame of the uprising and break the state of siege in which the enemy finds itself, and to beautify the plans which our people rejected and fought in the past."[11] The language of the leaflet was, however, less inflammatory, calling for silencing the voices calling for stopping the *intifada,* but making no mention of bullets.

This does not mean that the *intifada* has become an end in itself. Under certain circumstances the Palestinians would be willing to consider putting an end to it if they have sufficient evidence that their demands are going to be met, or if some of them are actually met. If an international peace conference in which the PLO is represented starts, or if even a date for the start of this conference is set, the Palestinians might stop the uprising (at least for a certain period of time) to give negotiations a chance. It is also possible that the *intifada* would end if Israel were to recognize the PLO, or if the US recognized the Palestinian people's right to self-determination. Leaflet No. 32 of the Unified Command of the Uprising, issued on January 9, 1989, stated: "The continuation of the uprising is not contingent upon the dialogue with the US or on municipal elections, but rather upon the political gains of our legitimate leadership, the PLO, and upon the evacuation of the occupation forces from our Palestinian land and our realization of freedom, independence and sovereignty."[12]

Competition among the various PLO factions or among competing trends within the same faction so far has not gotten out of hand. But in the absence of diplomatic progress it could do so. In addition, a specific plan for a political settlement to the conflict might result in serious differences. If the PLO leadership were to be divided over an issue of this kind, the division would likely creep into the occupied territories as well and cause a major split that would weaken the uprising or cause an internal fight. Some issues over which differences and splits could occur are the substance of the suggested confederation with Jordan, the issue of elections in the occupied territories, or the future conduct of the uprising itself. Although there is no sign of a situation of this kind on the horizon, the prospect remains a real possibility under certain circumstances.

The uprising may also be impeded if serious differences arise between the UNCU on the one hand, and the Islamic Resistance Movement (Hamas), on the other—even though Hamas cannot, in effect, sustain the uprising alone and without the participation of the UNCU, and cannot impede a political settlement of the conflict.

For Israel, the options are only a few. One is to attempt to crush the uprising in a very bloody fashion, in which thousands of people are killed and expelled. Israel has avoided this option because of its probably explosive repercussions. It would seriously polarize Israeli society, alienate the Arab community within Israel and strengthen its nationalist tendencies. Equally important, it would create dissent within the Jewish community abroad, which might in turn affect the flow to Israel of funds and immigrants. A bloody suppression of the uprising would also carry the relationship between Israel and the population of the West Bank and Gaza to a point of no return. The neighboring Arab countries might find themselves under strong popular pressure to act. The Egyptian government might, for example, find itself forced to reassess its now-normal relationship with Israel. Finally, a bloody suppression of the uprising might cause an international uproar and, in particular, alienate the United States. Despite these constraints, should the uprising continue or intensify, Israel might still try to crush it with much more massive force than it has used so far.

But Israel, in my view, is more likely to continue resorting to the option it is already pursuing: an increase in the harshness of its responses to acts of Palestinian resistance, without, however, resorting to high-profile massive retaliation. These measures include (among others) collective punishments, extended curfews, restrictions of movement, mass arrests and detention, shootings, house demolitions,

deportations, closure of educational institutions, and random harassment of the population.

Israel, in my opinion, is likely to increase and intensify such
measures. Israel is reconciling itself to the idea that the *intifada* may
continue for years, but many officials still appear to believe that they
can ultimately put an end to it the way Israel put an end to the earlier
armed resistance in the occupied territories in the late 1960s and
early 1970s.

But there is a major difference between the uprising and the previous
experience of armed resistance. The difference is the mass participation
of the whole Palestinian population in the uprising. The uprising has
put down solid roots and become truly institutionalized. It has sustained
itself and become a way of life. In spite of the multifaceted Israeli
measures to quell it, the *intifada* is becoming more intense and
all-encompassing. The relationship between the people and the Israeli
authorities is increasingly antagonistic as the Palestinians begin to
take charge of their own affairs. The instructions of the leadership of
the uprising are being increasingly strictly observed by the population.
Neither the severe Israeli measures, nor the political moves and gains
by the PLO have weakened the popular commitment to its continuation.
The Palestinians are convinced that nothing short of a sustained
uprising, no matter what the cost, will persuade Israel to recognize
legitimate Palestinian rights. The Palestinians in the West Bank and
Gaza now have a vested interest in the success of the uprising, both
as individuals and as a collectivity. Almost every member of their
society has paid, or is willing to pay, his or her dues.

Can the uprising continue, and for how long? As an expression of
rejection of a foreign occupation, the uprising will continue as long
as the occupation continues. This rejection can assume different
manifestations. While the objective conditions in the West Bank and
Gaza do not allow the Palestinians to sever all kinds of relations with
Israel, which might be the form taken by some civil disobedience
strategies, the Palestinians can overcome these problems by full
mobilization of their human potential and resources.

Leadership: The "Exterior" versus the "Interior"

The relationship between the UNCU and the PLO leadership in exile
has been characterized by close coordination. The UNCU is only an
organizational extension of the PLO leadership in exile, and depends

on the PLO leadership for guidance and instruction. There is, however, a division of labor. The UNCU leaders are the field marshals, while the PLO leaders in exile exercise leadership on the broader level. The input of the UNCU and that of the PLO leaders in leading the uprising has varied from time to time. At times the UNCU undertook responsibility for all or most leadership roles, such as determining the uprising's daily agenda, writing the leaflets, proposing or pushing for certain political moves to be adopted by the PLO, or even giving the PLO leadership a mandate over certain issues. At other times, the PLO would exert pressure and impose its wishes with regard to certain issues and solicit the required support from the UNCU.

The various PLO factions in exile view the role of the UNCU in slightly different ways. The factions which maintain a tight organizational structure in the occupied territories would like to see the UNCU playing a bigger role in leading and determining the agenda of the uprising. The role of the PLO leaders in exile in leading the uprising has, however, increased considerably. A leadership vacuum within the West Bank and Gaza has begun to develop owing to repeated Israeli waves of arrests, and the deportation of local leaders and cadres. This incipient leadership vacuum in the occupied territories has two implications, one internal and the other external. Internally, less experienced individuals have advanced in their respective organizational hierarchies to replace arrested or deported leaders and cadres. Externally, this thinning of the local leadership has enabled the PLO leaders in exile to have a larger input in running the affairs of the uprising and the situation of the occupied territories in general. This greater intervention has sometimes been motivated by a concern to continue the uprising. At other times, the vacuum has provided some PLO leaders and circles with the opportunity to consolidate their grip by neutralizing any side effects of the uprising which would undermine their influence.

Over the years of its occupation of the West Bank and Gaza, Israel has systematically hindered the emergence of an authentic leadership. Had this authentic leadership emerged it would have enjoyed at least equal weight to that of the PLO leadership in exile. While an authentic leadership would not compromise Palestinian national goals, it would have checked the PLO leaders in exile and worked for a close relationship between the "interior" and the "exterior." In the final analysis, the emergence of an authentic leadership in the "interior" could have been an asset to the PLO.

While Israel can mainly be held responsible for the non-emergence of an authentic leadership in the occupied territories, a number of other factors account for the failure of an alternative leadership to the PLO to emerge.

1. The PLO leadership managed through the years, in spite of setbacks, shortcomings, and corruption, to be accepted as the legitimate representative of the Palestinian people. The PLO and its leadership embody the national goals and national unity of the Palestinian people everywhere. No other organization in the occupied territories can claim to be the legitimate representative of all the Palestinian people.

2. The PLO has succeeded over many years in extending its organizational system to the occupied territories. For the people in the West Bank and Gaza, it has become the only political frame of reference. There is no alternative organized political presence. The religious leadership cannot be a substitute or even a parallel force to the PLO, since it lacks the national record, the sizeable following, and the appealing and realistic political program of the PLO—unless, of course, the PLO leadership fails to deliver.

3. The PLO leadership is representative of the Palestinian population socially and politically. The various Palestinian social classes believe that it represents their national and even their social class interests. Politically, the left, the right, and the center agree on the PLO as the sole legitimate representative of the Palestinian people.

4. Most Palestinians consider the PLO leadership to be democratic. Their view should be seen in context and in relative terms. The PLO represents groups with different political and ideological orientations. The Palestinian people can criticize their leadership, verbally and in writing, and get away with it, in the occupied territories, in Tunis and elsewhere. This democratic approach is a necessity for the PLO leadership, since it cannot force its will on the Palestinian people in the occupied territories and in the diaspora.

5. The PLO enjoys Arab and international recognition as the sole legitimate representative of the Palestinian people. If the emergence of an "alternative" leadership, perhaps more compliant with Israeli policy, in the occupied territories was scarcely possible before the uprising, it has become even less likely after the uprising. The uprising, as well as the US government decision to open a dialogue with the PLO, have written the death certificate for the idea of an alternative leadership to the PLO. There was a joke among some Palestinian cynics that, after the resolutions which were taken in the PNC session in Algiers, the PLO leadership had become the "alternative leadership" to the PLO.

Options for a Political Settlement

There are a number of alternative future prospects for a settlement.

1. *An Independent Palestinian State*

It is clear that both Israel and the US reject the option of an independent Palestinian state. Yet this is the option that the Palestinian people cherish, favor most and hope to achieve. But they also know that its realization can only take place in the framework of a comprehensive and lasting settlement of the conflict. An independent Palestinian state in the West Bank and Gaza could not materialize and survive politically, economically, and logistically without peaceful and cooperative relations with both Israel and Jordan.

The geography of a Palestinian state requires a corridor which cuts across Israeli territory. An independent Palestinian state cannot objectively be considered a threat to Israel. It would not be another Cuba or a spearhead for militancy and radicalism, since it would lack the material prerequisites for such a role. The state would also be created as a result of a negotiated settlement taking into account the security concerns of the other parties involved in the conflict, Israel in particular. It would therefore be subjected to a variety of political and practical constraints.

2. *A Palestinian-Jordanian Confederation*

While the Palestinian Declaration of Independence makes no reference to a confederation with Jordan, the final statement of the Nineteenth PNC declared: "The Palestine National Council confirms its previous resolutions concerning the distinct relationship between the two fraternal Jordanian and Palestinian peoples . . . the future relationship between the two states of Jordan and Palestine will be established on confederal bases and on the basis of the free and voluntary choice of the two fraternal peoples, consolidating the historical ties and common vital interests between them."[13]

In the leaflets of the UNCU, there has been no reference to the idea of a future confederation between an independent Palestinian state and Jordan. However, some of the leaflets have stressed the special relationship that should exist between the Palestinian and Jordanian peoples. While Leaflet No. 32 of the UNCU called for the adoption of a plan to Palestinianize institutions in the West Bank and Gaza to give substance to national independence, the leaflet affirmed that such a plan "does not contradict the strengthening of friendly and brotherly relations and the ambitions for unity with the brotherly Jordanian people and the Arab peoples in general."[14]

As far as the Palestinians are concerned, the Palestinian-Jordanian confederation is the second best option. What makes the option acceptable is the likelihood that it is more feasible than a separate Palestinian state, and that it corresponds to historical, geopolitical and practical considerations. There is a lot in common between the West Bank and the East Bank of Jordan. Furthermore, until 1967 the two Banks formed one country, and a close relationship continued to exist between their inhabitants after 1967.

Although the idea is less objectionable to the other parties than the independent fully sovereign state, as things stand now, neither Israel nor the US accepts a confederation between an independent Palestinian state and Jordan. It is also not certain that when Jordan and the PLO refer to a confederation between Jordan and the Palestinians, Jordan shares the Palestinian conception of a confederation between two full-fledged independent states.

Political analysts ask what stake Jordan has in a confederation of this kind. The Amman Accord of 1985 spoke of a confederation but made no mention of an independent Palestinian state. It also talked about the Palestinians' right to self-determination within the framework of the confederation. The Palestinians are concerned about being forced into a confederation established along the lines of the Amman Accord, which was not supported by a Palestinian national consensus. The substance of the Accord was a federation rather than a confederation, and this would not be acceptable to the Palestinians, who would wish to safeguard their right to return to an independent entity of their own in case the association with Jordan does not work in the long run. If that right were safeguarded, the Palestinians would agree, after the Israeli occupation ends, to the establishment of the state, and the establishment of a confederation.

3. *"A Fragile Entity"*

There is no need to stress the fact that the Palestinians reject autonomy as both a final settlement of the Palestinian problem and an interim solution. The aspiration to national independence and sovereignty has become an integral and irremovable component of Palestinian identity. It is extremely important, even if independence or sovereignty is only nominal and has a content that approximates autonomy.

Whether the Palestinians have a full-fledged independent state or a "fragile entity," they know that they are not a military match for

Israel and will do what they can to prevent Israel from attacking their state. The Palestinians realize today that a Palestinian state in the West Bank and Gaza cannot potentially be a security threat to Israel. All indications are that a Palestinian state will be coexisting with, and probably by necessity integrating into, a regional context formed by Jordan, Egypt, and Israel, the three countries which would have borders with the Palestinian state.

The Dialogue between the US Government and the PLO

The Palestinians inside and outside the West Bank and Gaza have welcomed the US government's decision to open an official dialogue with the PLO. However, they consider the move insufficient. Leaflet No. 32 of the UNCU stated that it was the uprising which had forced the US to start the dialogue with the PLO. Opening the dialogue, according to the leaflet, was a modest move and a minimum requirement for Palestinians to accept the political role of the US as an accepted mediator. If the US wished to enjoy this role, it should compound the dialogue with an official recognition of the PLO as legitimate, sole representative of the Palestinian people, and the recognition of Palestinian national rights: the right of return, self-determination, and the establishment of an independent state. The UNCU warned against stalling and undermining the substance of the dialogue.[15]

The Palestinians realize that for the US to open a dialogue with the PLO is one thing, and to recognize Palestinian national rights, especially the right to self-determination and the establishment of an independent Palestinian state, is another.

Although the Palestinians hope to induce the US to recognize these rights, they are still skeptical about US intentions. A statement issued by George Habbash, head of the PFLP, and distributed in the occupied territories shortly after talks began stated that "the attitude of the US in international forums and the UN is the test of its seriousness in responding to Palestinian national rights. The US voting against the convening of the international conference and giving the State of Palestine a seat in the UN General Assembly proves its hostile policy toward the Palestine question and its sole and legitimate representative, the PLO."[16] The PFLP warned against exaggerating the benefits of the American response and the significance of its acceptance of a dialogue with the PLO: "The US in collusion with its agents in the area, headed by the Camp David regime, will try to abort the uprising politically, while the Zionist enemy will try to quell it by its iron fist policy."[17]

There can be no doubt that the opening of the dialogue was mutually beneficial to both the PLO and the US government. The PLO viewed the American decision as a turning point, which brought the prospects for a political settlement closer. The decision also enhanced the status of the PLO and increased its respectability and legitimacy in the international arena. After being labelled a terrorist organization, the PLO's image has become one of an accepted and responsible party. In return, the American decision has put more constraints on the PLO to comply to a greater extent with acceptable international conduct.

Among the benefits obtained by the US government from its decision has been credibility as a broker of a political settlement. The decision made it easier for Palestinians to accept a settlement that is American-sponsored. It also made it easier for the US government to pursue its interests in the Arab world more freely, and freed pro-American Arab governments from embarrassment about their friendly relations with a United States that was hostile to the Palestinian cause.

The US decision to start a dialogue with the PLO provokes the question: Could the PLO not have met the US conditions to start the dialogue without the uprising? Theoretically speaking, opening the dialogue between the PLO and the US government should have been possible without the uprising. But in practice it was not certain that the US government would actually have opened a dialogue with the PLO without the uprising. The PLO feared that recognizing Israel's right to exist and accepting 242 would mean giving concessions beyond the ability of the PLO. The uprising enabled the PLO to meet US conditions without feeling that its hand had been greatly weakened.

By early 1990, however, the general feeling among Palestinians both inside and outside, as reflected by PLO official statements and UNCU leaflets, was that the dialogue had not achieved what the Palestinians had hoped for. The US was still viewed with great mistrust, especially after voting against the upgrading of the PLO status at the UN and against other international condemnations of Israel.

Conclusion

More than two years after the uprising started, the situation in the occupied territories was fluid and uncertain. The Palestinians were determined to continue the *intifada,* and the Israelis were equally determined to quell it.

Internally, the balance of political and social forces in place in the occupied territories before the uprising had been upset. The Islamic movement was growing in strength. A new breed of young leaders, cadres and activists was emerging in the villages, refugee camps, and popular urban quarters which were the main sites of the uprising.

Externally, the uprising continued to pose significant challenges to the PLO. To maintain its legitimacy and stature, it was necessary for the PLO and its leadership in exile to support the uprising and ensure its continuity, maintain Palestinian national unity, and engage in a political process that could produce tangible gains. While the PLO had been relatively successful in maintaining national unity and lending support to the uprising, it had not yet obtained major gains from the political process which the uprising had triggered. The continuing uprising was sure to be accompanied by a long and painstaking political process.

Notes

1. From a videotaped address by Salah Khalaf to a symposium of the International Center for Peace in the Middle East, Jerusalem, February 22, 1989.

2. *Journal of Palestine Studies,* Vol. 18, No. 2 (Winter 1989), p. 216.

3. Unified National Command, Leaflet No. 29, November 20, 1988.

4. The interview was originally published by *Al-Hayat.* It was reprinted in a leaflet and distributed in the occupied territories by the PFLP in January 1989.

5. *Journal of Palestine Studies, op. cit.,* p. 222.

6. *Jerusalem Post,* December 28, 1988.

7. The Islamic Resistance Movement (Hamas), "An Appeal to the Nineteenth Palestine National Council," November 10, 1988.

8. These remarks were part of an interview carried by the Kuwait News Agency on January 25, 1990. An English translation can be found in Foreign Broadcast Information Service, *Daily Report,* January 25, 1990.

9. *Jerusalem Post,* January 2, 1989.

10. *Jerusalem Post,* January 19, 1989.

11. Unified National Command of the Uprising, Leaflet No. 31, December 22, 1988.

12. Unified National Command of the Uprising, Leaflet No. 32, January 9, 1989.

13. For a slightly different translation, see *Journal of Palestine Studies, op. cit.,* p. 221.

14. Unified National Command of the Uprising, Leaflet No. 32, January 9, 1989.

15. *Ibid.*

16. Statement distributed by the PFLP in the occupied territories, late December 1988.

17. *Ibid.*

2 REVOLT OF THE PETITE BOURGEOISIE: URBAN MERCHANTS AND THE PALESTINIAN UPRISING

Salim Tamari[1]

> Q. Can you think of one major blunder you have committed [during the uprising]?
> A. Yes. Opening commercial stores by force. That was a mistake and we have learned the proper lessons from it.
>
> [Defense Minister Rabin, *Ha'aretz,* April 22, 1989]

Reflections about the *intifada* (and one can only reflect about a phenomenon that is still in flux) are permeated with the ideological predispositions of their authors. It invokes the parable of the blind men and the elephant: every perception reveals the perspective of the beholder. Because of its populist character, the social composition of the mass movement has lent itself to a multiplicity of interpretations. It has variously been assessed as the movement of the dispossessed in refugee camps (with the focus on the initial demonstrations in Gaza and the intensity of confrontations in the camps); as basically a rural insurrection (with the focus on the spread of the uprising to 88 villages in January, and over 200 by the end of February 1988);[2] and as a reflection of the leading role of workers in the national movement (highlighting the declining participation of Palestinian labor in Israeli firms, and workers' commitment to strike days).[3] There has even been a suggestion, despite evidence to the contrary, about the leading role of professionals and academics in the uprising.[4] The breakdown of data about those killed, injured, and arrested in clashes with soldiers was used to buttress claims as to the "weight" of various groups involved in the rebellion: predominantly refugees in Gaza, and predominantly workers and students from villages in the West Bank.[5] Most of these studies, however, say little about the process by which these groups became involved, or the relevance of their occupational identification ("women", "peasants," etc.) to their actual participation in the mass movement. Surprisingly, there has been a tendency to neglect the significance of the merchant community in general, and the role of urban shopkeepers in particular, in the consolidation of the uprising during the first three decisive months of its launching. One can only attribute this neglect to certain preconceptions about the "inert" conservatism of shopkeepers,[6] and to the absence of a heroic image that businessmen can project opposite the "children of the stones."

Based on interviews with shopkeepers and merchant-activists, and on an analysis of the clandestine leaflets of the mass movement, I will examine below the crucial role played by this traditionally conservative class, suggesting that it was the only social grouping which appears to have acted cohesively in the consolidation of the uprising in its earlier phase (Spring 1988). In its later development, what is usually referred to as the "institutionalization of the uprising," merchants' associations—acting within the Unified Command—determined the contours of the "economic war" between Israel and the resistance movement. The salient features of this confrontation were: the successful boycott of Israeli commodities, the non-payment of taxes, the pressure for the resignation of tax collectors and customs officials, and—to a lesser extent—the creation of an "alternative economy," based mainly on cottage industries. Finally, I will discuss the impact of the organizational crisis of the popular committees, as it affected the declining participation of merchants in the uprising at the beginning of its second year, and the emergence of differences between manufacturers, shopkeepers, and street peddlers.

Fifty years separate the two prolonged commercial strikes that consolidated the two great Palestinian rebellions of our century, the 1936 Revolt and the uprising of 1987-89. In both cases the participation of merchants in the national movement endowed the rebellion with a social weight and an urban character which would otherwise have diluted and fragmented its overall thrust. As in 1936, the urban general strike in 1987 preceded and set the tone for the spread of the uprising to the countryside. Then, as during the *intifada,* the primary objective of the colonial authorities in the initial stages of the rebellion was the dissolution of the general strike.[7] But there are significant differences between the two movements: the participation of merchants in the 1936 rebellion involved a substantial degree of coercion,[8] while the 1987-88 strike was basically—as I hope to show below—a *voluntarist* act. Moreover the Palestinian political elite which led the 1936 rebellion—a combination of urban notables and the coastal commercial bourgeoisie—was destroyed as a class by the war of 1948. That class has no hegemonic equivalent in the contemporary social structure of the West Bank and Gaza, its remnants having been dispersed among the professional and business strata of Jordan and the Gulf states. The current uprising was led by a strategic coalition of forces and social groupings which bear little resemblance to the elitist and semi-feudal character of the Higher Arab Committee of the 1930s.

Shopkeepers, Peddlers and Small Towns

Excluding the district of Gaza (which is not the focus of our analysis here), the urban sector of the Palestinian occupied territories (47 percent of the total population) is distributed among ll townships, the average size of which is 43,000 inhabitants (1987 data).[9] The economy of these townships is dominated by small traders and small workshops. The manufacturing sector is minuscule with the average number of employees per establishment amounting to 4.28 persons.[10] In a typical township like Ramallah, the ratio of commercial establishments (i.e., retail shops) to workshops and artisanal enterprises is 84:16, with an average of 38.6 retail shops for each one thousand inhabitants.[11] Virtually all the eleven Palestinian cities constitute regional markets, administrative and service centers for their rural hinterland in the manner described by Blake in his topology of Levantine small towns.[12]

Two features distinguish these townships from other urban centers in neighboring Middle Eastern states: the absence of one dominant urban center in the country, and—more significantly—the almost even growth rates in the size of the rural and urban population.[13] The first feature can be attributed to the absence of a state (and a bureaucratic state apparatus); to the absence of any substantial manufacturing sector; and to the wilful policy on the part of the Israeli military government of reinforcing the regional dependency of various district centers in the West Bank and Gaza on markets and services in Israel's metropolitan areas.

The second feature, the even demographic growth rates in urban and rural areas, can be explained by the low internal migration trends caused by the physical proximity of outlying villages to their district centers and the relatively good transport system that connects these villages to their townships. The result has been that the centers evolved not only as work and service centers for a rural population who continued to reside in their villages of birth, but also as locations of commercial investments and real estate transactions for rural entre-preneurs and potentates. Although there is scant empirical data on this subject, we know from Chamber of Commerce records for towns like Nablus, Ramallah, Bethlehem and Hebron that between 20 and 25 percent of all commercial establishments are owned by villagers from the district, and that the commuting daily population that uses the facilities of these townships exceeds the size of the urban population in each town.[14]

It is not my purpose in this study to discuss the consequences of this "ruralization" of Palestinian urban centers. I shall only point out here that a sizable population of shopkeepers and artisans do not live in the urban community where they work, and that in some townships like Ramallah, Tulkarm, Jericho, and Gaza City, a sizable proportion of the labor force come from families that became war refugees from the coastal cities in the war of 1948.[15] In each of those townships the local chamber of commerce (and in a few cases the "Chamber of Commerce and Industry") constitutes the framework that brings together refugee and "native" merchants. Under the impact of the uprising, and in part as a consequence of Jordan's dissociation from its historical links with the West Bank, representatives from eight Palestinian cities (including Gaza) established the Federation of Palestinian Chambers of Commerce and Industry in August 1989. This became the only corporate body representing the interests of Palestinian businessmen and shopkeepers on a national scale.

Nevertheless, the persistent division in each township within the middle classes along sources of origin (i.e., between refugees and "indigenous" citizens) continued to plague local political alliances. These were particularly evident in municipal and chamber of commerce elections where refugee and "native" candidates had to be balanced delicately in each competing slate. They were (and are) reinforced in marriage strategies between extended families, where refugee status continues to be as important as class background in the search for eligible spouses. Despite significant integration (and intermarriage) since the war of 1967, those divisions continue to be a primary obstacle to the social homogeneity of the middle strata in Palestinian urban society. They contributed significantly to the relative withdrawal of town merchants from active participation in the national movement until the eruption of the uprising in December 1987. One outstanding achievement of the uprising has been a noticeable decline in the social impact of these divisions, as evidenced by new intermarriage patterns and the willingness to waive "family rights" in the case of local feuds.

Finally, a distinction should be introduced here between shopkeepers and peddlers. While retail trade expanded considerably as a result of rural business ventures in the district centers, shopkeepers continue in the main to have urban roots, both refugee and local. Peddlers, on the other hand, are overwhelmingly of peasant origin. They predominate as street vendors of vegetable produce (mostly rural women who bypass kiosk rentals in the vegetable markets) and trinket salesmen on pavements. During the uprising the number of street peddlers increased several fold as unemployed workers, pauperized refugee camp dwellers, and tax-evading shopkeepers joined the ranks of peasant street vendors to eke out a living. As we shall see, they posed a formidable impediment to the ability of the national movement to organize a disciplined commercial strike.

Background: The Passive Agents of Resistance

Merchants and shopkeepers have always constituted the passive side of resistance to the military authorities. Commercial strikes have been a primary weapon of protest by the national movement since 1967. However, these have usually been one-day affairs, in observance of nationalist memorial days or in response to acts committed by the military government, such as the deportation of national figures or the punitive demolition of houses. They also were accomplished, in most cases, with a considerable degree of persuasion (to put it mildly) on the part of activists from the national movement.

The turning point was the imposition, in 1976, of the value-added tax (VAT) on all merchandise and services in the occupied territories as a means of financing the budget of the Israeli military government. In addition to being illegal by the terms of the Geneva Convention ("the occupier may not institute new taxes in the territory under its control"),[16] the tax was resented because merchants and manufacturers bore the brunt of its imposition. With the onset of the uprising, merchants readily responded to UNCU calls for a total commercial strike and the non-payment of taxes. Faced with a move for total civil disobedience, and a sharp drop in revenue for its civil administration, the Israeli authorities responded quickly:

. . . the granting of permits and licenses of any kind was made contingent on payment of taxes, among other required criteria (including obtaining a certificate of "good conduct" from the internal intelligence services, the Shin Bet). Such permits include, among others, drivers' licenses, travel permits, identity cards, birth certificates, permits to visit relatives detained [in detention centers], construction permits and import and export licenses.[17]

The forceful collection of taxes was used as both a means of revenue and as a method of subduing the rebellious population. The Jerusalem Arabic press daily reported the incursions of the "tax brigades." The following items were reported for an average day covering events for November 23, 1988:

> Last Wednesday the customs and tax bureau staff, accompanied by soldiers, raided the tailoring shop of Yusif Abdallah Shafiq and seized seven sewing machines whose value was estimated at 4,000 dinars [$8,000], for non-payment of taxes. A 1982 Renault belonging to Nasim Odeh was appropriated for the same reasons. A physician from Yatta [Hebron], Dr. Nayef Mahanbeh had his car seized; the condition for reclaiming it was the payment of 1300 dinars in back taxes. Tens of merchants in Khan Yunis were raided and their ID's confiscated. They were directed to reclaim them from the military government after paying the taxes imposed on them.[18]

The latter practice of confiscating ID's for non-payment of taxes was later declared illegal by the High Court; nevertheless, the practice continued.

The human rights organization, al-Haq, reported in its annual report the manner in which the army was used for these exactions:

> Typically, a curfew would be imposed, and the army would enter homes impounding property or summon property-owners to makeshift tax offices (usually schools) to present proof of payment for taxes. Al-Haq has documented confiscations of jewelry, vehicles and (occasionally exorbitant) sums of money, for example in the town of Beit Sahour at the beginning of July 1988. In addition, Palestinians have been stopped at roadblocks by police or army carrying lists; if their name appeared on the list, their car would be seized and returned only after the person had paid all outstanding taxes, as estimated by the authorities. In other instances, identity cards were confiscated and returned only after taxes had been paid.[19]

By the beginning of 1988 it became clear to the Israeli authorities that the December uprising was not limited in character or duration, as was the case in earlier outbursts. Defense Minister Rabin, who was quick to condemn the initial upheaval as the work of outside PLO inciters, announced a month later that "the disturbances reflect the tension that was building in the administered territories over 20 years and are not the result of the Palestinian organizations' call to violence."[20] The Chief of Staff, Dan Shomron, boasted on a tour of Gaza in December 1987 that "under no circumstances will we allow a small minority of inciters to rule over the vast majority—a majority which is, in general, pragmatic and wants to live quietly."[21] A few months later he made an about-turn, ". . . there is no such thing as eradicating the intifada because in its essence it expresses the struggle of nationalism . . . the participation of large number of civilians in violence has created what physicists call 'a critical mass'."[22]

The repressive measures listed above were thus intended not only to contain and isolate activists and inciters associated with the underground movement, but also to intimidate whole segments of the civilian population, including groups that had so far been immune. Mayors, mukhtars, heads of chambers of commerce, and leading businessmen and manufacturers had to spend hours under the sweltering heat, rubbing shoulders with youngsters summoned from refugee camps, and with peasants from curfewed villages asking for special permits to harvest their crops. Throughout 1987 and 1988 several prominent businessmen from Nablus and Ramallah were held and incarcerated for non-payment of taxes, a move unprecedented so far.[23] The army developed a special preference for commandeering the Volvos, Audis, and Mercedes of the rich (bearing blue West Bank licenses) to mount night raids against rebellious villages. They were often observed taking the vehicles afterwards for joy rides and returning them to their owners damaged and in need of major repairs.[24] Special yellow passes issued in the early eighties for dignitaries and businessmen to spare them the humiliations of excessive searches over border crossings were now abolished.[25] The Israeli satirist Philip Gillon encapsulated the situation succinctly: "They treat the Arabs like dogs, and they treat dogs like Arabs."[26]

In short, the *intifada* witnessed the dethronement of the Palestinian bourgeoisie from the relatively sheltered niche they had managed to occupy over the last two decades. A combination of increasing tax pressures, and a shift in the military government's perception of the urban middle classes to the idea that they were becoming a part of a hostile subject population and not a part of a "pragmatic majority that wants to live quietly" (a shift which was itself brought about by the ascendancy to power, and the staffing of the military government, by extreme right-wing elements) engendered a self-fulfilling prophecy. It hastened the process of involving the shopkeepers as wilful activists in the uprising.

Who Controls the Streets?

Within two weeks of the insurrection which marked the beginning of the uprising in the refugee camps of Gaza, Nablus and Bethlehem, the battle lines shifted from street confrontations between youthful elements and border police toward a general commercial strike in the urban centers. This shift marked the transition of the uprising from its initial spontaneous (and volatile) character to one in which control passed into the hands of the clandestine Unified National Command of the Uprising (UNCU). In this shift the cities of Ramallah, Nablus and (earlier) East Jerusalem played a crucial role. The UNCU (comprising the four main factions of the PLO in addition to the Islamic Jihad movement) began to direct and coordinate the daily activities of the popular movement through a network of popular committees, neighborhood committees, strike committees, and now merchants' committees. The instruments for diffusing these directives were the serialized communiques of the uprising (*bayanat*), as well as the occasional bulletins issued regionally by the popular committees.[27]

The battle for control over the streets of Jerusalem was the most protracted and perhaps, due to the centrality of the city in the Israeli strategy of control over the territories, the most crucial. It was sparked by General Sharon's transfer of his residence to the old city of Jerusalem on December 14, 1987, at the onset of the major demonstrations in Gaza. A commercial strike commenced in Jerusalem and continued unabated for 41 days, igniting a series of solidarity strikes in other West Bank townships, most notably in Nablus and Ramallah. The pattern which characterized the Israeli response to the Jerusalem strike established precedents for the behavior of the merchant community throughout the territories. This took the form of a cat and mouse game, which the Israeli press dubbed "the shopkeepers' war."[28] Throughout January and February 1988, merchants began to close their shops at 11 a.m., upon which soldiers would move in and force them to open their shutters. Activists of the "strike committees" would then engage the soldiers in a battle of stone throwing and compel the merchants to close the shops again. The scenario was reversed and the military authorities compelled the merchants to remain closed from 2:00-7:00 p.m. in response to a UNCU call for afternoon openings.[29] These confrontations turned into a contest of wills during January and February. The military authorities were determined to break the commercial strike as it became the most visible side of the institutionalized uprising. They may also have seen the merchants as the weak link in the organized national movement.[30] Soldiers began to smash the padlocks of striking merchants and leave the stores open overnight.[31] This last act boomeranged, however, as it generated unprecedented communal support. The *Jerusalem Post* reported at the end of January that control was slipping from the hands of the army:

> Shopkeepers say members of the local metalworkers union have been repairing damaged shop doors free of charge, in one of the first signs of communal self-help to maintain the strike. There have also been reports of collections and donations of money and food for needy people, who have been deprived of jobs and wages by the prolonged shutdowns.[32]

Within a fortnight the initiative passed into the hands of merchants' committees in the Ramallah-Jerusalem area. Merchants' representatives held their first public press conference on February 2, 1988 in which they exposed the army's attempts at the forceful breaking of their strike, and the widespread destruction of property.[33] In al-Bireh about 300 Muslim and Christian shopkeepers made a "blood oath" at the end of March in which they vowed not to pay their Israeli taxes.[34] Their act was saluted by the UNCU as a precedent to be emulated by other cities.[35] Significantly, the merchants also tied the ending of their commercial strike to national political demands: the annulment of unfair taxes, the ending of the deportation policy, the release of prisoners held during the December and January demonstrations, and the convening of an international conference to resolve the future of the territories.[36] On their part the Israeli Merchants Association in West Jerusalem voiced their opposition to the forceful opening of Arab shops—apparently wary of the effects on tourism.[37]

Following the mass resignation of the Arab police force in March, at the behest of directives issued by the UNCU, street committees and "popular guard committees" were formed to protect shops forcefully opened by the army.[38] In Hebron, bands of young men were observed manning observation points on strategic rooftops following settler attacks on Arab cars and shops. They later began to set up barricades to prevent armed settlers from entering the town.[39] By the early spring, the battle over the shops was won. The army and border police gave up interfering with storekeepers, and the directives of the Unified Command began to regularize opening hours. The commercial strike became the most visible daily feature of the uprising.

"Towers" of the Intifada

The victory of shopowners in the battle over the commercial strike marked a turning point in the formative phase of the uprising. It witnessed the ascendancy of the urban middle classes as leading elements in the confrontations with the Israeli army. For the first time during the two decades of Israeli rule, it demonstrated the ability of the national movement to control the streets, and sustain that control through the mobilization of the most self-conscious and individualistic sector of the urban population. The "war of the shops," in the view of a Palestinian historian, "brought the bourgeoisie into the fold, participating very fully and effectively in the uprising."[40] This occurred, in the analysis of one of the factions in the UNCU, when the uprising brought home the conclusion "to those segments of the bourgeoisie and the intelligentsia that it is impossible to continue coexisting with a 'liberal' occupation."[41]

This achievement would not have been possible without two essential ingredients: the wilful involvement of the merchants in the uprising after a brief period of hesitation and intimidation; and secondly, a decision on the part of the national movement—and the UNCU in particular—to give priority to the demands of merchants (and manufacturers) within the tasks of the movement as a whole. Concerning the first factor, there is no doubt that the imposition of taxes, the manner in which they were collected, and the generalized contempt displayed by the Israeli army and civil administration toward the middle classes since the early 1980s hastened the process of revolt. The shift in the attitude of the UNCU towards the merchants from one of patronizing exhortation (and on a number of occasions actual intimidation in the streets) to direct involvement in the concerns of merchants was realized through the establishment of the merchants' committees. The latter became the instruments of incorporating shopkeepers and small businessmen as direct participants in the uprising. These changes can be clearly monitored from the regional communiques of the national committees of the UNCU.

In an early political circular distributed by Fatah on February 20, 1988 ("the second month of the peoples' great rebellion") merchants were already identified as occupying "the paramount position [*makan al-sadara*] in support of the uprising" since the commercial sector has "the power and the ability *to paralyze the economy* in a general strike."[42] Merchants are targeted for mobilization in the following manner:

1. Merchants should be organized around the non-payment of taxes as *a matter of self-interest*. Otherwise a prolonged strike would not be sustained.

2. Merchants should be assured that their stores would be protected against looting in case the army opened their shutters forcefully. The national movement should repair damaged shops, and provide guard duties (at night).

3. Striking merchants should be supported and non-striking merchants should be punished severely.

4. The strength of the general strike lies in its implementation. Hence the duration of the strike should *be restricted* and coordinated with all the regions through the national communiques.[43]

This circular was remarkable for several reasons. First, it reflected the political weight accorded to the merchants by the largest of the political factions in the UNCU, identifying them as the primary mass base of the rebellion, *before workers and farmers*. Second, unlike the communiques issued by the UNCU for mass distribution, the *bayanat* of the uprising, it is completely lacking in any sentimental jargon; the political idiom used is concrete and straightforward, almost cynical. Finally the circular reveals the pragmatic positions that guided the leadership of the uprising, from the onset, in determining the timing and extent of its directives in a manner which clearly distinguishes it from the leadership of the 1936 general strike.

In the actual carrying out of these directives, however, considerable pressure was used, depending on the region and the issues involved. In the first phase of the commercial strike (lasting from January to April 1988) the main issue was the boycott of taxes and the regularization of strike hours. In the second phase (beginning June 1988 and intensifying in March 1989) the main issue became the boycott of Israeli goods and the expansion of the home market for native products. A circular addressed to the merchants of Qalqilya (a market town west of Nablus) by the "Qalqilya Popular Committee of the Uprising" (January 24, 1988) is typical of the patronizing stance which characterized UNCU circulars toward merchants in the first phase. After addressing shopkeepers to "assume your share in the national struggle, and to be *with* the people rather than *above* the people," it then proceeds to warn retailers who raise the prices of basic commodities of dire retribution: first the spoilage of their wares, and then the burning of their stores.[44] This balancing of exaltation with intimidation also characterizes the first three national communiques of the Unified Command, albeit with considerably more astuteness and sophistication. In communique 1 (January 8, 1988) reference is made to "our commitment to protect the interests of honest merchants from any attacks by the authorities . . . [while] we notify those weak souls of the repercussion of being seduced by collaborators."[45] Communique No. 3 (January 18, 1988) elevated merchants to prominence: "We salute you and salute your leading role in the making of our people's uprising," but the language is still condescending.[46] (This was just before the period, at the end of January, when the Unified Command intervened in the prolonged Jerusalem strike by making allowances for limited opening hours in the morning.)[47]

The turning point occurred in communique 5 (the beginning of February 1988). This is the only national communique that is almost entirely devoted to merchants and businessmen. More significantly, its formulation clearly reflects the elevation of merchants to a decision-making position within the leadership of the revolt. In its preamble it calls on "Merchants . . . towers of the intifada . . . its guardians, the bearers of its message and continuity. We salute your principal role as vanguards of the struggle."[48] This formulation corresponded to the formation of merchants' committees in Ramallah, Nablus, and Jerusalem whose task was "the escalation and coordination of the commercial strike within each city [i.e., through the UNCU] and the protection of striking merchants from retribution."[49]

Immediately after the success of the commercial strike the committees began to push for a tax boycott, and—in the words of a merchant activist from al-Bireh—"there is no doubt that the tax campaign was spearheaded vigorously by the merchants' committees, acting on the basis of their self-interest."[50] At the institutional level, the merchants' committees were expected to replace the disintegrating chambers of commerce as the organizational framework for representing their concerns, but this attempt apparently failed.[51] The chambers of commerce (and in the case of the Nablus region, of industry and commerce) had acted over the last two decades as the bodies for representing the grievances of the small merchant with the tax bureaus, and, with the dissolution of the nationalist town councils after 1981, as the main conduit between urban citizens and the military government. In the eighties they also assumed the task of validating official papers for the Jordanian government (such as passport papers, birth certificates, etc.).[52] For this reason, the chambers acquired the reputation of embodying a conciliatory, pro-Jordanian (but not collaborationist) leadership for the urban middle classes. Their demise ushered the collapse of these linkages with both Jordan and the military government. The failure of the merchants' committees to supplant them can be seen in this context not only as a failure of class representation, but also as reflecting the limitations inherent in *any* organs of the national movement performing an autonomous political function.

Merchants in Retreat?

In August 1988, the Palestinian uprising entered into an organizational crisis. While on the ground street confrontations were continuing unabated with the army, and while the commercial strike provided the backdrop for the "routinization" of the uprising, the *institutional* development of the *intifada* was not galvanizing around the popular committees, as anticipated by the Unified Command. "The danger of this period," wrote Ribi' al-Madhoun, "lies in the possible loss by the uprising of one of its distinctive features—namely, its mass character. It marks the regression of the movement to pre-*intifada* days, when revolutionary action was concentrated in the hands of students and rebellious youth in specified regions."[53] Two main institutional failures which can be mentioned here were the inability of the "popular education committees" to create a sustained alternative network to formal schooling (with the closing of most schools and universities in the West Bank); and the failure of the "agricultural committees" and the "domestic production committees" to create the much-heralded system of home production, based on cottage industries.

These issues reflected the general political malaise in the uprising itself. As the tempo of the movement was routinized and the popular committees were in retreat, the Unified Command sought to resolve the crisis by "heating up" street action confrontations.[54] At the root of the problem was the shift in the political strategy of the PLO after the Declaration of Independence in November 1988, when the leadership was seen as "investing" the political momentum created by the uprising in the search for sovereignty through a negotiated territorial settlement. Although this "investment" was acceptable in principle to the five factions of the Unified Command—as evidenced by Communique 29 (November 20, 1988)—it nevertheless created considerable controversy on how to proceed inside the territories.

Briefly stated, the controversy was highlighted in the internal debate about the nature of the campaign for civil disobedience (*'isyan madani*), which was generally seen by all political factions as the main instrument of mobilization as well as the strategic means of achieving total disengagement with Israel's political control over the West Bank and Gaza.[55] Commercial strikes, tax boycotts, and the mass resignation of police and tax-collectors, were all seen as steps toward a cataclysmic moment of separation when the system of colonial control would disintegrate. A necessary condition for this objective was that civil resistance should exclude armed activities (to avoid brutal liquidation by the army) and that mass participation should be sustained through the organizational work of the popular committees.[56] As the uprising escalated its momentum it would attain a new advanced plateau when these [popular] organizational networks would constitute an alternative power base to Israel's colonial administration.[57] It was the inability of the popular committees to create this alternative power base that was now seen as the essence of the crisis in the leadership of the uprising.[58] In effect, the diplomatic initiatives of the PLO to enter into a negotiated territorial settlement were seen as the new *alternative* strategy which would circumvent, rather than supplement, the political gains of the uprising.

In the ranks of the merchant community, this crisis was exemplified by three issues: (1) the retreat in the campaign for the non-payment of taxes, after some success; (2) the manner in which the boycott of Israeli commodities was carried out; and (3) the emergence of differences in the ranks of manufacturers, shopkeepers, and street peddlers (*bastat* owners).

The initial success of the tax campaign was no doubt connected to the resignation of tax collectors and Arab police officers in response to calls (and later threats) by the UNCU in March 1988.[59] In subsequent months, however, Israeli moves to take drastic measures against tax delinquents, and the forceful collection of taxes eroded the resistance of the business community. Factory owners and other manufacturers in Ramallah and Nablus received "special dispensation"—according to a prominent Ramallah accountant—from the Unified Command at the end of March 1988 to pay their taxes in order to keep their factories open and receive import licenses for raw materials.[60] The move was generally seen as necessary to sustain local industries, and expand the employment of workers laid off by Israeli firms. It nevertheless helped to a create a schism ("and considerable resentment")[61] between manufacturers and shopkeepers, and ultimately contributed to the collapse of the tax campaign. Since big merchants and manufacturers paid the bulk of the aggregate taxes the result was to minimize the losses for the Israeli treasury. By July 1988, it is estimated that 25 percent of the business establishments in the al-Bireh-Ramallah region (out of a total of 4520 establishments) had broken ranks and paid their taxes, amounting to 80 percent of the total Israeli tax levy.[62] An even higher payment rate was reported in Hebron, Bethlehem, Jenin, Tulkarm, and Nablus—the latter often referred to as the "citadel of merchants."[63]

The second issue which confronted the merchant community in this phase was the boycott of Israeli commodities. The boycott campaign was already addressed in some detail in the early communiques of the uprising. The Fatah clandestine directive (February 20, 1988), quoted above, laid down the conditions for boycott as follows: (a) Palestinian manufacturers should improve the quality of their products, to be on a par with equivalent Israeli items; (b) Arab products should not be priced higher than similar Israeli products; (c) local products should be diversified so as to offer the maximum possible replacement of Israeli goods.[64] "Strike forces" were directed in a number of UNCU communiques to enforce the demand for boycott.[65] This was usually understood to mean spoilage of Israeli commodities after initial warning to the storeowners, but only if there was a local substitute for the item. The spoilage campaign was accelerated in the spring of 1989 and reached its zenith in March, when masked squads of the strike forces raided hundreds of shops in several towns and held public bonfires of the offending items. In Nablus, excesses were widespread and no distinction was often made between commodities that have Arab substitutes and those that do not (such as Tnuva milk cartons); at least one shoe store was reportedly burnt down.[66] The "bonfire campaign" elicited widespread protests by merchants and the public at large and occasioned a reprimand of the strike forces by the Unified Command. In a rare directive issued by the UNCU to local committees, the roughing up of Nablus merchants was severely criticized, and they were commanded to treat violating shopowners in a more careful manner in future encounters.[67]

The third feature of the crisis was related to the uneven burden borne by shopkeepers in the conduct of the general strike, in contrast to the situation of manufacturers and street peddlers. There is now concrete evidence that Palestinian manufacturers, especially those who invested in food processing, soft drinks, sweets, cigarettes, pharmaceuticals, cleaning solutions and other items involved in the boycott campaign, benefited considerably during the uprising.[68] The increased demand for Arab products, despite a substantial drop in the public standard of living, allowed many Palestinian manufacturers to have a virtual monopoly on the local market. For this they received a special dispensation from the Unified Command to extend their working hours, and even—as mentioned—to pay taxes, to the chagrin of many storekeepers who demanded, through their merchants' committees, that a more even-handed policy be applied.[69]

The problem with street peddlers was more acute. In the earlier days of the commercial strike, petty street vendors, *falafel* stands, and small vegetable traders were allowed to sell their wares beyond strike hours in order to avail the public of emergency shopping facilities. It was also an economic safety valve which permitted an increasingly pauperized urban population a supplementary source of income in the form of "alley stores." As the uprising entered its second year, however, these enterprises mushroomed all over the country, blotting the urban landscape and considerably diminishing the already curtailed incomes of strike-bound merchants. More significantly, these peddlers threatened the integrity and the discipline of the general strike itself. It was in response to this last consideration, and under pressure from merchants' committees, that directives were issued calling for the regulation, then curtailment, of street peddling, charging "strike forces" with the task of enforcing this directive.[70] But the number of peddlers involved was apparently too large to control, and this measure could only be enforced during general strike days.[71] Subsequently, the friction continued between street vendors and storekeepers.

Conclusion

The Palestinian uprising marks the entry of the urban merchant community as active participants in the national movement. Until then, this conservative community had been used by the movement, with considerable reluctance on its part, in limited strikes to mark national days of protest and expressions of grievances. Subsequently, the use of taxes by the Israelis as a form of punishment, and the general Israeli humiliation of the urban middle classes, leading to their dethronement from their relative privileges, brought the merchant community to the forefront of confrontations with the army. They realized, in the words of a leading member of the Chamber of Commerce, that "co-existence with the Israeli presence was no longer feasible." And this was not a mere figure of speech. In the first four months of the uprising, shopkeepers were the single most decisive element in paralyzing the urban economy, and in consolidating the populist character of the insurrection.

For its part, the clandestine movement leading the uprising became aware of the limitations inherent in relying excessively on volatile street demonstrations and stone throwing as instruments for the realization of its political objectives. The leadership also realized that it was incapable of organizing Palestinian workers to desist from working in Israel, since the home industries could not sustain alternative employment for them. The commercial strike was seen, therefore, as an essential component for adding "class weight" as well as durability and urban depth to the uprising. The leadership's incorporation of the merchant community into the leadership of the revolt, through merchants' committees, received the blessings of both "left" and "right" factions of the UNCU.

A setback to this incorporation occurred as a result of the mishandling of the tax-boycott campaign and the provision of special dispensation to manufacturers and big businessmen to pay taxes while pushing the shopkeepers to take the heat. But the main obstacle leading to the retreat of merchants (as well as other organized groups in the uprising) from the forefront of events was political and not tactical. It had to do with the inability of the "popular committees" engendered by the *intifada* to create an alternative power (and in some sectors economic) base to Israeli rule. This shortcoming was enhanced and fed by PLO political initiatives abroad which were often seen (rightly or wrongly) as the culmination of political struggles in the occupied territories, rather than a supplement to them.

While the battle of the merchants constitutes part of the ebb and flow of the movement as a whole, it is a part that was decisive in the success of the uprising in its formative phase. Although merchants continue to exercise a visible role in the routinized features of the urban revolt, there is no doubt that the initiative is now located outside their hands.

Notes

1. This article is derived from the paper presented by the author at the Fourteenth Annual Symposium of the Center for Contemporary Arab Studies, Georgetown University, in May 1989. A modified version of the paper will also appear in Jamal R. Nassar and Roger Heacock, eds., *Intifada: Palestine at the Crossroads* (New York: Praeger, 1990).

2. Samir Barghouti, "Economic Preludes to the Uprising," *al-Ittihad* (Haifa), December 9, 1988 (special supplement).

3. Fayez Sarah, "The Social Structure of the Palestinian Uprising," *Shu'un Filastiniya,* No. 189, December 1988, pp. 8-9.

4. "It can be said without hesitation that these confrontations [during the uprising] were led mainly by revolutionary intellectuals, and politicized nationalists drawn from the ranks of students, and academics . . . ". Samir Barghouti, in *al-Ittihad, op. cit.*

5. Barghouti, *op. cit.;* Rashad al-Madani, "Statistics on the Martyrs and Wounded of the Uprising in the Gaza District," *al-Ittihad,* April 21, 1989; see also Ronald Stockton, *Intifada Death Patterns,* unpublished paper (University of Michigan, Dearborn, June 1988). The categories of "worker," "peasant," etc. used in these breakdowns should be used critically.

6. Ribi' Madhoun, *The Palestinian Uprising: Its Organizational Structure and Mode of Action* (Arabic, Akka, 1989), p. 32.

7. It is curious that little attention has been paid, so far, to these parallels in writings about the *intifada.* This might be related to the coercive character of the general strike in 1936, as well as its failure in reaching its economic objectives, namely the paralysis of the Jewish economic sector. Y. Porath, the Israeli historian of the 1936 rebellion, contrasted the more radical nature of the 1987 uprising with the 1936 rebellion: "This is the first time that there has been a popular action, covering all social strata and groups. True, the refugee camps are the vanguard. But remote villagers and the urban population are also involved, active." (*Jerusalem Post,* March 12, 1988.) For his analysis of the General Strike of 1936 see, *The Palestinian Arab National Movement: From Riots to Rebellion,* pp. 162-195.

8. Cf. Porath, *op. cit.,* pp. 177-178.

9. Israel, Central Bureau of Statistics, *Statistical Abstract of Israel, 1988* and The West Bank Data Project (WBDP), *The West Bank and Gaza Atlas* (Jerusalem, 1988), pp. 28-29.

10. United Nations Industrial Development Organization, *Survey of the Manufacturing Industry in the West Bank and Gaza Strip*; WBDP, *op. cit.,* p. 43.

11. S. Khayat, *Ramallah: 1985 Masterplan* (Jerusalem, 1985).

12. G.H. Blake, "The Small Town," in G.H. Blake and R. Lawless, *The Changing Middle Eastern City* (London, 1982), pp. 214-216.

13. WBDP, *op.cit.,* p. 28.

14. Khayat, *op. cit.*

15. In the case of East Jerusalem, though, they are regional migrants from the Hebron district.

16. Al-Haq (Law in the Service of Man), *Punishing a Nation* (Ramallah, 1989), p. 272.

17. *Punishing a Nation,* p. 281. These measures were subsequently given "retroactive legitimacy" through Military Order No. 1262.

18. *Al-Tali'a,* December 15, 1988.

19. *Ibid.*

20. "Rabin: Violence in Areas Indicates a 20-year Build-up of Tensions," *Jerusalem Post,* January 10, 1988.

21. *Jerusalem Post,* December 16, 1987, and December 9, 1988.

22. "Shomron: Intifada Can't be Eradicated," *Jerusalem Post,* January 1, 1989.

23. Interview with O.A.J., owner of a construction materials store, Ramallah, February 19, 1989.

24. I am writing here of incidents which I personally observed on numerous occasions in the Ramallah-Bireh regions during the months of December 1988 through April 1989. Car owners were allowed to apply for compensation to their damaged cars; in most cases, however, the Ramallah police would not process the claims, or would not respond to them. Similar cases were reported to me in Nablus, Jenin, Bethlehem and Hebron.

25. Interview with A.F., a leading member of the Ramallah Chamber of Commerce, December 22, 1988.

26. "Arafat Puts On His New Keffiyeh," *Jerusalem Post,* December 16, 1988. Gillon was referring to the live IDF dogs sent with remote-controlled detonation devices to the bunkers of Palestinian fighters in South Lebanon.

27. In the north, and in most villages, where the printing and distribution of leaflets were curtailed, minarets and portable loudspeakers were used to announce the directives.

28. See for example, Joel Greenburg, "The Battle Moves from the Streets," *Jerusalem Post,* March 18, 1988; and "Abnormal Becomes Normal in West Bank," *Jerusalem Post,* January 26, 1988.

29. Andy Court, "The Battle of Salah e-Din Street," *Jerusalem Post,* May 4, 1988.

30. Interview with S.J., striking merchant and member of the Ramallah merchants' committee, January 4, 1988.

31. Facts Information Committee, *The Palestinian Uprising: December* 1987-August 1988, pp. 139-140.

32. Joel Greenberg, "Abnormal Becomes Normal in West Bank," *Jerusalem Post,* January 26, 1988.

33. *Al-Tali'a* (Jerusalem), February 4, 1988.

34. Interview with S.J., January 4, 1989, *op. cit.*

35. UNCU, *Communique No. 12,* April 2, 1988.

36. *Ibid.*

37. "Jerusalem Merchants Oppose Forced Opening of Arab Stores," *Jerusalem Post,* April 26, 1988.

38. "The Formation of Popular Guard Committees in the West Bank," *al-Tali'a* (Jerusalem), March 17, 1988.

39. *Al-Tali'a, ibid.*

40. Mahmoud Ibrahim, Birzeit University medieval historian, quoted by Judith Gabriel, "The Economic Side of the Intifada," *Journal of Palestine Studies,* No. 69 (Autumn, 1988), pp. 205-206.

41. Palestine Communist Party, *Political Bulletin* [limited circulation], June 18, 1988, p. 17.

42. Fatah, *Political Circular # 2* [untitled], February 20, 1988, p. 17, emphasis added.

43. *Ibid.,* pp. 17-18, emphasis added.

44. Qalqilya Popular Committee of the Uprising, "A Communique to the Merchants of Qalqilya," January 24, 1988, reprinted in *al-Intifada: Basic Documents* (Nicosia: Beisan Publications, 1988), Volume 3, p. 433..

45. UNCU, *Communique No. 1,* January 8, 1988.

46. UNCU, *Communique No. 3,* January 18, 1988.

47. Madhoun, *op. cit.,* p. 35.

48. UNCU, *Communique No. 5,* [undated], distributed first week of February, 1988.

49. Interview with B.S., owner of a tailoring shop and activist in the merchants' committee, al-Bireh, February 19, 1989.

50. *Ibid.*

51. Madhoun, *op. cit.,* p. 35.

52. Interview with M.K., wood merchant and member of the Chamber of Commerce (Ramallah), March 3, 1989.

53. *Op. cit.*, p. 77.

54. Madhoun, *op. cit.*, pp. 77-78.

55. UNCU, *On Civil Disobedience*, [limited distribution], May 21, 1988.

56. UNCU, *On Civil Disobedience, ibid.*; and Nayef Hawatmeh, "Where the DFLP Stands," *al-Safir* (Beirut), reprinted in *Jerusalem Post*, April 18, 1989.

57. UNCU, *ibid.*, p. 2; see also the Popular Front, *Damir al-Intifada*, No. 5, January 1989.

58. PFLP, *Memorandum to Factions in UNCU* [undated, probably mid-March 1989].

59. UNCU, *Communiques Nos. 9, and 10*, dated March 3, 1988, and March 10, 1988. See also Joel Greenberg, "Screws Turned on West Bank Collection," *Jerusalem Post*, February 18, 1988; and *Jerusalem Post*, March 3, 1988.

60. Interview with F. K., accountant and prominent political activist, Ramallah, January 3, 1989.

61. *Ibid.*

62. *Ibid.*

63. *Ibid.*

64. Fatah, *Political Circular No. 2* [untitled], February 20, 1988, p. 23.

65. For example, UNCU, *Communique No. 19*, June 8, 1988.

66. Interview with S.M., Nablus money changer, April 10, 1989. The "bonfire campaign" was reportedly launched by one faction within the Unified Command.

67. UNCU, *General Directive* [limited distribution, undated], distributed end of March, 1989.

68. Hazem Shunnar, *Social and Economic Conditions during the Uprising* (Passia, Jerusalem, January, 1989, in Arabic), p. 42.

69. Interview with B.S., *op.cit.*, February 21, 1989.

70. UNCU, *Communique No. 19*, June 8, 1988, and *Communique No. 25*, September 6, 1988.

71. A date was even set by the Unified Command—February 28, 1989—to eliminate the presence of street vendors (and "roving money changers"), but no concrete action was taken in that direction. Cf. UNCU, *Communique No. 36*, March 16, 1989.

3 MASS MOBILIZATION AND THE UPRISING: THE LABOR MOVEMENT

Joost R. Hiltermann

When mass street demonstrations broke out in the Israel-occupied West Bank and Gaza Strip in December 1987, few observers realized that they were witnesses to the first manifestations of what would turn out to be a sustained popular uprising. The predominant perception at the time was that this was simply another wave of protest, a passing episode like the many which preceded it. With the advantage of hindsight, however, it can be argued that a prolonged mass uprising of the kind that has now materialized had become possible by the late 1980s. It was a logical extension of efforts by grassroots activists to build an infrastructure of resistance during the preceding two decades.

As recently as June 1985, a Palestinian activist stated in an interview in reference to trade unions:

> . . . the end of the occupation can [only] come about through a combination of forms of struggle: political, mass and theoretical. By theoretical I mean instilling a working class ideology in the masses. By political I mean diplomatic, propaganda and armed struggle, where armed struggle is the highest form of political struggle. By mass struggle I mean the daily struggle for bread-and-butter issues, but on the highest level this would be demonstrations, rock-throwing, strikes and commercial boycotts. A general strike/commercial boycott is highest on the agenda of the union blocs, but the masses must first be convinced through their daily struggle that these tactics are beneficial for them. We should not be adventurous and declare a boycott while we are not ready to enforce it. This would betray weakness, not strength.[1]

The fact that a prolonged partial commercial shut-down, regular stay-home strikes by workers, a boycott of Israeli-made products, a tax strike and a gradual disengagement from the administrative structures of occupation had become possible slightly over two years later, attests to the important changes that took place in Palestinian society during two decades of military occupation.

In this paper I seek to establish, through an analysis of the dynamics of mass mobilization in the occupied territories, how grassroots organizations, by their particular nature and through their particular activities, formed the basis for and sustained the popular uprising. For the sake of brevity, this paper will focus exclusively on the labor movement in the West Bank.

1. A Brief Historical Introduction

The origins of mass-based organizations in the West Bank and Gaza lie in the early and mid-1970s, when local activists, in many cases schoolchildren, began organizing volunteer efforts to address basic social and infrastructural problems in Palestinian society. They were motivated by two main considerations. In the first place, the occupying power not only appeared remiss in providing sufficient and adequate basic services to the population, but was perceived as inhibiting socio-economic development in the territories. Israel's policy in this regard was seen by Palestinians as a reflection of its political agenda in the occupied territories: Israel was not about to "trade land for peace," but had long-term designs of incorporating the territories into Israel through a gradual process of establishing facts on the ground. In the words of Rita Giacaman,

> The first ten years of occupation or so, everybody worked very hard to inhibit the breakdown of the infrastructure, the economic, social, health, educational and political infrastructures in the West Bank. It was clear to Palestinians that this attempt on the part of the Israeli military to break down social and economic infrastructures really meant a fight for survival. That infrastructure, we all knew, was crucial for the reconstruction of Palestinian society in the future. We knew that much. We knew that the Israeli military was out to possess the land without us people . . . . At the least, the military occupation failed to provide the basic services to people and at most, was out to destroy every attempt on the part of Palestinians to provide these services in a meaningful way.[2]

With regard to the second consideration, the ability of existing Palestinian institutions to provide the necessary services was limited by their urban charitable and therefore paternalistic nature, as well as their emphasis on curative rather than preventive action. This was not only so in the case of health,[3] but also education, social work, employment, conditions of women, and so forth. Such institutions, moreover, were dependent on the goodwill of the military authorities, who had the power to issue or withhold licenses for a variety of activities, and who have used this power liberally throughout the occupation in an effort to check the emergence of an autonomous Palestinian social sector.[4]

In the mid-1970s, the prevailing perception that the occupation would not last long started to fade as it was becoming increasingly clear that Israel was entrenching itself in the territories. A new realization emerged that Palestinians in the West Bank and Gaza would have to take their fate into their own hands and cease to rely on assistance, let alone liberation, from the outside. A new perception grew that there had to be a force that could counteract the actions of the occupier on a local level. The question was how to go about creating this force. According to Rita Giacaman:

> What we didn't know was how to mobilize under occupation, when it was becoming practically impossible to move and do anything at the political or other levels without being subjugated to arrests or attacks from the Israeli military . . . . By the mid-seventies it was becoming very clear that there was a large sector that was still unmobilized even at the political level, and actually it was the women who discovered this fact. A women's movement emerged that was trying to go to the villages instead of expecting the villages to come to it. This women's movement saw the necessity of mobilizing rural women . . . . That practical experience—the discovery of the villages—was the stepping stone for the Palestinians under Israeli military rule that proved to be crucial in developing a new movement, which is a movement of committees, the popular movement.[5]

Around the same time, the PLO became the driving force of the Palestinian national movement both inside and outside the occupied territories, gaining international legitimacy at the Rabat Conference in October 1974 and with Yasser Arafat's speech at the United Nations one month later. It adopted a new, transitional program calling for the establishment of a "Palestinian national authority in any Palestinian areas liberated from Israeli control," the embryo of the future Palestinian state.[6]

One of the PLO's objectives in the occupied territories was to forestall an attempt by Israel to implement an "administrative autonomy" scheme for which the occupation authorities needed pliable local Palestinian leaders. Through its local counterpart, the Palestine National Front, the PLO therefore encouraged efforts by Palestinian activists in the West Bank and Gaza to revive existing organizations and set up new ones, both as a counterbalance to the long-term designs of the occupation and as an infrastructure for the future independent state. The main idea was, in the words of Salim Tamari, that "when a Palestinian state arrives it will not arrive in a vacuum. It will already have an infrastructure of political and civic institutions to support it."[7]

Through the efforts of grassroots activists in the mid-1970s a generation of popular organizations was brought forth, ranging from voluntary work committees and student groups to trade unions, women's committees, medical and agricultural relief committees and, eventually, during the uprising, the more all-embracing popular committees. Their prime concern was to provide basic services to a population living under military occupation *as an alternative to the occupation,* all within the framework of Palestinian nationalism.[8] In the process they laid the groundwork for organized, institutional resistance to the occupation. This found its most articulate expression during the popular uprising in the late 1980s.

Trade unions formed an important part of this new generation of mass-based organizations. Some had survived from the British Mandate and the period of Jordanian control over the West Bank; others were set up in trades and locations where no unions had existed after 1967. The particular political and socio-economic context in the occupied territories lent the revived trade union movement the following idiosyncrasies, among others:

1. Both the migrant character of the labor force and the small size of Palestinian workshops in the territories caused unions to organize laborers in their places of residence rather than in their places of work, with the exception of those employed in the few large Palestinian companies and institutions. There is therefore a large number of small village-based unions in the West Bank, mostly "Construction and General Services Workers Unions," which recruit building workers and those employed irregularly in any trade, especially in Israel.

2. Because Palestinian unions cannot operate openly in Israeli workplaces on behalf of their members employed there, their activities remain limited to providing health insurance and legal services at reduced cost. For those employed in the territories, unions in addition negotiate collective agreements with employers concerning wages, benefits and working conditions.

3. Because of the military occupation which affects all Palestinians regardless of their economic position, unions have voluntarily "frozen" the class struggle and opted for a "national alliance" with employers. Considerable pressure is usually put on both workers and their employer in a labor dispute to reach a compromise solution. Moreover, because of the political situation, unions have placed great emphasis on political work in addition to their regular union activities on behalf of workers.

4. Because of the Israeli army's repression of any organizational activity, including trade union activity, in the occupied territories, unions have kept their leadership diffuse and easy to replace so that union activities could continue despite the frequent detention of union leaders.

5. The politicized nature of all grassroots activity in the territories, given the military occupation, has meant that divisions in the overall Palestinian national movement are strongly reflected in the labor movement in the West Bank and Gaza. In the 1980s, sharp divisions inside the national movement led to the emergence of three parallel trade union federations in the West Bank, after splits in the General Federation of Trade Unions in 1981 and 1985. Similarly, the move toward reconciliation among the various factions of the national movement during the eighteenth PNC in Algiers in April 1987 softened divisions between the various labor blocs in the West Bank, although no formal unity or reunification of the General Federation was achieved until March 1990.

The labor movement in the occupied territories thrived in the late 1970s and 1980s because of both the growth of a disenfranchised migrant labor force and the emergence of the PLO as the single representative and articulator of Palestinian national aspirations. To the extent that they were politicized at all, workers were imbued primarily with a nationalist rather than a socialist consciousness, although union leaders have espoused socialist views. Rather than a working class in the classic western sense of an industrial working class, the Palestinian workers constituted a nascent migrant-labor class with a primarily nationalist outlook and ideology. Through its activities, and given the conditions imposed by the military occupation, the organized representatives of this class, the Palestinian labor movement, became one of the pillars of the modern Palestinian national movement in the occupied territories.[9]

We now turn to an analysis of the role of the West Bank labor movement, as one segment of the popular national movement in the occupied territories, in laying the groundwork for the uprising that began in December 1987, by focusing on its main characteristics and contradictions.

2. Nationalism versus Trade Unionism

The nationalist orientation of trade unions in the West Bank and Gaza is not an accident or simply a function of the influence of the PLO over the lives of the Palestinians. The programs of the unions reflect the conditions under which they are forced to operate.[10] The prolonged military occupation has provoked unions, like other popular organizations, to articulate nationalist positions not just because they see themselves as representative organs of a particular section of the population, but also because workers experience the occupation in their everyday lives. In tracing the development of the working class, one of the union movements, the Workers' Unity Bloc, has stated:

> The occupied territories became annexed to the Israeli economy because they supplied cheap labor and constituted a consumer market for Israeli products preventing Arab commodities produced under severe competitive conditions from being sold. Consequently, the effects of the Israeli economic crisis (inflation and high prices) were reflected in the occupied territories, leading to an intensive exploitation and oppression of the working class, particularly those working in Israeli enterprises. So the working class suffered the most from occupation policy. Hence it badly needs and fights for the end of the occupation; it started to use its important role and influence among the ranks of the Palestinian people in the battle of liberation and national independence.[11]

An activist in one of the other union blocs, the Progressive Workers' Bloc, indicated what the implications are for the labor movement in an interview in 1985:

> Our main work is union work, but we believe that workers cannot get their rights as long as there is no independent Palestinian state . . . . That's why we are also involved in politics.[12]

In practice, this approach has meant a two-pronged effort to provide tangible services to workers while appealing to the workers' political sentiments. This combination has proven highly effective in recruiting workers to the labor movement, although both the impossibility of realizing political goals and inter-union quibbling have acted as constraints on the movement's growth.

In the territories themselves, as early as the late 1960s unions agreed to "freeze" the class struggle, opting instead for a "national alliance of classes" between workers and owners. The need for this alliance has been predicated on the belief that the occupation has distorted the structure of Palestinian society, erasing the dividing lines between the two main social protagonists while accentuating national oppression. Unionists have stressed, however, that within this alliance of classes, responsibilities should be distributed equitably. According to the WUB, "there can to some extent be negotiations with the national bourgeoisie. There can be compromise but not to the extent that everything will be loaded onto the workers' backs."[13] There is, in the words of another unionist, a "red line" which cannot be overstepped by employers.[14]

The uprising solidified this leitmotif of combined nationalism and trade unionism. However, during the early months of the uprising, the nationalist strand was accentuated as all normal activities were suspended and the Palestinian leadership, including its unionist elements, called on the masses to join in street demonstrations. The army's response, which included the shutdown of trade union offices, also temporarily precluded the continuation of regular trade union activities. As members of the general population, workers responded to appeals by the Unified National Command of the Uprising (UNCU), while many trade union leaders went underground, contributing to the direction of the uprising locally through the newly established popular committees. In Communique No. 2 of January 10, 1988, the UNCU addressed Palestinian workers, among others, promising: "Your prominent role in this comprehensive uprising is the best answer to the threats of the occupying troops and will defeat the policy of racial discrimination and constant oppression."[15] In Communique No. 3 of January 18, the UNCU praised workers for participating in a three-day general strike, and pointed to the specific role assigned to them during the uprising: "Let us paralyze the machine of Israeli production because enhancing the Israeli economic crisis is one of our weapons on the road to achieving our rights to return, to self-determination and to establish an independent state."

A few months into the uprising, the UNCU began the process of constructing the framework that would enable it to institutionalize and continue the uprising. Thus it alerted workers to the need to be organized as workers, so as to be more effective in carrying out the national tasks of striking and, increasingly, abandoning jobs on Israeli settlements in the territories and, when possible, in Israel itself. For example, in Communique No. 12 of April 2, workers were exhorted to "expand their workers' committees in their factories and in their places of residence, in order to organize themselves and consolidate their role in the struggle." In Communique 16 of May 13, workers were urged to "intensify the boycott against work in Zionist settlements and to refrain from giving any services to the settlers."

Toward the end of the first year of the uprising, the "national alliance of classes" was put to the test, and labor organizers were forced to re-focus on union activities as the economy took a sharp turn downward as a result of the commercial strike and Israeli economic punishments. As one unionist explained, Palestinian owners have claimed during the uprising that it is imperative that they stay in business in order to replace Israeli products with Palestinian ones, even if this takes place at the expense of the workers. In response, workers' committees and unions had to negotiate new agreements that reflected the conditions of the uprising.[16] One collective agreement that was being taken around workshops in the Ramallah area in December 1988 emphasized the need for workers and owners to work together in a "spirit of understanding and cooperation . . . in the framework of national interests." In January 1989, in the wake of the collapse of the Jordanian dinar, the UNCU (in Communique No. 33 of January 24) called on employers to raise their workers' wages by at least 40 percent, and urged workers' committees to enforce this demand.[17]

In summary, unions have carried out important trade union work throughout their existence. But they have been ready to suspend this type of work in times of emergency, and have at all times voluntarily tempered their struggle for the protection of workers' rights by their readiness to acknowledge and protect the interests of Palestinian owners who, like workers, were seen as economic victims of the military occupation.

3. The Formal versus Informal Nature of Trade Unions and Their Work

Israeli repression of Palestinian institutions and their leadership during the first decade of occupation motivated activists in the mid-seventies to build informal or semi-formal frameworks instead.[18] At the same time, the military authorities encouraged the informal nature of new Palestinian organizations by withholding licenses, apparently in an attempt not to confer legitimacy on them or grant them rights, however minimal, under the law. This was the case for student and voluntary work groups, as well as for the women's committees. Trade unions constitute a hybrid form. Those that existed before 1967 or were set up during the 1970s in most cases had or succeeded in obtaining a permit, since trade union organizations are provided for under the Jordanian labor law of 1965 which is applicable in the West Bank. Those unions, however, that were established from the late 1970s onward have generally been denied operating permits.[19] The majority of Palestinian trade unions in the West Bank do not therefore at present have a license.

Although trade unions are semi-legal and have operated informally, they developed strictly formal internal structures and regularly hold elections. Under the Jordanian labor law, any twenty or more workers in the same occupation or workplace may set up a trade union. Unions, in turn, may establish labor federations, which can affiliate with international union organizations.[20] According to West Bank unions' by-laws, card-carrying union members have the right to sit in the union's general assembly, which meets annually, or can be elected to the union council (the primary decision-making body) or to the executive committee.

The labor movement in the West Bank inherited a General Federation of Trade Unions (GFTU) from the period of Jordanian rule. New unions set up in the 1970s and 1980s applied for membership in the GFTU. Competition between the various union blocs, which are political tendencies within the labor movement, led to splits in the GFTU in 1981 and 1985. Between September 1985 and March 1990, there were three separate GFTUs, all using the same name. Unions have adhered to any one of the three federations, depending on which bloc dominated the particular union.[21]

Unions' activities have been of both a formal and informal nature. As long as they have operated in the West Bank and Gaza, they have been able to set up health insurance schemes and represent workers officially, in front of employers and in court. In addition, strikes have been organized openly by unions. In the Israeli workplace, however, Palestinian unions have no jurisdiction. They have therefore tended to operate indirectly through shop floor workers' committees. In the absence of effective Histadrut protection, especially in the case of undocumented workers, Palestinian strikes in Israel are usually spontaneous or organized informally and from a distance by Palestinian unions in the territories. Because of this, unions have experience in organizing workers informally, a skill that has proven useful during the uprising.

The closure of a large number of union offices and the detention of union activists by the Israeli military during the first months of the uprising forced the labor movement underground. In a number of cases, unions closed themselves down fearing punitive actions by the army.[22] Union activists joined the new popular committees and strike forces, temporarily forsaking regular union activities. In the village of Ya'bad in the Jenin area, for example, the local popular committee was reported to consist of "known village activists from the workers' union and youth groups in particular," although the committee itself was "a new formation, born of the uprising."[23]

Later during the uprising, union activities slowly began to resume, although still on an informal level. In late July 1988, workers at the Royal Crown Cola bottling plant in Ramallah organized a strike in protest against abuses of their rights in the first organized union activity since the beginning of the uprising. Negotiations took place informally at the plant, and were not coordinated from a union office. The strike was partially successful, even though the main organizer was promptly placed in administrative detention by the military authorities. Similarly, wage negotiations between workers and Palestinian employers that followed in the wake of the collapse of the dinar in early 1989 took place on an informal level, as most union offices remained closed. The three GFTUs continued operating, however minimally, limiting themselves to public relations exercises and receiving foreign trade union delegations.

Informal grass-roots activity, initiated in the 1970s and practiced throughout the 1980s, thus by necessity became a way of life during the uprising. This was as true for trade union work as it was for education following the closure of schools and universities. In the words of one union leader, "the important thing is not the university but the process of education: what the university can offer in terms of education despite its closure. For the union movement it is exactly the same."[24]

4. Factionalism versus Unity in the Popular Movement

Although the popular movement inside the occupied territories has its own characteristics, its main political trends copy currents in the overall Palestinian national movement. The differences between the various blocs are over political and strategic considerations concerning the national question more than methods of carrying out their day-to-day work in the territories. For example, four separate trade union blocs exist reflecting divisions in the national movement; on strictly trade union issues, however, they hardly differ from one another.

Relations between the political blocs in the popular movement have at times been difficult; depending on the overall political situation, or the occurrence of particular events like the war of the camps in Lebanon in 1987, blocs can be at complete loggerheads. Calls for unity, however sincere, therefore did not accomplish much prior to the uprising. In some organizations, divisions were more severe than in others, usually for historical reasons. For example, in the women's movement, a modicum of conviviality and cooperation has been possible, especially in cases of joint concerns, as in women's sit-ins protesting prisoners' hunger strikes. All four major women's committees were set up in a short period of about three years. They faced the same problems in recruiting women, and in the absence of an overarching federation, they did not have to work out differences within a single structure.

The trade union movement, on the other hand, has been racked by debilitating competition and schisms, with the various blocs each claiming to be the sole representative of the Palestinian working class. The reason probably lies in the fact that at the time of the revival of the labor movement in the mid-1970s, one trade union bloc already existed that had historically controlled the formal trade union structures and leadership. The appearance of new players on the stage was therefore seen by this bloc as a threat to its legitimacy and power, and many attempts were made, especially in the early 1980s, to prevent the new blocs from participating in existing unions and in the GFTU. This was done by barring the admission of new members to existing unions, and new unions to the GFTU, the latter in some cases on the pretext that the new unions did not have a license. The conflict led to the establishment of "parallel" unions in the same occupation, as well as to splits in the GFTU, in 1981 and 1985. Until March 1990, when the GFTU was reunified at least in name, three separate federations existed parallel to one another that did not recognize each other's legitimacy.[25]

Despite the strongly negative political atmosphere that prevailed in the territories from the mid-1970s until the mid-1980s as a result of factionalism, including attempts by Jordan to "buy" popular organizations and national institutions through selective but massive infusions of money, at least one commentator has argued that factionalism had the positive effect of spurring recruitment and therefore enhancing mass mobilization.[26] The truth is that despite the bitter feuds that have divided the political blocs, large sectors of the population were drawn into organizational frameworks in the 1980s, and these sectors were prepared to act collectively when called upon by a national leadership, as during the uprising.

The groundwork for cooperation during the uprising had been laid half a year before, during the 18th PNC in Algiers in April 1987. The admission of the Palestine Communist Party to the PLO and the fact that all major factions in the national movement chose to attend the session went a long way in reconciling blocs in the territories. According to Rashid Khalidi:

> This PNC session was numbered the 18th. This apparently innocuous fact signified the reunification of the historic factions and leaderships of the modern Palestinian national movement, after a split which lasted four years. It meant that all factions in attendance accepted the legitimacy of the 17th session in Amman, which many—notably the PFLP, the DFLP and the Palestine Communist Party—had boycotted. Besides Fatah, these are the only independent mass-based Palestinian organizations with a developed political infrastructure in both the occupied territories and the diaspora.[27]

Reunification in the PNC did not directly lead to reunification of grassroots organizations in the territories. Although calls were made to reunify the separate GFTUs, or at least two of them,[28] the labor movement remained divided on the organizational level.

During the first months of the uprising, popular committees replaced trade unions as effective organizational frameworks, representing all major factions present in the territories rather than a single one.[29] Later during the uprising, the UNCU called for the formation of separate workers' committees and the revival of trade unions, encouraging cooperation and unity. On the occasion of International Workers' Day 1988, the UNCU (in Communique No. 15 of April 30) called on workers to organize themselves and "to work for the unification of the labor movement." In Communique No. 19 of June 8, workers were urged to "complete the formation of unified workers' committees."

In practice, existing union structures remained as divided as ever during the uprising, even though workers stood side by side in non-unionist structures. In the words of one union leader:

> There is no agreement between the different factions. The absence of unity is a bureaucratic question. All unionists speak the same language, but it is a matter of control, of who wants to be the leader. Workers have no interest in divisions. On the shop floor they work together because *basic* issues are involved.[30]

However, on March 1, 1990, two of the three GFTUs announced their reunification, leaving two seats empty for representatives of the WUB, which did not immediately agree to join with them.

5. The Leadership versus the Base in Popular Organizations

Social processes in the occupied territories such as urbanization and education accelerated after the beginning of the Israeli occupation, marking the gradual erosion of traditional leadership structures. The power of local village notables, the *mukhtars,* was undermined by the migratory character of village labor, as young men employed in Israel or the Gulf returned to the native village with relative wealth. In addition, in many cases the *mukhtars* lost their legitimacy in the eyes of the population due to their association with either the Jordanian or Israeli regimes. In the towns, a new class of merchants and educated professionals challenged the power of traditional large families which had produced mayors and officials in the Turkish, British and Jordanian governments.[31]

The emergence of the PLO as the prime articulator of Palestinian aspirations on the international scene in the early 1970s hastened the eclipse of the traditional urban and village-based leaderships. Municipal elections in 1972 and especially 1976 brought to power an educated and fiercely nationalist leadership prepared to fight the PLO's political battle inside the occupied territories. Although this leadership clearly enjoyed mass support, the structures for active participation by the masses in decision-making did not yet exist.

The new orientation toward popular organizing in the mid-1970s therefore signaled a marked departure from existing political processes, and eventually generated an entirely new, broadly based level of leadership, which found its clearest expression in the popular uprising after 1987. Although the initiative for mass organizing came originally from university students and school children, one of the declared aims of the new generation of organizations was to mobilize the masses of the population, especially in the villages and refugee camps.[32] These organizations are highly decentralized, with branches extending throughout the West Bank and Gaza. Regular elections ensure representation of the branches in the central leadership. The leadership of mass organizations therefore increasingly derived directly from the masses themselves.[33]

Despite the emergence of the popular movement, leadership of the overall national movement in the territories remained, at least until the late 1980s, firmly in the hands of the urban elites who, in turn, deferred to the PLO leadership in the diaspora. Yet the trends set in motion in the mid-1970s—the growing strength of the masses through popular organizations, and the increasing relative weight of the Palestinian leadership in the territories over that in the diaspora—further crystallized during the popular uprising. The uprising firmly placed the initiative in Palestinian national decision-making with the PLO inside the territories, represented by the Unified National Command of the Uprising, although the PLO outside continued to play crucial political and diplomatic functions. Long-term changes heralded by the uprising are not yet fully visible, but the clandestine and diffuse nature of the UNCU (as opposed to the earlier Palestinian National Front and the National Guidance Committee), as well as the power of the popular committees and strike forces in setting local daily schedules for the uprising, are indications that the days of elite urban-based middle-class leadership in the occupied territories may have passed.

6. Repression versus Resistance in the Occupied Territories

In realizing its agenda of *de facto* annexation of the West Bank and Gaza, Israel faced the task of bringing an entire population to heel that was (1) foreign, and (2) directly hostile to Israel's perceived intentions. Military repression of the popular movement should be seen in this context. The dialectic of repression and resistance in the occupied territories has therefore had a holistic quality: this has been a struggle not merely between two political actors, but two populations. The rationale of army repression has therefore not been self-protection against individual acts of resistance, but attacks on the obstacle to integrating the territories into Israel, i.e., the Palestinian population itself.[34]

The methods used to realize this objective have been two-fold: (1) Economic and administrative strangulation, so as to "spirit out" the population in the Herzlian sense; and (2) The type of collective punitive measures that by their nature affect everyone, whether directly through actual imprisonment, or indirectly by instilling fear, since everyone by definition is "guilty" of obstructing Israeli objectives.[35] Repressive measures have been carried out on two levels: against the general population on one hand, and against its institutions and leadership on the other.

Generally, the population in the occupied territories has been denied the right to freedom of expression. Political organizations are banned, and formal publications are subjected to strict censorship. By declaring the territories a closed military area, the military authorities have effectively restricted the population's movement, and made it contingent on acquisition of a permit, which is given only upon proof of "good conduct." Curfews and economic punishments, like bans on marketing and exporting, are imposed on areas that challenge the occupation. All these punishments have been abundantly documented in the twenty-one years preceding the uprising and therefore do not need elaboration here.[36]

To prevent organized resistance by the hostile population to the occupation, the Israeli authorities have attempted to stamp out any local form of organizing, whether political or not. Since the authorities have been singularly incapable of forestalling the emergence of a Palestinian civil society, they have singled out Palestinian institutions and popular organizations for specific repressive measures. On an administrative level this has entailed delegitimation, (1) by withholding permits, forcing organizations to operate informally, thereby reducing their rights and leverage under the law; and (2) by temporarily closing institutions and offices, or banning organizations outright. On the level of membership, repression has consisted of harassment and intimidation in an effort to deter actual and potential activists from carrying out their work. On the level of the leadership, repressive measures have included arrests and administrative punishments (i.e., outside the military courts), including town arrest, administrative detention and deportation. All popular organizations have suffered from these measures since the beginning of the military occupation in 1967, in particular the student and labor movements.[37]

Palestinian resistance to the occupation has never simply been an expression of opposition to foreign rule, but also, more importantly, a method of survival.[38] In order to prevent the breakdown of Palestinian civil society and its socio-economic infrastructure, activists in the 1970s gave the impetus for the formation of popular organizations which aimed at (1) providing basic services to a population in need, and (2) mobilizing the population in order to ensure national survival, as part of a strategy of "institutional resistance." In the words of Salim Tamari:

> One aspect of this strategy of institution-building was . . . the notion of survival: until the Israelis withdraw, and they're going to be here for a long time, we need both the political will and the institutional fabric to help us survive these years of land confiscation, repression and deportation. This strategy of informal resistance, if you like, or institutional resistance, was actually far more successful than even its own designers envisioned. By the late 1970s it had established the complete political hegemony of Palestinian nationalism and the PLO as the single articulator of Palestinian aspirations.[39]

In light of the previous experience of Israel's repression of Palestinian attempts at institution-building, the popular organizations were nurtured in an informal sphere of semi-legality, with an amorphous, broad-based and largely invisible leadership that was easily replaced if arrested. More importantly, because the occupation had affected everyone from the very beginning, these organizations gained a truly mass membership, rendering army efforts to root them out futile.

This was the situation before the uprising. Events since December 1987 have demonstrated that the strategy of institutional resistance was extremely well-conceived. Although Israel's repression has increased many-fold during the uprising, it has also become increasingly less effective in accomplishing its long-term goal of bringing the population to heel. Telling symbols of the Palestinians' success in devising an effective response to the occupation and all it entails are the emergence and survival of the UNCU as a strong legitimate local leadership, the formation of active popular committees in all localities, and the ability to maintain regular communication between the various levels of leadership through periodically issued leaflets, whose contents are read and whose calls are observed by the population to the extent possible.

7. Conclusion

In a pamphlet distributed in the fall of 1988, one of the women's committees in the occupied territories, the Federation of Palestinian Women's Committees, claimed that the uprising constituted the "historical embrace" between the objective factor of forty years of occupation, dispossession and repression on the one hand, and the subjective factor of popular mobilization on the other: "The popular uprising was not the result of a one-day struggle, but it is the climax of continuous Palestinian struggle, a struggle rooted in and supported by political awareness and mobilization in popular committees, [mass] organizations, [labor] unions, etc."[40]

Such a claim constitutes a fair assessment of the antecedents of the uprising. As I have sought to demonstrate in this paper, a number of factors contributed to the emergence of a popular movement in the occupied territories in the 1970s that was able, by the late 1980s, to take the initiative inside the Palestinian national movement by virtue of its singular ability to lead and sustain a popular uprising beyond its first stages of wild euphoria. These factors include: a direct and immediate need to institutionalize the provision of basic services to the population as a strategy of survival; the mobilization of all sectors of society under the banner of Palestinian nationalism, encouraged by the Palestinian leadership in the diaspora; a blurring of class lines in the face of a common enemy whose policy of dispossession affected all; the need to operate informally to protect oneself against Israeli attacks on the Palestinian infrastructure; the Israeli repression itself, which by its quality of punishing all regardless of particular offenses committed provoked a collective response from the population; and reconciliation of the main factions inside the Palestinian national movement in 1987, a few months prior to the uprising.

The combination of performing real work at the grassroots of Palestinian society while appealing to Palestinian nationalist aspirations has proven to be dynamic, crystallizing into a strategy of informal, institutional resistance aimed at creating *faits accomplis* as alternatives to the facts being created by the occupier. The infrastructure of resistance that came about in turn succeeded in organizing, directing, sustaining and institutionalizing a popular uprising in the occupied territories so as to turn it into a new way of life in Palestinian society. It has marked an acceleration of the effort to provide alternatives to the Israeli reality, and made it possible, in 1988, to start the process of disengagement from the structures of occupation as a first stage in rolling back the occupation itself.

Notes

1. Interview, Jerusalem, June 6, 1985.

2. "An Interview with Rita Giacaman: Women, Resistance, and the Popular Movement," *Palestine Focus*, No. 24 (July-August 1987), p. 3.

3. See Mustafa Barghouti and Rita Giacaman, "The Emergence of an Infrastructure of Resistance: The Case of Health," draft manuscript, forthcoming in Jamal R. Nassar and Roger Heacock, eds., *Intifada: Palestine at the Crossroads* (New York: Praeger, 1990).

4. *Ibid.*

5. "An Interview with Rita Giacaman," *op. cit.*

6. See, for example, Helena Cobban, *The Palestinian Liberation Organization: People, Power and Politics* (Cambridge: Cambridge University Press, 1984). See also Ibrahim Dakkak, "Back to Square One: A Study in the Re-Emergence of the Palestinian Identity in the West Bank, 1967-1980," in Alexander Schölch, editor, *Palestinians Over the Green Line: Studies on the Relations Between Palestinians on Both Sides of the 1949 Armistice Lines since 1967* (London: Ithaca Press, 1983), pp. 64-101.

7. Salim Tamari, "What the Uprising Means," *Middle East Report*, No. 52 (May/June 1988), p. 26.

8. For an overview of the emergence of the popular movement in the two decades preceding the uprising, see Lisa Taraki, "The Development of Political Consciousness Among Palestinians in the Occupied Territories, 1967-1987," draft manuscript, forthcoming in Nassar and Heacock, *op. cit.*

9. For a detailed overview of the development of the labor movement in the occupied territories, see Joost R. Hiltermann, "Before the Uprising: The Organization and Mobilization of Palestinian Workers and Women in the Israeli-Occupied West Bank and Gaza Strip" (Ph.D. thesis, University of California at Santa Cruz, 1988: forthcoming from Princeton University Press, 1991).

10. A similar argument can be made for women's organizations in the territories, whose feminist agenda is limited and has as a rule been subordinated to the requisites of the nationalist struggle. See, for example, Rita Giacaman, "Reflections on the Palestinian Women's Movement in the Israeli-Occupied Territories" (unpublished paper, May 1987).

11. *Workers' Unity Bloc in the West Bank and Gaza Strip* (Workers' Unity Bloc, April 1985), p. 5.

12. Interview, Hebron, December 2, 1985.

13. Interview with a unionist, Ramallah, December 8, 1985.

14. Interview, Ramallah, November 2, 1985.

15. The UNCU, being a branch of the PLO, is a banned organization under Israeli military law, and its periodic communiques are therefore not publicly available. However, a number of the UNCU communiques cited in this essay have appeared in English translation in *Facts Weekly Review*, an underground weekly update of events relating to the uprising. In September 1988, a number of these reviews were included in a full-length report analyzing the uprising, entitled *Towards a State of Independence: The Palestinian Uprising, December 1987-August 1988*, published clandestinely in East Jerusalem.

16. Interview, Jerusalem, January 9, 1989.

17. For the activities of trade unions during the uprising, see Joost R. Hiltermann, "Work and Action: The Role of the Working Class in the Uprising," draft manuscript, forthcoming in Nassar and Heacock, *op. cit.*

18. See Taraki, *op. cit.*

19. See, for example, International Labor Office, "Appendix III: Report on the Situation of Workers of the Occupied Arab Territories," *Report of the Director-General* (Geneva: International Labor Organization, 1987), p. 34.

20. "Provisional Labor Law of the Hashemite Kingdom of Jordan (Law No. 21 of 1960)," *Official Gazette*, No. 1491 (May 21, 1960), Articles 68-9.

21. See Hiltermann, "Before the Uprising," *op. cit.*

22. At least 24 unions, in addition to one of the GFTUs, which itself housed 6 unions, have been closed down by the authorities since the beginning of the uprising. See Al-Haq, *Punishing a Nation: Human Rights Violations During the Palestinian Uprising, December 1987-December 1988* (Ramallah: Al-Haq, 1988), pp. 318-19.

23. Penny Johnson and Lee O'Brien with Joost Hiltermann, "The West Bank Rises Up," *Middle East Report*, No. 152 (May/June 1988), p. 12. One of the leaders of the union, Ahmad Kilani, was shot dead by the army on October 8, 1988.

24. Interview, Ramallah, December 15, 1988.

25. See Hiltermann, "Before the Uprising," Chapter 3.

26. Taraki, *op.cit.*

27. Rashid Khalidi, "PNC Strengthens Palestinian Hand," *Middle East Report*, No. 147 (July-August 1987), p. 38.

28. See, for example, the statements by two union leaders, each a deputy secretary-general in a GFTU, in the Palestinian press at the time of the 18th PNC: "Unionist Movement Should Unify Its Ranks to Contribute to National Struggle," *Al-Fajr Jerusalem Palestinian Weekly*, April 26, 1987.

29. Ironically, Fatah, which was never particularly interested in organizing Palestinians in frameworks such as trade unions, was strongly represented in the popular committees owing to the majority support it has enjoyed among the masses of the population.

30. Interview, Jerusalem, January 9, 1989.

31. See, for example, Joel S. Migdal, *Palestinian Society and Politics* (Princeton: Princeton University Press, 1980).

32. See Lisa Taraki, "Mass Organizations in the West Bank," in Naseer Aruri, editor, *Occupation: Israel Over Palestine* (Belmont, Mass.: Association of Arab-American University Graduates, 1989), pp. 431-63.

33. In the cases of the labor and women's movements, see Hiltermann, "Before the Uprising," *op. cit.*, Chapters 3 and 4, respectively.

34. For a more detailed analysis, see Joost R. Hiltermann, "Human Rights and the Palestinian Struggle for National Liberation," *Journal of Palestine Studies* (Winter 1989), pp. 109-18.

35. For economic policy, see Brian van Arkadie, *Benefits and Burdens: A Report on the West Bank and Gaza Strip Economies Since 1967* (Washington and New York: Carnegie Endowment for International Peace, 1977); Antoine Mansour, *Palestine: Une économie de résistance en Cisjordanie et à Gaza* (Paris: Editions L'Harmattan, 1983); Sarah Graham-Brown, "The West Bank and Gaza: The Structural Impact of Israeli Colonization," *MERIP Reports*, no. 74 (January 1979), pp. 9-20; and the various reports published by Meron Benvenisti's West Bank Data Base Project. For military repression, see Raja Shehadeh, *Occupier's Law: Israel and the West Bank* (Washington, DC: Institute for Palestine Studies, second edition 1988), and the various reports published by Al-Haq in Ramallah.

36. See note 35, *supra.*

37. For a detailed account of repression of popular organizations, see Joost R. Hiltermann, "Mass-Based Organization in the West Bank and Gaza: Offering Services Because of and Despite the Military Occupation" forthcoming in Emma Playfair, editor, *The Administration of Occupied Territories* (Oxford: Oxford University Press, 1991).

38. This idea has been elaborated most recently by Barghouti and Giacaman, *op. cit.*

39. Tamari, *op. cit.*

40. "Women in the Uprising," undated pamphlet distributed by the Federation of Palestinian Women's Committees in the fall of 1988.

4 THE EVOLUTION OF THE POLITICAL ROLE OF THE PALESTINIAN WOMEN'S MOVEMENT IN THE UPRISING*

Islah Abdul Jawwad

Since its inception in the early twenties of this century, the Palestinian women's movement has been a product of the nationalist movement that emerged in response to the idea of creating a Jewish National Home in Palestine. From its early stages, the movement has been influenced by Palestinian political life and been part of it. The movement followed a peaceful and reformist path of struggle against the British Mandate policy toward the Arabs and focused on putting an end to colonialist domination. Its class nature was similar to that of the leadership of the Palestinian national movement under the Mandate, and was limited to women from upper urban classes. This influenced the nature of the roles they played. They saw social change in charitable form, or as a matter of the rich helping the poor. Thus, women operated through various charitable organizations, by providing aid to needy families, putting competent girls through the school system, and by providing childhood and maternity services.

At the political level, some members of the women's charitable organizations participated in some of the demonstrations in the cities on national occasions, such as those held in February 1920 and March 1921.[1] The women's role became increasingly visible with the intensification of conflicts between the Palestinians and the vanguards of the Jewish immigrants. In the Aqsa conflict (the Buraq incident) in August 1929, nine women villagers were killed by the British soldiers. This led to the creation of the Arab Ladies Committees in 1929. The creation of these committees was considered a major development, since it formally organized women's political activities. Nevertheless, women were generally kept out of existing political organizations and parties due to segregation between genders and the social unacceptability of mixing between the two sexes. This was reflected in the nature of women's participation in the public demonstrations, where they used to be surrounded by boy scouts or put in the rear of demonstrations, behind the men, for protection.

---

* Translated and edited by Ibrahim Ali.

Despite the increase in the number of women's demonstrations and conferences after 1933 and during the 1936-39 Revolt, women's activities in general were limited to women from narrow sectors of the urban rich, students, and some villagers. They frequently helped in transporting arms and food or in contributing with their jewelry for the purchase of arms. This kind of participation was spontaneous and without supervision or organization by any party or women's organization.

After the setback of 1948, when the war had uprooted thousands of Palestinians from their villages and cities and led to the emergence of the refugee camps, many Palestinians were driven to join the ideological Arab nationalist or Marxist parties. Palestinian women were not detached from these trends. They joined the existing secret political parties, especially in Jordan, where the largest Palestinian population in the diaspora had taken refuge. Thus, some Palestinian women joined the Jordanian Communist Party, the Ba'ath, and the Arab Nationalist Movement. This new kind of militant woman functioned through mixed political parties, in contrast to the previous situation, where women's activities were pursued through women's societies. Nevertheless, these political parties paid little attention to the question of women's liberation. Women's activities within these parties did not go beyond the recruitment of new female members, or talking in general terms about equality between men and women, and there were no specific programs for women.

Despite the fact that these political parties were mixed, most of them created special cells for women as an extension of the prevalent segregation between the two genders. In most cases, women were assigned secretarial duties and services like typing leaflets, carrying letters, collecting signatures, and the distribution of leaflets.[2] Most female members were recruited from among the students or the educated. Female membership was unstable and subject to the woman's social circumstances. Secrecy and government crackdowns were factors impeding the deep expansion of political activity among women in refugee camps or the poor neighborhoods.

The significance of women's participation in these parties lay in the training of a number of women cadres who played an important role in confronting the Israeli occupation after the 1967 war. The creation of the General Union of Palestinian Women in 1965 came as a major step forward in the political organization of Palestinian women. It provided women with an alternative to joining the charitable organizations or to individual involvement in political parties. Nevertheless, several factors restricted its effectiveness among women.

One of these was the crackdown by the Jordanian authorities on activists, which forced them to resort to semi-secret activities. Another factor was the prevalence of a tendency focusing on propaganda and public relations, due to the leadership of women from the urban middle class and previous activists in charitable organizations and women's unions. Nevertheless, the Union confirmed the Palestinian identity of Palestinian women. It became "a base for mass organization" in the PLO, declaring its mission as "the liberation of the usurped homeland."[3]

The 1967 Defeat

The defeat of the Arab armies in 1967 played an important role in enhancing the popularity of the Fatah movement as a "revolutionary alternative" and as a mass organization relying on "armed people" rather than the conventional armies. In spite of the ambiguity and the generality of the slogans raised then, they drew attention to the need to mobilize the potential of all Palestinian social classes and sectors. Leftist political parties, in particular, paid attention to the mobilization of women.

Nevertheless, none of the Palestinian political organizations, despite the difference in their views regarding women's questions, articulated any gender agenda for women to be part of the general agenda of the revolution. They only repeated general slogans like "women will only be liberated by the liberation of society," or "men and women side by side in the battle."[4] This was reflected in the representation of women in PLO institutions since the beginning. Attention was focused on female students and the educated to attract them towards political and military activities. The image of women as military cadres was projected as the highest form of struggle.

Palestinian women played a revolutionary role in confronting the Israeli occupation immediately after 1967, through the expanding channel of the General Union of Palestinian Women and through the charitable organizations. Both were in direct contact with the first National Guidance Committee.[5] This Committee was established in early 1968 to lead the struggle of the Palestinian people inside the occupied territories until it was dissolved in 1969. The practices of the occupation, such as collective arrests of men, administrative detention, and the humiliation of people, particularly males, had led many women to protest such practices. An Israeli policy of leniency with women in the first years of the occupation soon changed owing to the increase of women's involvement in the resistance. In 1967, only ten women were arrested and a number were fined. The number of female prisoners in 1968 reached 100 and kept increasing in the following years. Most of the charges which women faced were contacts with Palestinian commandos, hiding weapons, agitation against the occupation, and/or affiliation with armed organizations.

With the increase in the number of female prisoners, which reached 3,000 by 1979,[6] it became clear that there were two forces attracting women and pushing them toward joining the resistance. The first consisted of the various political organizations that worked among women individually to recruit them for military operations, transportation of arms, and carrying letters. The second included the charitable organizations and/or the General Union of Palestinian Women, whose activities concentrated on the media, strikes, demonstrations, and delivering letters of complaint to foreign consulates. Both forces lacked specific gender agendas for women or previous knowledge of their situation. They focused on general national slogans calling for the end of occupation and for independence, and demanding that more women join the resistance.

The formation of the National Front in August 15, 1973 helped to expand women's participation for several reasons:

1. The presence of a woman in the leadership of the front.
2. The presence of young and radical elements in the leadership.
3. New methods for mobilizing women, like voluntary work camps.
4. The circulation of news concerning the heroism of Palestinian women prisoners who remained steadfast under torture in Israel prisons (e.g. Amina Dahbur, who got a 12-year sentence in 1969, and Rasmiyyeh Audeh, who received a life sentence in 1969 until she was deported in 1979).

All of these things had an important impact on changing the traditional views of society toward women as being weak creatures incapable of surviving the burdens of political activities and their problems.

The various political factions provided moral and political support for women prisoners to mitigate the effects of their arrest on their families by highlighting the heroism of their daughters to boost the pride of their families. This attitude helped in creating various examples of heroic women who gained the attention and the respect of society, which mitigated the pain of torture and molestation in prison.

Starting from 1978, a new force emerged, led by women with political affiliations who were armed with their experience inside

Israeli prisons and inside political parties. Most of them had a clear ideological affiliation with leftist parties who saw extending help to women not as an end in itself, as it is in charitable organizations, but as a means of changing women's consciousness of themselves and their positions in society. This view began to materialize after 1978 with the appearance of four different women's organizations: the Women's Action Committee in 1978, the Committee of Working Women in 1980, the Committee of Palestinian Women, and the Women's Committee for Social Work in 1982.

The literary production of Sahar Khalifeh, Khadija Abu Ali, Ghazi al-Khalili, *al-Dayariq* (a magazine), and the theater group "Cinema," all emphasized the role of women in the resistance and the necessity of social change. In addition, the atmosphere of political escalation which prevailed in the West Bank and Gaza after the success of the nationalist blocs in the 1976 elections helped to permeate the women's committees. In those elections, women had acquired the right of voting for the first time. From among 32,548 eligible to vote, 21,948 actually participated in the elections (approximately 67. 5 percent).[7] This participation helped the nationalist blocs to win the elections and led to the defeat of the conservatives and moderates. The elections guaranteed the failure of any autonomy plan as an alternative to Palestinian political independence. Furthermore, they helped to show the inability of the leadership of women's charitable organizations to organize large numbers of women. They underlined the necessity to create a new women's movement that linked the national struggle and feminist social questions.

This idea was encouraged by the strategic approach of the major factions in the PLO, which emphasized the creation of large mass organizations for the mobilization of students, professionals, and women. The new form of organization is very hard to destroy, in contrast to the previous forms, which relied upon a limited number of cadres and national figures who enjoyed the support of the masses without having any organized bases to mobilize the people against the occupation.

With the emergence of the various new women's groups, whose programs are largely similar, there appeared a new caliber of women leaders from different social origins. The main measure of their influence was ideological affiliation with a political faction and not their family origin or relationship with political notables. They had entered politics under more flexible conditions for membership (such as attending meetings, acceptance of an organization's goals, and participation in decision-making).

Different Programs

Although one of the reasons for forming the various organizations was to establish a link between the national struggle and the question of social liberation for women, the committees used their various centers for political means and not for women's education. The linkage was not translated into detailed social programs. Demands for women's liberation were limited to calls for equality between men and women in general, sometimes taking a specific form, like equal payment and the improvement of women's conditions in the work place. It is important to stress that in spite of the lack of the formulation of social programs for women, questions relevant to the status of women, the reasons for their inferior position in Palestinian society, and the necessity for creating a new consciousness to change this position were discussed. Such questions were often raised in the internal meetings of the various feminist groups. The internal leaflets and publications which were circulated among the members of various women's organizations, regularly in most cases, played a very important role in this respect.

In general, it is possible to say that the emergence of a feminist framework can be considered a qualitative change in the evolution of the political role of Palestinian women's movements. This change is particularly important in terms of the increase in the number of women cadres inside the nationalist movement. Practical feminist achievements have been difficult due to the prevalence of the nationalist question. However, with the expansion of the nationalist struggle during the uprising, it is important to emphasize that the presence of social feminist consciousness will become one of the important factors which will prompt feminist leaders to publicly demand the articulation of social programs to improve the social conditions of Palestinian women.

The Evolution of The Political Role of Palestinian Women

Palestinian women participated intensively in the uprising from its early days. As mentioned earlier, it was not new for Palestinian women to play a political role in society, especially in times of crisis. The change lay in the extent of this role and its diversity, which included demonstrations, building road blocks, participation in various popular committees, the preparation and the transfer of stones, raising the Palestinian flag, and preventing the arrest of young men. These kinds of activity were first performed in the refugee camps and the poor neighborhoods in cities. They were characterized by a degree of violence that reached the level of physical confrontation between the army and women demonstrators.

The first communique that appeared in Gaza indicated the extent of participation by women. The communique aspired to direct their role, and called for its continuation. The communique, distributed in Gaza on December 16, 1987, was signed under the name of the "National Forces in Gaza Strip." It urged women, children, the young and the elderly in every refugee camp, village, and city to participate in the peaceful funeral on December 16 to commemorate the first week of the murder of the four Gaza workers whose killing caused the uprising. These demonstrations soon spread to include the villages and the cities of the West Bank. They were accompanied by the appearance of similar communiques signed under the name of "The Unified National Command" (UNC). Their purpose was to organize the resistance in the West Bank and Gaza.

What is noticeable in these communiques is that women were called upon to participate in all capacities. This became a permanent part of the text of subsequent communiques.

Specific leaflets for women began to appear after January 10, 1988. On that day, a leaflet with a general political nature, signed by the four women's organizations, was distributed. It called upon women to participate more fully. However, until March 8, 1988, International Women's Day, an overt gender agenda for women had not yet been articulated by the various women's organizations. This matter was left to the leaflets of the UNC of the uprising. Women's organizations followed the various instructions in these leaflets like everybody else. Their activities involved demonstrations, strikes, and political rallies. The number of demonstrations reached 115 each week in the West Bank and Gaza. By March 8, 1988, the date of the first overt gender agenda for women, 16 women of various ages had been killed.[8]

A New Gender Agenda

The leaflet signed under the name of "Palestinian Women in the Occupied Territories" on March 8, 1988 can be considered the first serious effort by the Palestinian women's leadership to develop a gender agenda. It directly addressed women by appealing "to the large masses of heroic women, e.g., the mothers of martyrs and detainees and the wounded, their wives, their sisters, their daughters, and all women of our people in all refugee camps, villages, and cities of Palestine who are united in confronting the policies of oppression and terror." The leaflet emphasized the appreciation of the new quality of women's participation by mentioning "all of our sisters in the smoke of battle, where all theories against women have been burned." This leaflet specified the following various forms of participation which women should follow:

1. Participation in various popular committees in the neighborhoods, villages, cities, and refugee camps in order to escalate the uprising.

2. Helping with the collection of funds.

3. Joining labor unions in order to increase their coordination with workers, and the boycott of work during the general strike days.

4. Calling upon women teachers in particular to confront the policy of de-education and the closure of learning institutions, by participating in popular alternatives for education.

5. Urging mothers in all locations to prevent the arrest of young men by considering any man arrested or injured as one of their sons and trying to rescue him.

6. Calling upon women to develop the concept of home economy by producing food and clothes locally as a step toward a total boycott of the products of the occupation.

If we analyze this program, some observations can be made about the two most important demands concerning activities of women, the popular committees and the home economy.

The Popular Committees

The formation of the popular committees at the beginning of March 1988 came as a direct response to collective punishments that burdened the daily life of the people. Such punishments were represented by the closure of markets, isolation of villages and cities from each other, the closure of stores for the whole day, and the closure of all schools. Generally speaking, women in the cities responded positively to the invitation to participate in the various popular committees, especially the committees of agriculture, education, food, and health.

Was this participation a mere assignment of women by men, or was there women's participation in decision-making and in specifying the assignments? Were these committees means of changing the structure of political, economic, and social authority, or only means of expanding the sphere of the mass political organizations?

To answer these questions, it is necessary to discuss the way the committees were formed. Usually, the initiative was made in city neighborhoods—especially Ramallah, al-Bireh, Jerusalem, Bethlehem, and Beit Sahur—by a small number of cadres among the active and politicized young men and women. The primary consideration in those committees was the political affiliation and the level of education of members, which mostly prevailed over sexual differences.

Differences in political affiliation often led to an authoritarian tendency for decision-making to become concentrated in the hands of men with political affiliations. The main driving force behind the formation of the popular committees was the expansion of the sphere of influence of the various mass political organizations. Moreover, the Israeli authorities outlawed the popular committees in their embryonic stage, thus preventing participation in them with the accompanying experience.

The popular committees in the refugee camps and villages were mostly composed of young males. Their secret meeting places, in coffee shops and mosques, made it difficult for women to participate. This is due to the prevalence of more conservative traditions restricting mixing between genders in the villages.

It is difficult to answer the question of whether the committees played an important role in changing the position of women by allowing them more participation or by reeducating them to eliminate the social obstacles facing them. Nevertheless, the expansion of the sphere of influence of each mass political organization and the increase of its membership were clearly the primary objectives of the committees. The role of women remained an extension of their traditional roles in such fields as education and social services. There does not appear to have been much difference in this respect between committees dominated by leftist or rightist elements.

The Home Economy

Instead of focusing on the different meanings of the concept of the home economy, it is important to emphasize that its main objective was to minimize the consumption of Israeli products, particularly where there was a local substitute. This usually meant attempting to reach the highest level of self-sufficiency, and returning to the land through adopting the "family farm" in order to create a more self-sufficient family economy, through the wide participation of women. What is important is that the national leadership and feminist leaders realized that women have an important role in the success of this objective and in the support of "positive steadfastness" until independence.

Was the role which women were asked to fulfill a new one or not? The answer is contained in one of the women's publications, which reads "The reactionary nature of the home economy can be eliminated from the framework of serving reaction into the framework of serving the progressive, by transforming it into other forms outside the home like women's cooperatives."[9] The feminist leadership actively began to create various forms of cooperatives so as to find new methods of productive work for women, and consequently minimize dependency on the market and curb its role in controlling mass resistance.[10]

These kinds of cooperatives took two forms. The first concentrated on attracting women to work outside their homes in their free time. This kind of work provided them with income in a context in which women were in control of production, marketing and the administration of their cooperatives.

The second form encouraged various groups of women to produce foodstuffs inside their homes. These cooperatives sought to change the position of women, but not at the expense of their home duties.

Demonstrations

The role of women trying to "rescue" males from arrest gained prominence over other roles played by women. Because it was practiced very often, examples of female courage emerged and were given a lot of attention by various women's organizations. The result was the development of a new kind of female role model. In the beginning of the Palestinian women's movement (during the 1930s), female role models were represented by the "ladies" of society. Later, and in the beginning of the resistance, the role models were as "sisters of men" or as the mothers of martyrs. It was made clear in the gender agenda of March 8, 1988, however, that the role of women should be a more dynamic one. The mere fact that a woman was a mother or a sister of a martyr or a detainee should give her more incentives to act and demonstrate and confront soldiers to prevent them from committing atrocities.

Many heroic titles pertaining specifically to women started to appear, like al-Harbajiyya (warrior) and Hubub al-Rih (the fast wind), which was the title of Manal Samura, who was killed in the Shatti' Refugee Camp on October 25, 1988.

Palestinian women have played a very important role in mobilizing the people, in general, and young males, in particular, to participate in demonstrations. It is now very hard to find a general demonstration without women in the front, despite the restrictions that prevent a lot of girls from participating publicly. This can be considered a major political development.

Women's participation during the 1920s was limited to small groups of women going in their private cars to join a march where they were surrounded by boy scouts to protect them from mixing with men. In contrast, women now take part in mixed demonstrations in accordance with the directives of the Unified National Leadership. In many cases the demonstrations are started by women to protect men and not vice versa.

The regular participation of women in the various demonstrations at the funerals of martyrs in the villages and camps had an important effect on political awareness. This is reflected in the slogans raised by women at the funerals. For instance, during a funeral in Kufr Ne'ama near Ramallah in February 2, 1988, women immediately made a circle to lament the martyr in accordance with the traditions in the villages. A woman soon voiced the slogan "with our soul, with our blood we sacrifice for you, our martyr," followed by others. The funeral was turned into a huge women's demonstration.

The participation of women in demonstrations has also played a very important role in changing the concept of woman's honor.[11]

The Palestinian Women's Movement

Most women activists involved in the *intifada* aimed at linking the national struggle against the occupation to the question of women's liberation.[12] However, most of the questions related to women's liberation related to the issue of the rights of working women, or the creation of projects for the vocational training of women to enable them to become active and productive workers.[13] Despite the fact that some leaflets and publications addressed social problems like divorce, control over women's income, and the position of women at home,[14] the Palestinian women's movement does not yet have a complete gender agenda. There is a feeling that the articulation of a full program can be postponed until a later stage, when the "articulation of individual status laws will be ready in the period following independence."[15] Thus, we find feelings of certainty that Palestinian women will gain legal rights after independence.

Several factors, however, raise doubts about whether this feeling of certainty is justified. The Palestinian women's movement is a product of the Palestinian nationalist movement. Its political participation during the present stages of national evolution therefore makes it a hostage to the positive and negative developments in the political leadership of the movement. This is reflected in the division of the Palestinian women's movement into four parts parallel to the prevalent division in the leadership of the Palestinian nationalist movement. There is an absence of social content in the Palestinian national liberation movement, which is particularly apparent in the theoretical direction of the largest political organization, Fatah.

One of the most important theoretical texts which governs the actions of the Fatah movement reads, "The Palestinian nationalist movement in its regional framework represents a stage of liberation for a people who lost their social and political being, and so no longer have a problem of peasants and workers, because the peasants and the workers are no longer part of the class hierarchy of the Palestinian society which was destroyed by the diaspora." A similar sense that there is no real division between the interests of Palestinian women and men has dominated Fatah's attitude toward women's issues. Another factor affecting the future of the women's movement has been the emergence of political forces with an Islamic ideology inside the West Bank and Gaza.[16] The role of women, as seen by these forces, is at home and in natural reproduction. These forces do not object to the education of women. In the charter of the Islamic Liberation Movement (Hamas), we read the following under the title of "The Armed Woman," article 17: "The armed woman in the war of liberation has a role not less significant than that of the man, since she is a maker of men. Her role in guiding generations and educating them is a very big one." The educating of generations in this context is linked to the religious pillars such as studying the Holy Book and the Sunna. We can also learn from the practices of Islamic forces in other Muslim countries that the status of women and the laws that govern family relations are heavily emphasized in the programs of Islamic movements.[17]

The position of the Palestinian feminist movement is that women's liberation can be achieved by the future leadership of the Palestinian state, as a reward for the role which women have played in the national struggle. It is ironic that the movement aspires to this objective while feminist consciousness is very weak and while the vast majority of women prefer a division of labor between genders, as a result of an education and upbringing which makes it seem normal.

Notes

1. "Al-Haraka al-Nasawiya" (The Women's Movement), in *Al-Mawsu'a al-Filastiniya* (Palestinian Encyclopedia), Part 2, p. 211. The encyclopedia is published in Damascus by the Palestinian Encyclopedia Committee.

2. Khadija Abu Ali, *Muqaddima Hawl Waqi' al-Mar'a wa Tajrubataha fi al-Thawra al-Filastiniya* (Introduction to the Reality of the Experience of Women in the Palestinian Revolution), Beirut: General Union of Palestinian Women, 1975, pp. 44, 54-55.

3. Maysun al-Wahidi, *Al-Mar'a al-Filastiniya wa al-Ihtilal al-Isra'ili* (The Palestinian Woman and the Israeli Occupation), Jerusalem: Arab Studies Society, 1986, pp. 8-9.

4. Ghazi al-Khalili, *Al-Mar'a al-Filastiniya wa al-Thawra* (The Palestinian Woman and the Revolution), Beirut, 1977, p. 133.

5. The president of the General Union of Palestinian Women, Zalikha al-Shihabi, was deported on September 6, 1968. She was later allowed to return for humanitarian reasons.

6. Soraya Antonius, "Femmes prisonnières pour la Palestine," *Revue d'Etudes Palestiniennes*, (Paris), No. 1 (automne 1981).

7. Moshe Maoz, *Al-Qiyadat al-Filastiniya fi al-Difa al-Gharbiya* (The Palestinian Leadership in the West Bank and Gaza), p. 39. Here we have to observe the differences between the communiques of the uprising and those issued earlier by the National Committees or the Arab Higher Committee, which usually addressed males without any mention of women.

8. *Toward a State of Independence: The Palestinian Uprising, December 1987-August 1988* (Jerusalem: Facts Information Committee, 1988), pp. 147, 159-162.

9. See the leaflet, *Al-Intifada Mustamirra* (The Intifada Continues), a one-time publication by the Union of Palestinian Women's Committees, March 1988.

10. *Ibid.*

11. In many cases the Israeli soldiers used to show their sexual organs and make degrading gestures in order to humiliate women.

12. *Tatawwur al-Haraka al-Nasawiya al-Falastiniya* (the Evolution of the Palestinian Women's Movement), published by the Palestinian Federation of Women's Action Committees (n.d.) p. 12.

13. *Ibid.*

14. See, e.g., the publications "Kifah al-Mar'a," "Tariq al-Mar'a","Nidal al-Mar'a","Sawt al-Mar'a," and "Darb al-Mar'a," published by the Federation of Women's Action Committees in various years. See also the publications of the General Union of Palestinian Women.

15. The representative of the Federation of Women's Action Committees in a symposium held at Birzeit University on the Palestinian Women's Movement in January 1989.

16. The Islamic forces were involved in the distribution of communiques parallel to those of the UNC of the uprising, both at the political level and at the level of women's

issues. It is difficult for women in Gaza to go out without covering their heads. If their heads are not covered they are threatened with punishments which could include the throwing of acid at their faces.

17. Fuad Zakariya, "Mawqif al-Jama'at al-Islamiya al-Mu'asira min Qadiyat al-Mar'a" (The Attitude of Contemporary Islamic Movements to the Women's Question), a chapter in *Al-Tahadiyat allati Tuwajih al-Mar'a al-'Arabiya fi-Nihayat al-Qarn al-'Ishrin* (The Challenges Confronting Arab Women at the End of the Twentieth Century), Cairo: Manshurat Tadamun al-Mar'a al-'Arabiya, September 1986.

5 THE POLITICS OF CULTURAL REVIVAL

Hanan Mikhail Ashrawi

When a national culture faces the threat of annihilation, distortion or absorption—as has been the case with the culture of colonized nations—it runs the risk of resorting to one of two opposing extremes for self-preservation. The assertion of authenticity may lead to a reactionary, xenophobic defensive stance. This reaction tends to convolution and self-absorption generally expressed in revivalism (of folklore, folkgeist, heritage), super-nationalism (in symbols, signs, focus) and exclusive purism (in linguistic structures and forms as well as in perceptions and concerns). Such a protective impulse toward the indigenous as an end unto itself is countered by another extreme reaction which views universality as an escape from the confines of the particular, modernism as a response to revivalism, and foreignization as an antidote to chauvinistic nationalism. Cultural escapism, with its inherent loss of identity or emulation of the conqueror/oppressor culture, is sometimes perceived as the ultimate defeat of the national spirit. Defensiveness, on the other hand, signals an alarming weakness in the self-perception of a culture and its capacity for endurance.

At one time or another, the Palestinian experience has exhibited symptoms of both extremes in its response to Israeli attempts at negating Palestinian national and cultural identity. A significant and self-sustaining level of Palestinian self-consciousness and confidence has been achieved as a qualitative outcome of the cumulative history of the Palestinian people. The cultural expression of the Palestinian people has always been inextricably interwoven with political realities and developments, embodying a dialectic of change and development directly proportional to its objective context. It has simultaneously become part of the momentum for resistance and transformation, as well as an expression of (or a semiotic reference for) developments on the ground. Consequently, the *intifada,* coming as a result of the cumulative history of resistance of the Palestinian people everywhere, has developed a culture which is both an expression of its own uniqueness and an inseparable component of its own process of resistance and social/political transformation. As a period of acceleration and condensation, the *intifada's* motivation, velocity, and compression of experience have become the salient characteristics of the Palestinian *intifada* culture. In this context, the term "revival" is perhaps only partially applicable to the cultural components of the *intifada,* most appropriately in its suggestion of renewed vigor or revitalization. The term "politics" is relevant both to the self-perception and objectives of Palestinian culture as a force of commitment and transformation.

The most noticeable quality of contemporary Palestinian culture is its emergent nature. Like Palestinian society (and reality as a whole) it is in a state of being or becoming, its forms and substance emerging from the particularity of its conditions. As such, it is neither static nor completed, but primarily dynamic in its search for the fullness of action and expression to enhance, capture, and convey the process of the *intifada* itself. The literature of the *intifada,* in its constant experimentation and search, in its constant awareness of the changing nature and the mutability of its structures and modes, consciously articulates its perception of its emergent role as unfolding within the quest of the *intifada* itself:

. . . The grinding, searing daily event; the lucid, flowing blood, the naked, blazing stone; the glorious, obstinate barricade; and the sacred flag—all are juxtaposed with the word: faithful, despite its sorrow; joyful, despite its wound; opening its windows wide, in spite of the smoke and haze, releasing its secrets in defiance of the truncheons and the siege—so that we may all arrive at the gate of our approaching collective chant.[1]

At the same time, Palestinian theater, music, art and other cultural activities persist in showing their wholeness in a state of dynamic change, with the same intensity and concentration that is distinctive of the *intifada* as a process of revolution and transformation. Consequently, they display a focus of immersion rather than the perspective of distancing, and the action of involvement rather than the contemplation of implications and significance. In contemporary Palestinian theater, for example, it is difficult to distinguish between the substance of the play and the actions taking place in the street,[2] while in the popular songs of "commitment," the lyrics and melodies are no more than extensions of the chants and popular slogans of demonstrations and other collective acts of resistance.[3]

The popular nature of these cultural activities necessarily lays a greater emphasis on their informal and collective tone, at once reflecting the democratic, grass-roots nature of the *intifada* and reinforcing its spirit of unity and cohesion. The individual voice is conspicuously absent from all forms of cultural expression and discourse unless it conveys a collective significance rather than a narrow personal focus. In addition, there is a clear aversion from the "elitist" forms and expressions of culture in favor of a more "mass-oriented," communal sub-culture. Not only should this activity be physically, financially, and intellectually accessible to the public as a whole; it should also be perceived as actively relevant to the *intifada* and its objectives.[4] Here, commitment to the national cause and assertion of national identity have become the basic components and goals of cultural activities and the acid test of their "relevance." Frivolity and levity are viewed as serious distractions and diversions which may undermine the "earnestness," the seriousness of intent and endeavor which characterize the *intifada*. Thus, humor is admissible primarily as satire, satire being the tool which is capable of disarming the enemy and negating the component of fear on the part of the oppressed and power on the part of the oppressor.[5]

Popular culture further expresses the austerity of Palestinian life under occupation. Severe economic restrictions have been imposed on the population as a whole as a form of collective punishment and pressure. Consequently, the Palestinians of the *intifada* have had to survive on a subsistence level which leaves no room for "luxuries'" (however modest) and social trimmings. While the *mahr* (the dowry) has been reduced to a minimum, all public celebrations have been curtailed if not altogether eliminated. Feasts are limited only to religious rites, while weddings and other social festive occasions have become modest and private affairs. Since these traditionally formed the occasions and outlets for the expression of popular folk-culture, alternative outlets have had to be devised in a distinctly more politicized context.[6] By necessity also, austerity has been extended to the manner of presentation and the cost of participation in these activities.[7] Furthermore, with the closure of movie-theaters and all other forms of public entertainment, formal, organized cultural events have been concentrated in East Jerusalem (mainly in Al-Nuzha El-Hakawati Center). On the other hand, Israeli closure of all institutions— academic, social, cultural, and professional—has further deprived the Palestinians of their traditional formal venues and outlets for cultural self-expression, thus contributing directly to the process of popularization and democratization of the cultural event as it seeks expression in less structured and more mass-based popular activities— many of which have remained underground.[8]

Inevitably, the creation of alternative or appropriate means of cultural self-expression as part of the dynamic of the *intifada* itself is nowhere as significant as in the field of communication. When electrical blackouts, army sieges, curfews, censorship, and other Israeli measures have rendered technology (radio, television, telephones) and the officially printed word (newspapers, magazines, books) entirely unavailable or unreliable, counter-measures and means, true to the nature of the *intifada,* have been devised. Underground leaflets have become the most reliable and authentic methods for disseminating information and mass mobilization.[9] Alternative, popular communication is also carried out by means of graffiti appearing overnight in key places and areas, and by a vast network of contacts transmitting information orally. Understandably, Palestinian discourse has developed an economy of style which is essentially cryptic and highly symbolic. This style is gradually infiltrating the literary output of the *intifada,* imbuing it with originality of expression and structure in keeping with the urgency and dynamism of perception and substance.

From the barricade to your eyes we rise for the sky is a crystal
In which secrets are revealed . . . .
Between bullet and funeral is a green oasis
Oh, my homeland, how sweet the call![10]

Popular, oral history has been incorporated as well into the literary movement, whether in the form of *zajal*[11] or colloquial rhymed verse.[12] Recorded cassettes in the poets' own voices have become another vehicle for transmitting poetry, further reinforcing the oral popular nature of the genre.[13] The fusion of formal and popular literary forms has produced a wealth of familiar songs, chants, and slogans while creating a versatile and vital literary movement in the making.

In all different forms of activities and expressions, the word, whether written or spoken, remains dominant. Visual arts and graphics rely heavily on the incorporation of calligraphy,[14] while the lyric is more significant than the music of the song.[15] Dialogue, more than action, is the vehicle of significance in Palestinian theater, while folkdance groups are increasingly becoming reliant on lyrics and verbal motifs to give meaningful coherence to the union of *dabke,* music, and words.[16] This verbal bias is on the one hand an extension of the traditional reliance of Arab and Palestinian culture on the word as the central embodiment of religion, art, and identity, while on the other hand it reveals most directly the didacticism and versatility of contemporary Palestinian culture as one of commitment and change.

The spirit, focus, and tone of this culture exhibit a predominantly youthful slant with a predilection for the glorification of the young as the primary forces of the *intifada*. With a vast majority of the population of the occupied territories below thirty,[17] the concerns and aspirations of this age group, as well as its dominant and visible role in the *intifada,* have understandably transformed Palestinian culture, shaping its characteristics, defining its objectives, and constituting its main audience.[18] Similarly, the emerging role of women in the *intifada* and the increasing recognition of the gender agenda as a significant factor in the struggle for national independence are gradually creating a feminist perspective which had been noticeably absent in Palestinian culture. Women's leaflets, magazines, and one-time publications have become familiar expressions of the gender issue as an integral component of the political struggle for freedom and independence. The grass-roots work and organizational significance of the women's committees in the social and economic transformation of society (in addition to their overtly political activities) has bestowed on the women's movement credibility and legitimacy which have made the articulation of feminist theory not only acceptable, but also desirable. The formation of the Higher Council for Women (or Higher Feminist Council) has qualitatively altered the work of women's committees both as an expression of national unity and as a reorientation toward a consciously feminist analysis and discourse.[19]

A nationalist popular culture with a clear political substance and role, the culture of the *intifada* displays a tone of assertion and affirmation as an articulation and expression of authenticity. Thus, the Palestinian identity, in its historical, cultural, and political dimensions, is the source and objective of this assertive tone. If, in some cases, the affirmation of authenticity has led to a narrow regressive focus and attitude,[20] it has on the whole exerted a revitalizing influence toward the creation of an original and experimental cultural movement with its own unique and distinctive flavor.[21] The fusion of the familiar and the novel, of the indigenous and the foreign, of the traditional with the futuristic, has led to a redefinition of authenticity as a dynamic process based on paradoxical synthesis.

Ultimately, Palestinian culture is an expression of and a vehicle for national and political legitimization in the context of the *intifada* as a process of de-legitimizing Israeli occupation while affirming the legitimacy of Palestinian rights and realities. The *intifada*'s rejection of Israeli attempts at creating a counterfeit and abnormal reality of occupation by imposing norms and structures external to the genuine Palestinian experience and self-definition, lies at the center of the substance and role of Palestinian culture. The *intifada's* political, social, and economic "disengagement" from Israeli occupation as a negation of its authority is expressed in the emergence of an essentially "engaged" Palestinian culture which draws upon its own authentic resources and frames of reference. The integrity of its vision is reinforced on the one hand by its distinctive "separateness" and on the other by its "commitment" to a universal set of principles and ideals. Thus, self-determination in the Palestinian experience is not an abstraction nor an expression of political aspiration only, but a concrete reality embodied in a culture growing toward its own self-realization. The legitimacy which the political struggle seeks to attain, the methods and characteristics of the *intifada* itself, and the energy which propels the process of resistance and social transformation all form the progressive and unifying motivation, identity, and vision of the cultural reality of Palestine today.

Notes

1. Al-Mutawakkil Taha, Intro. to Atallah Qattoush, *Shams al-Layl* (The Night Sun), Jerusalem: Union of Palestinian Writers, 1988.

2. This is least applicable to the plays of the "El-Hakawati" theater group, with their high degree of stylization and spectacle. The plays of "Al-Masrah al-Filastini" remain the most direct and immediate mirror-image of external reality.

3. In particular, cf. Mustafa Al-Kurd's cassette recording "Atfal al-Hijara," 1988.

4. A striking example is the controversy which surrounded whether folk-dancing (the *dabke*) may be performed publicly without being perceived as a frivolity in the present context. The debate was resolved in favor of "authentic" *dabke* performances by "committed" groups and clubs.

5. In demonstrations, for example, children often "make fun" of Israeli soldiers and challenge them in word and gesture in order to bring them "down to size." Much Palestinian theater and art tends to present satirized versions of the "invincible" Israeli army to expose its moral weakness and assert the moral ascendancy of Palestinian popular resistance.

6. The establishment of centers like "Markaz al-Funun al-Sha'biya" in Bireh-Ramallah in March 1989 has been a conscious means of providing progressive alternative cultural collectives.

7. Admission to art exhibitions is free, and the price of paintings has been reduced. All public performances of plays, folklore, and song or dance festivals are either without charge or subject to a ceiling which is minimal.

8. Popular committees in all their forms (educational, political, social, cultural, economic, agricultural, etc.) have been declared illegal by the Israeli occupation authorities. Membership or support of such committees is an offense punishable by up to ten years' imprisonment.

9. The underground Unified National Command of the Uprising regularly issues numbered leaflets (*nida'*), which manage to reach the whole Palestinian population. Other leaflets

are also secretly distributed by different political groups or social organizations to provide specific analyses or perspectives.

10. Khalil Touma, "Al-Nida," from *Maqali'* (Slingshots), Jerusalem: Union of Palestinian Writers, 1988. Note here that *nida'* or "call" also refers to the underground leaflets of the UNCU.

11. See Rajah al-Salfiti's contribution to the same collection, *ibid.*

12. "Sidi Harkash" [pseudonym], *Hilm al-Sabi* (The Boy's Dream), Jerusalem: n.p., 1988.

13. For example, Hussein Barghouti and Yaqout al-Bahri [pseudonym], *Aleph, Nun, Ta* (Anta or *intifada*). Jerusalem: n.p., 1988.

14. In March, 1989, the Association of Palestinian Artists held an exhibit in "El-Hakawati" Center. The invitation card itself was a graphic representation of the word "Adhar" (March), and within it were the terms for the different events commemorated in March (Women's Day, Karameh, Mother's Day, and Land Day).

15. This is especially true of the audience reaction to the songs of Walid Abdul-Salam and Mustafa Al-Kurd. "Sabrin" relies on a more complex interaction between lyric and music, thus requiring greater audience sophistication.

16. Cf. the performances of "Al-Funun al-Sha'biya" group.

17. It is estimated that 70 percent of the population is below 30 years of age, while about 60 percent were born after the 1967 occupation.

18. For example, Suhail Khoury's musical cassette "Marah" (Jerusalem, 1988) is geared towards children and sung in their own voices; a vast majority of Palestinian paintings have the young as their major theme; and all music and *dabke* groups are made up of young adults.

19. The formation of the Higher Council for Women was formally announced on November 15, 1988. The second leaflet was issued on International Women's Day (March 8, 1989), which was marked by women's marches, demonstrations, and sit-in strikes.

20. Such manifestations include the rejection of all "foreign" elements associated with modernism, the obsessive pursuit of folk expressions, or the resort to traditional modes of propriety and decorum.

21. The music of "Sabrin," for instance, is a unique blend of Western jazz and blues with Eastern rhythm and melody; of acoustic guitar and string bass with the "oud" and "qanun"; and colloquial idiom with classical structure. Similarly, the paintings of Taysir Barakat, Nabil 'Anani, and Sulaiman Mansour express an original interaction among medium. motif, color and perspective, motion and frame. The plays of "Al-Warsha al-Faniyya" and "Al-Sanabil" are an adaptation of international masterpieces and Palestinian reality.

PART 2: THE INTIFADA AND THE WORLD

6 THE PALESTINIAN CHALLENGE TO US POLICY

Michael C. Hudson

If American Middle East policymaking could be likened to a glacier, the Palestinian *intifada* and acceptance of a two-state solution might be viewed as a heat wave. Glaciers not only are cold but have a structure and momentum of their own; heat waves can be intense or mild, brief or enduring. To assess the effects of the Palestinian warming trend, we need to take its temperature, which means examining its influence on the Middle Eastern political environment as well as its specific impact on Washington.

Many analysts have concluded that the *intifada* has significantly altered the political equation in the region; some even believe that it has made a Palestinian state inevitable.[1] But that is only half of the analytic task. We also must take a close look at the glacier. What is its melting point? Some say that US policy is locked into largely unchanging basic interests: Israel, oil, and anti-communism. Others see it as permanently captive to the powerful Israel lobby. Neither of these views foresees much change, no matter what Palestinians might do. But there are also less deterministic interpretations of the Middle East policy "machine." Day-to-day observers insist that a great deal depends on who the "key players" are, and liberal analysts argue that shifts in public opinion can change policy. Which analysts are right— those who foresee little significant change in US policy, or those who believe that because the Palestinian factor is altering Middle Eastern realities it is also beginning to melt the US Middle East policy glacier, with its reflexive pro-Israel bias?

I believe that the *intifada* and related developments are stimulating a much-needed reassessment of the American stance by opinion-makers and officials inside and outside the government. The *intifada* has rendered the old status quo of Israeli occupation untenable, and the PLO's diplomatic initiative has opened the way for a non-violent compromise solution to the persistent problem of Palestine. As the *intifada* enters its third year, American public opinion and officials are more aware of these new regional realities. The attitude of American Jewry and the non-Jewish community supporting Israel has become more complex and ambivalent as Israel's liberal reputation declines under the pressure of the *intifada*. The foreign policy opinion-making

87

elite, including influential news media figures, has if anything turned in a pro-Palestinian direction. On the moral plane, more Americans recognize that Palestinians have at least some legitimate political grievances and deplore Israeli repression; and on the practical level, more Americans now favor a compromise solution that would finally end the tension and danger to international stability that has always been characteristic of the unsolved Arab-Israeli conflict.

Yet despite all these signs of potential thaw, American policy after the first year of the Bush Administration remained essentially frozen in the mold set during the Reagan presidency. In substance and spirit, Washington bent over backwards to accommodate an unbending Israeli government while trying to marginalize the authentic leadership of the Palestine Liberation Organization in every possible way. In method and style, the American stance is passive and, at best, incrementalist; and the State Department excuses itself from a more vigorous role on the grounds that the problems between Israel and the Palestinians are too intractable. This negative orientation, which persists in spite of the growing understanding of the new realities outside the top decisionmaking circle, could result in a historical opportunity to solve the Palestine-Israel problem being missed. The PLO, led by Chairman Yasser Arafat and his centrist constituency, has staked its political future on a strategy based on the audacious and perhaps mistaken proposition that the Palestinians can play an "American card." Certainly, a year after making the historic concessions, Arafat could not claim that his "American strategy" had even begun to succeed; and Arafat's militant critics, like *Hamas* (the militant Islamic movement in the occupied territories), were beginning to agitate again for an approach of uncompromising, armed struggle aiming at the liberation of all of Palestine. The question for Arafat, and for all of us, is perhaps not whether the US will discover evenhandedness but rather whether it will do so in time to avert a new cycle of violence and instability in the region.

The Legacy of the Reagan Administration

President Ronald Reagan assumed office in January 1981 with a mixed inheritance. For Jimmy Carter, the Middle East had been the scene of his greatest foreign policy triumph—the Camp David Agreements—and his greatest failure—humiliation at the hands of the leader of the Iranian Islamic revolution, Ayatollah Ruhollah

Khomeini. One goal of Camp David, an Egypt-Israel peace treaty, was achieved; but the second goal, securing a Palestinian-Israeli agreement, was not realized. President Reagan, despite his unfamiliarity with the Middle East, could hardly ignore the region: Iran's hostility to the American "Great Satan" and its threat to neighboring oil-rich, conservative, and pro-American Arab governments required close attention; and the issue of Israel's security against Arab "terrorism" was too high on the agenda of American domestic politics for him to ignore. Reagan came to power promising to restore bruised American prestige in the area and to settle, or at least "manage," the main conflicts. He failed in most areas: Palestine/Israel, Lebanon, Iran, and even Libya. His Administration succeeded to a significant degree, however, in helping bring about a cease-fire in the Iraq-Iran war and mitigating to some extent the Iranian threat to the Arab oil kingdoms.

On the Palestine problem, the Reagan Administration's main contribution was the "Reagan Plan" of September 1982, which called for negotiations to settle the fate of the Israeli-occupied West Bank and Gaza Strip. Having asserted that Israel's occupation was not an acceptable permanent solution but that an independent Palestinian state was also unacceptable, the President's plan—like Camp David— envisaged a principal role for Jordan in the future administration of the territories, in some kind of collaborative or confederal association with Palestinians from the territories.[2] Following the commitment made in 1975 to Israel by then Secretary of State Henry Kissinger, Reagan ruled out a role for the PLO until it recognized Israel's right to exist and renounced terrorism. In 1985 and 1986, Jordan and the PLO (with indirect US government involvement) came close to working out a confederal agreement for the territories, but the negotiations broke down. Jordan and the US castigated the PLO for rejecting a US offer to accept the idea of an international conference and PLO attendance, in return for unconditional PLO acceptance of UN resolutions 242 and 338. The Palestinians blamed the US and Israel for demanding the PLO's unqualified recognition of UN resolutions 242 and 338, despite their lack of reference to Palestinian national rights.[3]

Two conclusions may be drawn about the Reagan Administration's approach to the Palestine problem. Although committed to the famous "land for peace" formula of UN Resolution 242, it did not accord consistent high priority to the issue. Preoccupied with other world and Middle Eastern issues (Lebanon and the Gulf), it did not ener- getically push its own 1982 plan. And the Jordanian-Palestinian negotiations of 1985-86 revealed American rigidity—indeed, hostility —toward Palestinian self-determination. Thus, when President Reagan and Secretary of State George Shultz authorized an official US-PLO dialogue in the waning days of their Administration in December 1988, the general reaction was one of great surprise. Which party had blinked? Had the PLO given away a cherished principle? Or had the glacier of the American policy process thawed a bit?

At a news conference in Geneva on December 14, 1988, PLO Chairman Yasser Arafat finally succeeded in convincing the US government that the PLO accepted UN resolutions 242 and 338 without qualification, that it now specifically recognized Israel's right to exist, and that it totally renounced all forms of terrorism, including individual, group, and state terrorism.[4] The US immediately named its official representative for the dialogue, Ambassador to Tunisia Robert Pelletreau, and set about organizing the first meeting. Secretary Shultz insisted that the American position had not changed; yet less than three weeks earlier, he had shocked world diplomatic opinion by denying Arafat a visa so that he could speak before the United Nations General Assembly in New York. Arafat and his aides, helped by Swedish government intermediaries and a group of American Jewish private citizens, clarified their language meticulously,[5] but these were minor points compared to the fundamental and public shift in the PLO position over the previous year. That shift would have been impossible had not the Palestinians in the territories launched their *intifada* in December 1987. The *intifada,* among other things, persuaded King Hussein to remove Jordan as a possible surrogate ruler of the Palestinian territories, thus nullifying the Reagan Administration strategy. More importantly it gave the PLO the courage and sense of urgency to take a bold step to induce the US to play a more evenhanded and active role.

The lackadaisical approach of the Reagan Administration is not difficult to explain. Clearly the influential Israel lobby cast a long shadow over the White House as well as the Congress, but it would be simplistic to claim that the policy was made *in toto* by AIPAC. Neither the Reagan Plan nor the opening of the US-PLO dialogue were to the liking of the mainstream lobby groups—not to mention the Israeli government, which reacted in fury to both of these initiatives. The lobby was effective, however, in imposing sufficient domestic political costs on the Administration to wear down the advocates of a more positive approach.

A second factor was President Reagan's personal orientation. He was not very knowledgeable about the Arab-Israeli conflict. But what he did understand was shaped by his strong sympathy for Zionism and Israel, which was perhaps a result of his past political and social milieu in California. Moreover, his adherence to the cold-war mindset of the conservative wing of the Republican Party disposed him to accept the idea that Israel is "a strategic asset" in the struggle to contain Soviet and Communist influence. Most scholars of American Middle East policy would agree with William Quandt that "the quality and courage of presidential leadership will be an essential element" in any US-led resolution of the Arab-Israeli conflict.[6] But according to Steven Spiegel, Reagan was "a passive and even uninvolved chief executive who was surrounded by competing and frequently changing players."[7]

A third consideration was the competing pressure of other problems in the region and in the world. Lebanon and Iran (especially the Iran-contra scandal) were major distractions. In Lebanon, President Reagan's first Secretary of State, Alexander Haig, appears to have given Israeli Defense Minister General Ariel Sharon an "amber light" to invade Lebanon in 1982. Sharon's intention was to destroy the Palestine Liberation Organization and install a pro-Israeli, right-wing Maronite Christian government in Beirut, while Haig was mainly interested in striking a blow for "the West" against the Soviet-based Syrians. Israel's adventure came to be judged by most Israelis, and others, as a failure which cost over 17,000 Palestinian and Lebanese lives. When the US sent in Marines as part of the multinational peacekeeping force, they got caught up in Lebanon's civil war. President Reagan's special emissary, Ambassador Philip Habib, achieved a qualified success in helping negotiate the withdrawal of PLO fighters from Beirut, but the US failed in its larger goals of protecting Palestinian civilians, restoring order among the Lebanese factions, and working out a Lebanese *modus vivendi* acceptable both to Israel and Syria. In October 1983 a truck-bomb killed 241 Marines sleeping in their barracks at the Beirut airport, and before long the US military force withdrew without having accomplished its mission.

Libya proved to be a politically convenient distraction from the disasters of Lebanon. President Reagan and his key advisors wanted to punish Colonel Mu'ammar Qadhafi, regarded by them as perhaps the principal organizer of "international terrorism." Responding to Libyan-inspired threats and attacks against US diplomats and friendly Middle East governments, the US bombed Tripoli and Benghazi in 1986, the culmination of a series of military challenges to the Libyan leader. Although some terrorism experts think that the American attack crippled Qadhafi's support of terrorism, it is more likely that the Colonel's subsequent turn to a low profile in his foreign policy was due more to falling oil prices and his own growing domestic unpopularity. The general volume of international terrorism did not notably decline.

But it was the scandal involving secret arms sales to Iran to fund the secret and illegal military assistance to the *contra* rebels opposed to the Sandanista government in Nicaragua that overshadowed all other foreign policy concerns in the last years of the Reagan Administration. Ironically, the only Middle Eastern problem in which Reagan enjoyed some success was the Iran-Iraq war and the larger question of Gulf security. His projection of an American military presence in the Gulf (and the deepening of military cooperation with the conservative Arab Gulf states) probably contributed to Iran's acceptance of a cease-fire in the summer of 1988. The reflagging of Kuwaiti oil tankers was an important symbol of American determination to help preserve the security of the Arab gulf states against Iranian expansionism. Even this success was marred by the accidental shooting down of an Iranian civilian airliner, a tragedy which probably inspired the destruction of a Pan American airliner over Scotland in December 1988. But at the same time the US was trying to constrain Iran, a small group operating virtually out of the White House was carrying out a policy diametrically opposed to the official one. Once discovered, the covert Iran-contra operation, organized in the President's National Security Council, preoccupied and nearly destroyed the Administration in its last three years. The fact that Israel was directly involved certainly compromised the Arab regimes that Washington was trying to protect from Iranian extremism.[8] Many believed that President Reagan had intended to exchange arms for American hostages being held in Lebanon; and two indeed were freed, but as of 1990, eight were still being held, along with four hostages of other nationalities.

The Reagan Administration's performance on the Middle East, and especially on the Palestine problem, was hampered by the Israel lobby, the President's limited grasp of Middle Eastern realities, his inability to lead and discipline the cumbersome "policy machine," and the bureaucracy's inadequacy in coping with the region's multiplicity of problems. Would the incoming Bush Administration fare any better?

The Bush Administration

Even before the inauguration, the Bush team had assigned foreign policy advisor Dennis Ross the task of formulating Middle East policy options. The public perception, however, was that the Administration was inattentive to the region, except for the sharp criticism of Israel in the State Department's annual report on human rights, issued in February 1989. The President and Secretary of State reacted defensively to press criticism of their slowness in assembling their foreign policy team for the Middle East and other regions. From the Arab world there was also criticism that the US-PLO dialogue was going nowhere. Then, when Shamir came to Washington in April with a plan for elections in the territories that came nowhere close to minimum Palestinian demands, the Administration hastily and eagerly embraced it. This move was met with dismay by all who had hoped for a new evenhandedness. But the damage was mitigated on May 22, 1989 when Secretary Baker delivered a major statement of the Administration's policy. Appropriately, the forum was a meeting of AIPAC. While Baker's position basically reiterated existing US policy, the tone of the speech was unexpectedly blunt in its advice to Israel:

> For Israel, now is the time to lay aside, once and for all, the unrealistic vision of a greater Israel. Israeli interests in the West Bank and Gaza—security and otherwise—can be accommodated in a settlement based on Resolution 242. Forswear annexation. Stop settlement activity. Allow schools to reopen. Reach out to the Palestinians as neighbors who deserve political rights.[9]

The reaction of the Israeli government to this advice was even blunter. "It's useless, it was useless," said Prime Minister Shamir, "We cannot agree to what he said about some positions of Israel in the future, or even issues not related directly to the peace initiative— for instance, what he said about a greater Israel or the settlement problem and so on."[10] At the same time, Ambassador Pelletreau was reported to have upgraded the level of his PLO contacts in Tunis by talking with Salah Khalaf (Abu Iyad), one of the most senior Palestinian officials.

The US, however, took pains to reiterate its special and cordial relationship with Israel. In February 1989, it vetoed a UN resolution deemed too critical of Israel. The question of transferring the US embassy in Israel from Tel Aviv to Jerusalem was another issue on which the new Administration showed signs of possibly beginning to accept Israel's legal sovereignty over the city, in contravention of existing US policy which regarded the city as a "corpus separatum" under the 1947 UN Partition Plan. The US, it will be recalled, maintains a consulate-general in Jerusalem, independent of the embassy in Tel Aviv, much to the discomfort of the Israeli government. An amendment written by Senator Jesse Helms had called on the State Department to transfer the US embassy to Jerusalem. On the last day of the Reagan Administration, January 19, 1989, the US and Israel signed a Lend Lease and Purchase Agreement to acquire "new diplomatic facilities." The US would purchase one piece of land in Tel Aviv and lease a second piece of land in West Jerusalem for this purpose, and (in a compromise with the Helms amendment) it would be up to the President to determine which of them might be the site of the US embassy. Queried in the Security Council by the Palestinian representative about this matter and a US suggestion to remove the customary expression "including Jerusalem" from a reference to the occupied territories in a draft resolution, the American delegate, Ambassador Pickering, insisted that "We haven't changed our policy with respect to Jerusalem in any way at all . . . .Our policy for Jerusalem is a long-standing one that in this respect we have always considered the occupied portion of Jerusalem as part of occupied territory."[11] It could be argued, however, that the very act of signing a lease agreement over Jerusalem land implicitly signaled a change in US policy, whether or not the President decided to relocate the embassy itself to that spot. Moreover, by introducing a distinction between "occupied" Jerusalem (the eastern part seized by Israel in 1967) and the western part of the city captured by Israel in 1948, the US might be construed as having altered its longstanding position that Israel has no permanent legitimated claim to the whole of Jerusalem. Any such policy shifts could have momentous political repercussions.

But most importantly, Bush and Baker had aligned American and Israeli approaches by instantly endorsing Prime Minister Shamir's April 1989 proposal for elections in the occupied territories, thus relegating other modalities—such as an international conference—to secondary status. And when Shamir accepted a set of limiting conditions on his plan demanded by his Likud bloc's rightwing critics, the US first threatened to send out a special envoy to investigate this unhelpful development but then quickly backed down. Then, in July, when Israel precipitated the Administration's first foreign policy crisis by kidnapping a Shi'ite leader linked to the Hizballah movement and endangering American hostages in Lebanon, the Administration stifled its initial criticism of Israel and sought to work with the Israelis to resolve the situation.

How can we explain the new Administration's initial approach to the Middle East? Can we identify factors that might shape its future behavior? The classical approach to the study of international relations views foreign policy as a rational intellectual process, in which policies are devised as instruments for achieving goals, or national interests. If this approach is overly abstract and often self-serving of official interests, it has the virtue of emphasizing the central role of power and influence in the shaping of policy. An alternative approach, which we may label "empirical" or even "behavioral," insists that foreign policymaking is a political, not just an intellectual, process, and that the values and preferences held by participants in the process—some of whom enjoy greater influence than others—define not only the national interests but also shape the policies and their implementation. Foreign policy decisionmaking is seen as embedded in a sociopolitical structure whose main features must be identified and understood: social classes, ethnic groups, lobbies, bureaucracies, and officials. The interplay—often rivalry—among participating groups with differing degrees of influence may decisively and consistently "bend" policy in a particular direction. An empirical approach to President Bush's Middle East policy might focus on key officials in the Executive Branch, the role of Congress, the political parties, interest groups, and public opinion.

The Policy Process: Actors and Actions

The Bush Administration took office inheriting both the burden of failed Reagan policies and the unexpected asset of the US-PLO dialogue. During the 1988 election campaign, Bush and his Democratic Party rival, Governor Michael Dukakis, vied with each other in expressing extravagant support for Israel. Although the *intifada* was raging throughout the campaign season, however, the Middle East did not emerge as a major issue. All the candidates for both parties made the obligatory gestures toward Israel (the exception being Democratic candidate Jesse Jackson, who expressed sympathy for the Palestinians as well as for Israel), but none sought to highlight the conflict except before Jewish audiences. An Arab lobbying group accused the candidates of avoiding the issue.[12] In something of a breakthrough, however, Democratic Party organizations in seven states adopted resolutions calling for Palestinian self-determination; and at the Democratic Party nominating convention in Atlanta in July 1988, candidate Jesse Jackson proposed a Palestinian self-determination plank in the national platform that created a furor among pro-Israel Democrats. AIPAC led a successful counterattack to eliminate any mention of Palestinians from the platform.[13] Bush committed himself to the policies of his mentor, President Reagan, and virtually rejected the idea of an independent Palestinian state.[14] Most of the Jewish vote, however, went to Dukakis (who had supported moving the US embassy in Israel to Jerusalem), thus loosening slightly the theoretical leverage the Israel lobby might otherwise have enjoyed over the Bush White House. Advocates of a more evenhanded approach were also encouraged by the new President's apparently greater knowledge of, and contact with, the Arab world, compared to his predecessor's. Similar hopes were expressed about the incoming Secretary of State, James Baker, and the new head of the National Security Council, Brent Scowcroft. Pro-Israel groups were not happy about the appointment of John Sununu, former governor of New Hampshire and Bush's campaign chairman, as White House Chief of Staff, because of his Palestinian-Lebanese family background, and his suspected sympathy with Palestinian grievances.

But the new Administration's appointees to key Middle East policy positions were, on the whole, not reassuring to advocates of a less pro-Israel policy. Lawrence Eagleburger, a protege of Henry Kissinger, became Deputy Secretary of State. (Kissinger had advised the Israelis to "put down the insurrection as quickly as possible—overwhelmingly, brutally and rapidly" and ban all television coverage.)[15] Dennis Ross, director of Near Eastern and South Asian Affairs in Reagan's National Security Council, became director of the State Department Policy Planning Council, and was given a special responsibility for the Arab-Israeli "peace process." Richard N. Haass, a former lecturer at Harvard without substantial Middle East experience, became the NSC Middle East specialist. All of these individuals had been members of a "presidential study group on US policy in the Middle East" convened during the election campaign by the Washington Institute for Near East Policy, a think tank sympathetic to Israel and headed by a former deputy director of research for the American-Israel Public Affairs Committee (AIPAC), the spearhead of the Israel lobby. The report of this study group called, first, for reiterating Israel's special and favored relationship with the US; curbing the *intifada*; encouraging "responsible" Palestinian leadership primarily from the occupied territories (the PLO having "repeatedly failed" to be responsible); rejecting any unilateral PLO initiative for an independent Palestinian state, even if it included also accepting a Jewish state; preserving a role for Jordan; scaling down the US role from that of seeking a "breakthrough" (which might involve unacceptable pressures on Israel) to assisting in a "process"; advocating a long transition period of limited Palestinian autonomy to "test" the Palestinians' sincerity in co-existing with Israel; and expressing studied ambiguity as to what the final outcome and "legitimate Palestinian rights" might be.[16] Clearly, the recommendations were proffered as a kind of damage control against the *intifada* and the evolving PLO diplomatic offensive. Perhaps more significant, however, was the high degree of access to power symbolized by the membership of the study group itself. Heavily weighted with well-known pro-Israeli academics, writers and former officials (although with a nod or two toward "balance"), it not only included virtually the entire future senior Middle East policy group, but also representatives of the Democratic Party candidates. Had Dukakis or even Jesse Jackson won the presidency, this report would still have had some influence.

At the second level within the Executive Branch, two of the most important appointees had extensive Middle East experience: Ambassador Thomas Pickering as US representative to the United Nations, and Ambassador Robert H. Pelletreau, Jr. as ambassador to Tunisia with special responsibility for the US-PLO dialogue. The designation of Ambassador John Kelly as Assistant Secretary of State for the Near East and South Asia elicited mixed reactions: an Arab observer in Washington, for example, faulted his relative lack of Middle East diplomatic experience and wondered whether he could effectively present the views of foreign service officers in the field in the policy process.[17] In keeping with the new team's cool and incremental approach, Kelly was known to reject the thesis of some Middle East specialists that the conflict, untended, could lead to new and dangerous explosions in the territories and elsewhere in the Arab world.[18] The abrupt replacement of all six deputy assistant secretaries for the Near East in May 1989 appeared to some Middle East hands as a "Saturday Night Massacre" engineered by a close-knit group around the Secretary of State and his deputy in order to weaken "Arabist" influence at State.

On the Congressional level, although overall support for Israel remained very solid there was some criticism of Israel's brutal tactics in trying to repress the *intifada* and Shamir's rejection of the "land for peace" formula supported by the US—exemplified by an unusual open letter to Prime Minister Shamir in March 1988 signed by 30 senators.[19] The Democratic chairmen of the Senate and House Appropriations Committees, Senator Patrick Leahy and Congressman David Obey, warned that future aid appropriations for Israel might be jeopardized unless the Israelis reduced their coercion in the territories. Interestingly, the Administration's decision to open the dialogue with the PLO did not elicit a storm of Congressional opposition, perhaps because American Jewish organizations were ambivalent on this development. In May 1989 a concurrent resolution was introduced in the House of Representatives by Congressman Howard Nielson (a Utah Republican), joined by 26 cosponsors, calling on Israel to open schools in the West Bank.[20]

By far the dominant trend in Congress in the election year, however, was continuing vigorous support for Israel. It succeeded, over White House objections, in closing the PLO's information office in Washington. In the November 1988 elections the Democratic Party (traditionally more pro-Israel than the Republicans) captured majorities in both the House of Representatives and the Senate, so there was no diminution in Congress's strong sympathy and generosity toward the Jewish state. A perusal of Middle East-related statements in *The Congressional Record* during the period of the *intifada,* both before and after the 1988 elections, reveals a preponderance of legislative expressions of support for Israel, and scarcely a word of criticism. The Bush Administration, true to its own inclinations and aware of this bedrock congressional commitment to Israel's welfare, presented its fiscal year 1990 foreign aid request for Israel in March 1989—$3 billion ($1.8 for military spending, and $1.2 for economic support). This was at the same level as the three previous years, although there were enhancements that would provide additional indirect benefits above the $3 billion total.[21] At the same time, by comparison, the Administration requested $12 million for development assistance in the occupied territories. As for foreign aid and military sales to Arab countries, Egypt was the only one to receive largesse comparable to that of Israel ($2.2 billion for fiscal year 1990). This was a continuing reward for its peace treaty with Israel, and reflected continuing concern that Egypt's parlous economic condition could endanger that treaty. For other Arab countries, aid levels were less than $100 million (e.g. $85 million for Jordan, $15 million for Lebanon). Israel's friends in Congress continued to oppose major weapons sales to Arab countries other than Egypt, although certain Arab Gulf states, such as Bahrain, Kuwait, and Oman, were allowed modest purchases, owing mainly to the Iranian threat. The Israel lobby's particular hostility to Saudi Arabia, perhaps because it was the Arab country with the most significant economic and strategic relationship with the US, had thwarted major arms sale requests from the Kingdom in 1987 and 1988 amounting to at least $30 billion and perhaps as much as $68 billion. When Saudi Arabia concluded a huge arms deal with Britain in 1988, there was virtually no congressional reaction, despite the negative implications for US influence with this strategically vital country, and also of course for the US defense industry. Notwithstanding its strong pro-Israel stand, the Reagan Administration had strongly backed these military sales, and presumably the Bush Administration was of a similar disposition. It could not, however, override AIPAC's hold on Congress.[22]

Notwithstanding their continuing hegemony over Middle East policy, Israel's backers in Congress were disturbed at what they perceived as a cooler attitude on the part of Bush and Baker toward the Jewish state. They had been relatively quiescent throughout the first year or so of the *intifada,* recognizing that Israel's image in American opinion was tarnished by the severity of its response. Indeed, several senators were reported to have warned the visiting Israeli foreign minister, Moshe Arens, that there were signs of erosion of support for Israel in American public opinion, even though congressional support remained solid.[23] They allowed the US-PLO dialogue to begin, despite their misgivings, perhaps because the Reagan Administration had been so scrupulous in insisting that the PLO make an ironclad commitment on the issues of Israel's right to exist and terrorism. In the words of one of Israel's strongest congressional supporters, Rep. Mel Levine of California, Arafat "uttered the magic words."[24] After Shamir presented his election plan, they seized on it as Israel's diplomatic counterattack and praised it vociferously, while at the same time castigating the PLO.[25] Baker's May 22 speech also elicited concern on Capitol Hill. Although there was some praise for its "evenhandedness," some Congressmen took Baker to task for being too harsh on Israel; and in a show of muscle, ninety-five Senators signed an open letter to Secretary Baker, urging that "the United States must be fully supportive, both in fact and in appearance" of the Israeli government's "peace initiative."[26] It was also reported that a delegation of eleven pro-Israel senators, headed by Senators George Mitchell and Robert Dole, the Democratic and Republican party leaders, respectively, had met with Bush at the urging of American Jewish organizations to express concern that escalating US-PLO contacts were damaging Prime Minister Shamir and his election initiative among hardline factions in Israel. They urged the President to write a friendly and supportive letter to Shamir, which the President agreed to do, "while grumbling about the continued creation of Jewish settlements on the West Bank."[27]

A more serious matter, amounting to a direct assault on the Administration's opening to the PLO, was an amendment to a State Department authorization bill submitted by North Carolina Republican Senator Jesse Helms in July 1989. Helms, one of the most contentious of the pro-Israel congressmen and a bitter foe of the PLO, sought to bar official talks with any PLO representative whom the President could not certify had not participated in, conspired in, or been an accessory to the planning or execution of a terrorist action resulting in the death, injury, or kidnapping of an American citizen. Interestingly, the Administration not only recognized that the amendment would severely weaken the PLO dialogue (making it impossible, presumably, to deal with important PLO leaders, such as Salah Khalaf), but it also mobilized all its resources to defeat it. Both the President and the Secretary of State directly intervened, and with the cooperation of both the Democratic and Republican leadership, were able to substitute a substantially weakened version giving the President discretion to report to Congress about known terrorist participants in the talks.[28] The AIPAC-inspired Helms amendment clearly was welcomed, if not encouraged, by Prime Minister Shamir and the far right in Israel, as well as by the largest Jewish organization, B'nai B'rith International. Interestingly, however, at least two other major American Jewish organizations, the American Jewish Congress and the Union of American Hebrew (Reform) Congregations, opposed the amendment, and the *Washington Post* expressed guarded apprehension over efforts to terminate the US-PLO dialogue.[29] The incident showed two things: first, that the Israeli government and the Israel lobby would fight tenaciously against any perceived threat to Israel's privileged position in the US Middle East policy process; but, second, that the lobby no longer had the field entirely to itself. Alternative views, both inside and outside the American Jewish community, were being expressed in public; and for that reason the lobby was at least occasionally finding itself on the defensive.

Israel and its American supporters were also embarrassed, temporarily at least, over Israel's kidnapping of a Lebanese Shi'ite cleric in

July 1989, in the hope of bargaining his freedom for the release of three captured Israeli soldiers. This action, however, apparently led to the execution of an American hostage in the hands of a pro-Iranian group in Lebanon and the threat to execute another American if Israel refused to release the cleric and 450 other prisoners. The hanging of Marine Col. William Higgins led Senator Robert Dole, Republican leader of the Senate, to criticize Israel for endangering American lives. "A little more responsibility on the part of the Israelis one of these days would be refreshing," he said.[30] Upon being deluged with critical mail, Senator Dole softened his criticism somewhat, but refused to retract it; and one of his aides said that he had received "a lot of thumbs up" support from fellow lawmakers privately, even though almost none would do so publicly. Other congressmen insisted that there was little deterioration in support for Israel. Speaker of the House Thomas Foley accused the terrorists of trying to drive a wedge between the United States and Israel, while Representative Lee Hamilton, chairman of the House Subcommittee on the Middle East and Europe (and himself a critic of the Israeli abduction) doubted that it would lead to a congressional cut in aid to Israel, observing that "there is an unusual durability and permanence to the US-Israeli relationship."[31]

But as if to remind us of how the unexpected can happen, the revolutionary upheavals in Eastern Europe in the autumn and winter of 1989 prompted Senator Dole, in January 1990, to propose trimming US foreign aid commitments to the major recipients by five percent, in order to free up funds to assist the new governments there. As the largest recipient by far, Israel saw itself as the main target, just at the moment when it was planning to ask Washington for an increase in aid, so that it could support the new influx of Soviet Jews. Newspaper accounts suggested that Senator Dole had the Bush Administration's tacit approval to challenge publicly the sacred cow of aid to Israel.

In October 1989, after Israel rejected an Egyptian proposal to break the impasse that had developed over Shamir's election plan, Secretary Baker put forward a five-point compromise plan proposing, on the basis of certain "understandings," that the foreign ministers of Egypt, Israel, and the US should meet in Washington to hammer out the modalities of a subsequent Israeli-Palestinian dialogue in Cairo.[32] Israel accepted the plan conditionally, but with a series of "assumptions," including Israeli approval of the Palestinian delegation, restricting its members only to residents of the West Bank and the Gaza Strip, no role for the PLO, and limiting the substance of the dialogue strictly to Shamir's election plan. For its part, the PLO did not officially reject the Baker points but conditioned its acceptance with its own "assumptions," which included its approval of any Palestinian delegation and the right to link discussions of an election plan to a process for determining the final status of the occupied territories. As Salah Khalaf, the second-ranking PLO official, put it: "The United States is asking the PLO to hide its presence so Israel will accept it [the Baker proposals]. Who is the crazy one, to accept that?"[33] In the face of this renewed impasse, Baker let it be known in January 1990 that he was becoming impatient with both parties, but particularly with Prime Minister Shamir; and his spokeswoman observed that "there are many other areas in the world clamoring for his attention . . . ."[34] Before Shamir's coalition government fell in March 1990, US-Israeli tensions increased as Baker warned that the US would not provide aid to settle Soviet Jewish immigrants in the occupied territories and Bush described East Jerusalem as occupied territory. Yet the Administration was obviously reluctant to undertake a comprehensive, energetic and evenhanded action—a reluctance surely nurtured as much by the fear of incurring domestic political costs as by the intractability of the Palestinian-Israeli situation.

Given the political realities of the Middle East policy-making process in the Bush Administration, one might reasonably ask whether there are forces at work strong enough to enable the US to play a more constructive, less biased role in the resolution of the Palestinian-Israeli conflict. As we have seen, an examination of US policy behavior since the beginning of the *intifada* in December 1987 suggests that the hegemony of the Israel lobby is not total and that it may in fact be weakening slightly. But are these just random incidents of evenhandedness or are they supported by more significant political trends? The record of Bush's first year does not offer much evidence for change. But there are two structural trends that may be significant in the future. One is the growing openness of the American news media and public opinion toward the Palestinian side of the story. The other is the pluralism that increasingly characterizes the political debate on Israel in the American Jewish community.

The News Media and Public Opinion

The *intifada* made its most powerful impact in the United States through television news coverage. It was extensive and, on balance, quite damaging to the stereotypical image of Israel as a virtuous but beleaguered country. Similarly, the press—and certainly the "elite" newspapers such as the *New York Times,* the *Washington Post,* the *Christian Science Monitor,* the *Wall Street Journal,* and the major newsmagazines—brought considerable depth and objectivity to their coverage.[35] Unfortunately, as the *intifada* continued, it became less newsworthy and the coverage declined. The killing of three or four Palestinians would have made the front page during the first three months or so, but after a year and a half, such news was often relegated to a paragraph at the back of a story on the inside pages.[36]

It was probably the news media's need for fresh news that was mainly responsible for this shrinkage, although efforts by the Israeli military to curb media coverage and complaints by some pro-Israel groups in the United States also may have contributed to it. Nevertheless, the story remained alive. The editorial and opinion columns, historically preponderantly pro-Israel, exhibited considerable diversity of views on the *intifada.* If there were dyed-in-the-wool defenders of Israeli policies—columnists like George Will, Jeane Kirkpatrick, and William Safire—there were articulate voices sympathetic to the Palestinians too: for example, Anthony Lewis, Mary McGrory, Georgie Anne Geyer, Philip Geyelin, and Joseph C. Harsch. The editorials in the *Times* and the *Post,* although firmly supportive of Israel, did occasionally criticize Israeli excesses; but they were usually hostile, suspicious and patronizing toward the PLO. Even their approval for the PLO's peace initiative was grudging.

Is American public opinion changing toward Israel, the Arabs, and the Palestinians? What impact have the *intifada* and the PLO's peace offensive (acceptance of Israel's right to exist, acceptance of UN resolution 242, and renunciation of terrorism) had on American attitudes? The data do not reveal any very dramatic changes in traditional sympathy for Israel and antipathy toward the Arabs, but there are some interesting shifts nonetheless. Some of them pre-date the *intifada.* In his examination of Gallup polls between 1981 and 1986, Fouad Moughrabi found an increase in pro-Palestinian sympathy and a decline in sympathy toward Israel: when asked if they were more sympathetic to the Palestinian position than they were a year ago, 22 percent said "more sympathetic" in 1981 while 39 percent said "more sympathetic" in 1986. For Israel, 37 percent said "less sympathetic" in 1981 and 51 percent in 1986.[37] Polls taken in the first weeks of the *intifada* indicated some modest slippage in sympathy for Israel: in February 1988, 30.1 percent said they sympathized with

Israel more than with the Arabs (only 12 percent sympathized more with the Arabs), compared to 48.8 percent a year earlier. But Israel's "sympathy" score went up to 51 percent in April (to 12 percent for the Arabs), which compared closely with its score in 1979.[38] Interestingly, when asked to compare sympathy between Israel and the Palestinians (and not the Arabs), the differences narrowed: in April 1988, 55 percent for Israel and 22 percent for the Palestinians. Based on a comparison of polls taken between January and May 1988, Eytan Gilboa concluded that there was no significant or constant shift in support away from Israel, and while there was some increase in general sympathy for the Palestinians, this was not carried over into support for the PLO or for a Palestinian state.[39] Moughrabi, however, reached somewhat different conclusions. Citing a *Chicago Tribune* poll in April 1988, he reported that 38 percent of those who had been following events in the media said that their opinion of Israel had decreased in recent months.[40] He also cited a *Los Angeles Times* poll in April 1988, indicating that 50 percent favored giving the Palestinians "a homeland of their own in the West Bank and the Gaza Strip," while 33 percent simply favored "more autonomy" for them.[41] Moughrabi, in addition, draws our attention to the findings of a poll commissioned by the American Jewish Congress in April 1988 indicating that while the general public is almost evenly divided on the desirability of an independent Palestinian state, the more affluent and well-informed respondents support this option by a two to one majority, a pattern replicated by other polls as well. Despite his general conclusion of "no significant change," some of the poll data presented by Gilboa suggests a certain improvement in the Palestinian position. For example, when asked in 1980, 1981, and 1982 whether Israel should permit a Palestinian state in the West Bank if the PLO recognizes Israel and renounces terrorism, 39 percent of the respondents said yes in all three polls, but when asked in April 1988 the percentage was 57.[42] And the survey results he has assembled on "sympathy" for Israel or the Arabs reveal considerable variability: for example, a Roper poll commissioned by the American Jewish Committee and carried out between April 16 and 29, 1988, discovers only 37 percent sympathizing with Israel (in sharp contrast to the 51 percent and 61 percent figures cited above from other polls taken the same month), which represents a drop of eleven points from a similar poll taken in February.[43]

The surveys mentioned above were conducted within the first five months of the *intifada*. What of more recent polls? The PLO's new moderation and the US decision to open a dialogue with it drew strong but qualified support in a *New York Times*/CBS poll conducted in mid-January 1989. Fully 64 percent of the respondents backed the US-PLO talks. The percentage rose with levels of education: 76 percent of college graduates and 84 percent of those with postgraduate degrees. But only 24 percent thought that Arafat and the PLO "want peace in the Middle East enough to make real concessions to the Government of Israel," and 56 percent thought that they didn't; and only 28 percent thought that Israel was ready to make real concessions, while 52 percent thought that it wasn't.[44] Considering the longstanding and extremely negative view of the PLO in US public opinion, this poll and others marked the beginning of a more positive evaluation: now, at least, the PLO and the Israeli government were regarded as more-or-less equally intransigent. In truth, Americans remained very skeptical about PLO intentions: only 36 percent felt that it had really accepted the idea of coexistence with Israel, while 33 percent felt that it still aims to destroy Israel. As negative as these opinions are, they nevertheless represent a certain upturn in the organization's reputation. A year earlier, fully two thirds of the American public thought it was a terrorist organization.[45] Harris polls in 1977 and 1978 had found that only 9 to 13 percent thought the PLO "really wants peace"; in 1982, 75 percent labeled it "a force for war"; in 1985, only 9 percent thought Arafat "sought peace"; and in January 1988—a month into the *intifada*—the percentage believing that the PLO was sincere had doubled, but was still only 18 percent.[46] A *Washington Post*/ABC News poll in early April 1989 found that eight out of ten Americans had an unfavorable impression of the PLO, despite its "peace offensive"; but eight out of ten also believed that peace would not be possible without direct talks between Israel and the PLO.[47] Suspicion of the PLO clearly remained deeply ingrained, but Americans appeared to be recognizing it at least as a necessary evil.

A Media General/Associated Press survey in January 1989 discovered that 62 percent believe that the Palestinians "should have their own country." This may be compared with polling data compiled by Gilboa, which found that to the question "Should a Palestinian state be established somewhere?" the affirmative percentages were 71 percent in 1980 and 72 percent in January 1988. The comparison reveals no change (possibly even a decline), but the more remarkable fact is that around two thirds or more of Americans find the principle of Palestinian statehood acceptable. Gilboa tries to explain the strong response by noting that the question doesn't state *where* the Palestinian state would be. When Americans were asked in early 1988 "Should a Palestinian state be established in the West Bank and Gaza?" the responses in four separate polls ranged between 35 and 43 percent.[48] It is not unreasonable to suppose that the respondents to the Media General survey a year later were assuming that the "country" of the Palestinians would be the West Bank and Gaza (would many of them still be thinking of Jordan or some other place?). If the questions are comparable, then of course the differences are quite dramatic. The April 1989 *Washington Post*/ABC News poll reported that "half of those interviewed said they support the establishment of a homeland for the Palestinians in territory occupied by Israel."

How has the US public viewed Israel after a year and more of the *intifada* and the PLO's new moderation? As noted above, Israel's "sympathy" rating has remained generally high but it has had its ups and downs. The April 1989 *Washington Post*/ABC News poll found that support for Israel had rebounded about to its pre-*intifada* levels and was higher now than at any time since it began measuring it in 1982. (It should be noted that Israel's invasion of Lebanon in 1982 caused its popularity to sink dramatically.) At the same time, however, criticism of Israeli policies was also widespread: half of the sample was critical of some aspects of Israel's response to the *intifada,* notably Israel's destruction of the houses of Palestinians accused of anti-Israeli activities, and eight out of ten said that the harsh Israeli countermeasures would weaken American support for Israel. When half the sample was asked whether the US should increase or decrease its aid to Israel, two thirds said it should remain about the same, while 26 percent called for a decrease. But when the other half was asked the same question preceded by information about the actual level of assistance (some $3 billion, as we have noted), 43 percent called for a decrease and only 51 percent felt it should remain the same. To the revealing question "Do you think Israel is a reliable ally of the United States?" the American public's response in 1989 was surprisingly negative. A February 1989 *Washington Post*/ABC News poll found that 56 percent feel that Israel is not reliable; in April, the figure was 46 percent; and in August—in the midst of the hostage crisis precipitated by Israel's kidnapping of Shaykh Obeid and the apparent killing of Col. Higgins—the figure had jumped again to 53 percent. Fifty-one percent of the April sample had called Israel reliable, but in August that level had fallen to only 29 percent.[49] For a country whose American partisans tout it as a "strategic asset," it was not exactly a vote of confidence. Politicians reading the poll results might reasonably conclude that while generalized sympathy for Israel remained quite high, the American public could be highly critical of Israeli actions; and while public suspicion of the PLO remained deeply ingrained, public sympathy for Palestinian grievances was steadily increasing. The opinion climate was not such that a President or even a Congressman should expect a tidal wave of public anger (apart from the organized protest of the Israel lobby) in criticizing Israel's behavior or adopting policies displeasing to the government of Israel or to its faithful American supporters.

In his collection of public opinion studies, *The Arabs in the Mind of America,* Michael Suleiman observes that negative stereotyping has "practically made a non-people" out of the Palestinians.[50] "Nevertheless," he goes on to say, "it is, to say the least, paradoxical that Palestinians are in the news almost every day, yet they are treated as if they do not exist." He observes that public opinion on the Middle East changes slowly. Recognizing that public opinion usually does not have the same impact on foreign policy as it does on domestic policy, and that there is some evidence that "opinion follows policy" in foreign affairs, he suggests "that the primary change has to take place at the highest level of government in its attitudes to the Middle East and to Arabs in particular." But he contends that "in a democracy, the existence of intense and widespread views on any issue can set limits which policy-makers may violate only at the risk of popular and electoral displeasure." His conclusion is that there is a need to develop influential organizations "representing the Arab side or general American interests" to counter-balance the Zionist lobby, as well as a need for strong Presidential leadership.[51] One should bear in mind, however, the view of a former high State Department official with extensive Middle East policy experience, that it is not so much public opinion but the Israel lobby's ability to use election campaign financing to reward or punish congressmen that accounts for Congress's virtually ironclad pro-Israel stance.

The American Jewish Community

The *intifada* and the PLO's new diplomatic stance generated concern, anguish and not a little confusion in the American Jewish community. The TV pictures of Israeli brutality against Palestinian teenagers, women, and even small children were profoundly disturbing to

American Jews. The tradition of abstaining from public criticism of Israel clashed with the desire to speak out against such behavior. A poll of Jews in New York and Long Island in January 1988 found that 39 percent thought that Israeli tactics were too harsh while 38 percent thought them about right and six percent too lenient.[52] Hyman Bookbinder, the veteran pro-Israel lobbyist, said in March 1988, "Yes, we're anguishing, but we're not spending all of our energy anguishing . . . We're trying to help Americans understand why there are riots . . . Don't point the finger of blame at Israel alone."[53] Prominent Jewish liberals such as Rabbi Arthur Hertzberg, a former president of the American Jewish Congress, were openly critical of the Israeli tactics. Michael Lerner, editor of a liberal Jewish magazine, *Tikkun,* intended as an alternative to the neo-conservative *Commentary,* wrote: "The path of least resistance—privately criticizing Israel but publicly supporting it or remaining silent—is actually a dramatic betrayal of the interest of our people . . . Americans must use every possible means to convey to the Israelis . . . that Israel is in deep jeopardy and that the occupation must end."[54] Several prominent mainstream Jewish figures, including Rabbi Alexander Schindler, a leader of Reform Jewry, and Rabbi Balfour Brickner, also voiced their unease; and Morris Abram, president of the Conference of Presidents of Major American Jewish Organizations, reportedly expressed concern directly to Israeli Prime Minister Shamir. AIPAC and the neo-conservative Jewish leadership, however, represented by figures such as Norman Podhoretz, editor of *Commentary,* were generally supportive of the Israeli crackdown. On the extreme right, the Jewish Defense League and similar militant organizations reflected the defiant attitude of the Israeli settlers in the occupied territories. Groups of this kind may have been responsible for threatening telephone calls and obscene mail sent in May and June 1988 to prominent liberal Jewish Americans who had signed an advertisement in the *Jerusalem Post* calling on Israel to change its policies toward Palestinians.[55] If the *intifada* created anguish among many American Jews, it also appeared to increase fundraising for Israel: for example, at a "super-Sunday" fundraiser in Miami in January 1988, the United Jewish Appeal raised 62 percent more than it had in the previous year, and in Boston the increase was 23 percent.[56] But the small Jewish groups critical of Israeli policy also received increased contributions: the American Friends of "Peace Now" reported that donations had doubled since the uprising began, and membership had risen from 12,000 to 20,000. Many more Jews (48 percent) than non-Jews (26 percent) felt that the TV coverage of the *intifada* was biased against Israel, according to a late January 1988 poll.[57]

It should be noted that American Jewish criticism did not begin with the *intifada,* even though the *intifada* may have made such criticism more acceptable. A small movement called "Breira" (Hebrew for "Choice") was created in 1973 to encourage Israel to explore nonviolent and just alternatives for peace with the Palestinians, but it was vilified by mainline Jewish organizations and soon withered. But establishmentarian American Jews began criticizing former Prime Minister Menahem Begin's rigid policies as early as 1979, when 59 prominent Jewish figures, such as Saul Bellow and Leonard Bernstein, expressed distress to Begin over new settlements.[58] Israel's invasion of Lebanon in 1982, and its indirect involvement in the Sabra-Chatila refugee camp massacre, triggered strong American Jewish as well as non-Jewish criticism. Edward Tivnan, in his study of the Israel lobby, reports that a 1983 poll conducted for the American Jewish Committee showed that there was very widespread American Jewish disagreement with the policies of Begin and Shamir, and that almost half the sample disagreed with AIPAC's policy of opposing negotiations with the PLO and the idea of a Palestinian state next to Israel.[59] The conviction in 1987 of an American Jew, Jonathan Pollard, for spying for Israel, elicited a strong reaction from American Jews: 61 percent of a sample polled reacted to what he had done with anger or embarrassment, while only 13 percent were sympathetic; and when asked in the same poll whether American Jews automatically stick up for Israel and if so is it appropriate, 18 percent replied yes-appropriate; 14 percent said yes-not appropriate; and 58 percent replied no, they do not.[60] And in the autumn of 1987, just before the *intifada* broke out, American Jewish organizations expressed acrimonious opposition to the efforts of Israeli religious parties to exclude Reform and Conservative Jews (the branches to which most American Jews belong) from being considered as eligible for automatic citizenship under the Law of Return. At the same time, the American Jewish Congress broke with Israeli government policy by calling for an international conference on the Arab-Israeli conflict. Despite these growing signs of independence, AIPAC continued to convince American congressmen that it represented an American Jewish community basically united around Israeli policies. Yet it seemed clear that ferment was growing among American Jews.

Perhaps the ambivalence in the American Jewish community over Israel's response to the *intifada* accounts for the surprisingly muted response of major Jewish organizations, including AIPAC, to the US decision to open its dialogue with the PLO. The active involvement of a group of American Jews in the negotiating process that led Arafat to utter "the magic words" also helped legitimize the step.[61] The fact that Secretary Shultz, such a staunch and proven friend of Israel, had approved the dialogue, doubtless also helped prevent what some State Department officials had predicted would be a firestorm of protest. An official of the American Jewish Committee said that they had "not received a single angry call"; and representatives of other major groups, such as the Conference of Presidents of Major American Jewish Organizations and the American Jewish Congress, as well as influential personalities across the political spectrum, including Morris Abram, Howard Squadron, Representative Mel Levine, Norman Podhoretz, and Leon Wieseltier took at least a "wait and see" attitude. This mild response was all the more remarkable in light of the bitter hostility expressed by Israeli officials and politicians to the development.

That there is a new pluralism among American Jews on the Middle East and a more critical attitude toward Israel seems beyond doubt, but whether this trend will lead to a weakening of American Jewish commitment to Israel and a weakening of the Israel lobby's influence on US Middle East policy formation remains to be seen. Within the Jewish community itself there is disagreement. Michael Lerner, the editor of *Tikkun*, put the pluralist case forcefully:

> The Bush Administration will soon face heavy lobbying from the Jewish organizations that claim to speak for all American Jews. In fact, they don't . . . . There is another sector whose voices have been stifled inside "the organized Jewish community" and whose members are appalled by Israel's brutal repression of the Palestinian uprising. They reject Mr. Shamir's attempts to perpetuate the occupation of the West Bank . . . . Political and social conservatism, the absence both of democratic mechanisms for choosing national policies and of real debate, and the replacing of authentic Judaism with empty ethnicity, have alienated young Jews from most Jewish organizations that claim to represent them . . . . In the years ahead the silenced majority will increasingly refuse to be hushed . . . . The Administration and the media must not allow themselves to be misled by today's Jewish leaders. Mr. Shamir has no blank check from American Jews to perpetuate the occupation indefinitely and to refuse to participate in serious negotiations.[62]

Steven M. Cohen, a sociologist specializing on the Jewish community, found that younger Jews "are just more remote from Israel," and that there has been a fundamental change in the image of Israel since the middle-1970s. He cited a survey he had conducted for the American Jewish Committee which found that 56 percent of Jews aged 25 to 34 felt close to Israel compared to 78 percent of Jews 65 and older. But establishment Jewish leaders rejected such views. In another expression of the pluralist ferment, a new group intended as an alternative to AIPAC, the Jewish Peace Lobby, was founded in May 1989 by Jerome M. Segal of the University of Maryland, a liberal activist calling for Israeli-Palestinian reconciliation.[63] And in November 1989, a group of 41 prominent Jewish leaders, most representing mainstream organizations, published an open letter to Prime Minister Shamir on the occasion of his visit to the US, expressing their "profound differences" with him on his conduct of the peace process, especially his rejection of the "land for peace" formula. But they reiterated their unwavering support for Israel's security.[64]

Encouraging as these signs are, it must be admitted that they have not by any means revolutionized the stance of American Jews on Palestinian political aspirations. A prominent American Jewish liberal, involved in private discussions with the PLO, concedes that the dovish view is still marginal in American Jewish life. At a conference in Washington in December 1989, marking the second anniversary of the *intifada,* an official of B'nai B'rith insisted that most American Jews have come to feel that the *intifada* is nothing but a new chapter in the perennial Arab effort to destroy Israel.[65]

An Interim Balance Sheet

After only one year in office, to make predictions about the Bush Administration's Middle East policy directions is perhaps premature. On the other hand, the first year of an Administration offers more opportunities for innovation, more room for maneuver, and more freedom from political pressures—especially in controversial areas such as the Middle East—than is likely to be the case later on, as electoral considerations loom larger and policy lines and bureaucratic configurations are hardened. Furthermore, the regional situation in this particular year offered more of an opportunity for peaceful settlement than at any time since the early 1950s. Thus, what happened—or did not happen—in 1989 may be of special significance.

There are certain structural givens in the US Middle East policy-making process that possess remarkable durability. The most important is the highly institutionalized Israel lobby with its deep entrenchment in the halls of Congress. It is simplistic to contend that the lobby alone makes policy. As I have tried to show, Middle East realities create conditions which force certain reactions on the part of Washington. Two of the most important changing Middle East realities involve the two main antagonists: the Palestinians and the Israeli government. The *intifada* and the new PLO "moderation" are having some impact on some elements of secondary importance in the US policy process. Likewise, the perceived intransigence and recklessness of the Israeli government is eroding traditional sympathy for Israel both inside the US government and in American public opinion. On the domestic front, there are several actors besides the lobby who exercise great influence: the President and his chief policy executives obviously are foremost among them. The first year of the Bush Administration provided some indications that the President and Secretary of State might be more sensitive to Middle East realities, and more open to balance, than their immediate predecessors. Other players, somewhat more removed from the levers of policy, also are important: these include the foreign policy opinion-makers in the "elite" news media, the Jewish community apart from AIPAC, and that amorphous phenomenon of the pollsters, "public opinion." I have suggested that there are modest trends in the elite media, public opinion, and the Jewish community, toward a more balanced discussion of the Palestinian-Israeli conflict.

It is tempting for liberal and optimistic analysts to read more into these changes than is warranted. The Bush Administration's journey toward evenhandedness—if such it be—is at best painfully slow and marked by reverses and detours. To make it clear just how slow it is, I would like to conclude with the comments of a leading Palestinian-American intellectual and four senior State Department officials familiar with the Middle East. We have dwelt at some length on Secretary Baker's speech on May 22, 1989, suggesting that it was unexpectedly critical in tone of Israeli expansionism and noting how much unease it caused among the mainstream backers of Israel in Congress and in AIPAC. Lest one suppose that the Baker speech was a definitive example of evenhandedness, it is worth pondering the reaction to it of a leading Palestinian-American moderate, Professor Edward Said:

> . . . what he said was not really new and, in fact, given his
> underlying adherence to the Shamir "peace plan," was outright

rejectionist . . . .Without an admonishing word about a "peace plan" that rejects any possibility of negotiation with the PLO or any real change in the military occupation itself, he repeated formulas about US and Israeli love for "democracy" which took the discourse back several decades . . . .Without holding Israel to a timetable for elections, without specifying concretely what conditions had to obtain for them to be useful and free, without allowing that Palestinians would be justifiably apprehensive about elections for "self-government" held under a more and more brutal Israeli occupation, Baker's speech advanced the already extensive complicity between the United States and Israel a good deal further, thereby sanctioning more, rather than less, Palestinian suffering . . . .Thus, Baker's speech in context gives Israel yet another chance to do what it and the United States clearly want: to postpone Palestinian claims for as long as possible, with the idea that under more pressure they might dissolve entirely, or become once again subservient to Jordanian ambitions.[66]

The second sobering note emerges from the reactions of four present or former senior State Department officials with Middle East responsibilities and familiar with the Congress to the thesis advanced here that "evenhanded" tendencies in the Jewish community and in public opinion could lead to a reorientation of US policy. According to one of these informants, Congress remains unshakably in the grip of the Israel lobby, and there are no signs that liberalization in American Jewry or American public opinion are having any impact on the bedrock support for Israel on Capitol Hill. It has been a struggle (against ferocious opposition from the pro-Israel congressmen) simply to keep the US-PLO dialogue alive. In the opinion of another senior official, to expect a major shift in Washington's pro-Israel tilt, given the predispositions of the Bush-Baker Middle East team, would be extremely naive. A third official insists that American policy in the Middle East is doing quite well, and that there is no urgency about changing it. And a fourth diplomat argues that there is very little that any party, including the US, can do to resolve the Palestinian-Israeli conflict, because of its historical intractability and the durability of Israel's privileged place in US domestic politics. That being the case, the outlook for a major American role in bringing peace (with justice) to the Palestinian-Israeli struggle is slim, and "realism" suggests an incremental, "conflict-management" approach. It is not surprising, then, that some observers who support a two-state solution attentive both to Palestinian rights and Israeli security believe that the US should disengage itself altogether from peacemaking, since it seems incapable of playing a fair and constructive role. For those, however, who believe that without a major American role, the likelihood of renewed conflict in the region has to be considered substantial, such a withdrawal would be a mistake in spite of the present disappointing signs. Yet for those who believe in the pluralist model of American politics, there are also enough indications of positive change to warrant continuing public efforts to improve US policy.

Notes

1. See, e.g., a study commissioned by the office of the Secretary of Defense, by Graham E. Fuller, "The West Bank of Israel—Point of No Return?" Santa Monica, CA: The Rand Corporation, August 1989 (RSD-3777-0SD).

2. For the text of the Reagan Plan, see the *New York Times*, September 2, 1982, p. A11. ". . . [I]t is clear to me that peace cannot be achieved by the formation of an independent Palestinian state in those territories. Nor is it achievable on the basis of Israeli sovereignty or permanent control over the West Bank and Gaza . . . .[I]t is the firm view of the United States that self-government by the Palestinians of the West Bank and Gaza in association with Jordan offers the best chance for a durable, just and lasting peace."

3. Palestinians argue that the PLO showed good faith and flexibility by offering two compromise proposals that would have enabled it to endorse the two UN resolutions: one, by the US, publicly recognizing the Palestinians' right of self-determination; the other by the PLO agreeing to recognize "pertinent" UN resolutions, including 242 and 338. See Daoud Kuttab, "PLO: breaking out of the 'no win, no-peace' initiative," *Christian Science Monitor*, March 11, 1987.

4. The text of Arafat's statement and Shultz's announcement authorizing the dialogue may be found in the *New York Times*, December 15, 1988, pp. A18-19.

5. Having failed to satisfy the American conditions in his speech before the UN General Assembly in Geneva on December 13, Arafat—on the insistent urging of the Swedes, Egyptians, and Saudis—agreed to call a news conference the next day to "clarify" the PLO position. He succeeded in clarifying three points: first, the PLO chairman was persuaded to "renounce" rather than simply "condemn" terrorism, "including individual, group, and state terrorism." Second, he also agreed to state the PLO's acceptance of UN resolutions 242 and 338 without adding any implied conditions about Palestinian self-determination. Third, he spoke unambiguously of "the right of all parties concerned in the Middle East conflict to exist in peace and security and, as I have mentioned, including the State of Palestine and Israel and other neighbors." See the text of his statement in the *New York Times*, December 15, 1988, p. A19; see also the various accounts in the *New York Times* and the *Washington Post* of December 15 and 16, 1988. On the Swedish role, see Françoise Nieto, "Swedish 'midwife' to the US/PLO rapprochement," *Manchester Guardian Weekly* (*Le Monde* English section), December 25, 1988.

6. William B. Quandt, *Decade of Decisions: American Policy Toward the Arab-Israeli Conflict, 1967-1976* (Berkeley: University of California Press, 1977), p. 36. See also Seth P. Tillman, *The United States in the Middle East: Interests and Obstacles* (Bloomington: Indiana University Press, 1982), pp. 288-89. Even Steven L. Spiegel, who insists (untenably,

in my view, in light of his own evidence) that the Israel lobby's influence is vastly overrated, rightly emphasizes the importance of the President and "the people at the top." See his *The Other Arab-Israeli Conflict: Making America's Middle East Policy, From Truman to Reagan* (Chicago: University of Chicago Press, 1985), pp. 390-93.

7. Spiegel, *op. cit.*, p. 395.

8. On Iran-contra, see *The Tower Commission Report: The Full Text of the President's Special Review Board* (New York: Times Books, 1987), and *Report of the Congressional Committees Investigating the Iran-Contra Affair* (Washington, November 1987). See also Bob Woodward, *Veil: The Secret Wars of the CIA* (New York: Simon and Schuster, 1987); James A. Bill, *The Eagle and the Lion: The Tragedy of American-Iranian Relations* (New Haven: Yale University Press, 1988), esp. Ch. 8 and pp. 410-14; and Michael C. Hudson, "From Lebanon to 'Irangate': A Review of Recent American Middle East Policy," (Washington, D.C.: Georgetown University Center for Contemporary Arab Studies, CCAS Reports Series, 1987).

9. Secretary Baker, "Principles and Pragmatism: American Policy Toward the Arab-Israeli Conflict," an address before the American-Israel Public Affairs Committee (AIPAC), U.S. Department of State, Bureau of Public Affairs, *Current Policy*, No. 1176.

10. Thomas L. Friedman, "Israeli Leaders Rebuff Baker on Call to Forgo Expansion," *New York Times*, May 24, 1989.

11. United Nations Security Council, S/PV 2867 (June 9, 1989). Ambassador Pickering's statement was made during the discussion of this issue in the Council on the previous day.

12. "The Deadly Silence: A Report on the 1988 Presidential Candidates and Where They Stand on the Middle East," (Washington: The Arab American Institute, 1988). See also, Gerald F. Seib, "Majority of US Presidential Candidates are Turning a Blind Eye to Mideast Riots," *Wall Street Journal*, February 29, 1988.

13. William E. Schmidt, "Democrats Back Palestinians at 7 State Party Conventions," *New York Times*, June 23, 1988; and David E. Rosenbaum, "In Setting Platform, Party Puts Aside Palestinian Issue," *New York Times*, July 20, 1988.

14. In a campaign speech before B'nai B'rith in Baltimore on September 7, 1988, Bush said, "Anyone who has trouble making up his mind on this issue [of a Palestinian state], or who proposes to leave it open, just doesn't understand the dangers to Israel and to the United States, just doesn't understand the very real threats that continue to exist. My Administration would not support the creation of any Palestinian entity that would jeopardize the security of our strategic ally Israel."

15. Robert D. McFadden, "Kissinger Urged Ban on TV Reports," *New York Times*, March 5, 1988.

16. *Building For Peace: An American Strategy for the Middle East*, report of the Washington Institute's Presidential Study Group on US Policy in the Middle East. Washington, D.C.: The Washington Institute for Near East Policy, 1988.

17. Raphael Calis, "The Bush People and Palestine: High Hopes Dashed?" *The Return* (March 1989), pp. 6-9.

18. Kelly's meeting with Palestinians in the occupied territories in August 1989 was described as "stormy." He was said to have "flatly told the group the United States opposes the creation of a Palestinian state." He was also said to have been angered by the group's handing him a letter asserting that its members considered themselves only agents for the PLO. "US Official Meets with Palestinians," *New York Times*, August 4, 1989.

19. Neil A. Lewis, "Senators Criticize Shamir's Position on Mideast Peace," *New York Times*, March 5, 1988. Noting that Secretary Shultz's diplomacy was rightly predicated on the formula of land for peace, the senators wrote: "Accordingly, we were dismayed to read in the *New York Times* of February 26 that Prime Minister Shamir had said that 'this expression of territory for peace is not accepted by me.' "

20. On July 12, 1989 Israel announced that it would begin a phased reopening of West Bank schools, and the resolution was amended to commend Israel for its decision and to express the hope that the schools would not be used for political purposes.

21. "FY 1990 Assistance Request for the Middle East," Statements by Deputy Assistant Secretaries Edward S. Walker and A. Peter Burleigh, March 1 and 2, 1989, *Department of State Bulletin*, May 1989, pp. 61-63. In addition, American private contributions to Israel may amount to nearly $1 billion, bringing the total annual aid coming from the US to around $4 billion. These private contributions include some $450 million from individuals and institutions through the Israel bond drive, United Jewish Appeal tax-deductible gifts amounting to some $350 million, and other smaller fundraising efforts. See Steven Pearlstein, "What Israel Needs Most—Independence," *Washington Post*, March 12, 1989, Outlook Section, p. D1.

22. In a strongly worded speech that was all the more remarkable for having been delivered less than three weeks before the election, Defense Secretary Frank Carlucci made what journalists described as "a stinging attack on pro-Israeli lobbying groups and congressional factions," blaming them for the loss of tens of billions of dollars worth of jobs by blocking military cooperation with Arab states. *Washington Post,* October 22, 1988.

23. Thomas L. Friedman, "Public Support for Israel Slipping, Foreign Minister Told by Senators," *New York Times,* March 15, 1989.

24. E.J. Dionne, Jr., "US Jews' Muted Reaction Said to Reflect New Uncertainty," *New York Times,* December 18, 1988.

25. See, e.g., the statements in *The Congressional Record* on May 18, 1989 by Senator McCain (S 5733); Senator Grassley (S 5740); Senator Lieberman (S 5750); Senator Hatch (S 5751); Senator Lautenberg (S 5752); Senator Levin (S 5753); and Representative Barney Frank (E 1790).

26. For the text and signatories see the *Washington Post,* July 11, 1989. It was noted that 228 members of the House had signed a similar letter.

27. Daniel Schorr, "Bush's Ill-Advised Letter to Shamir," *New York Times,* July 25, 1989. According to Schorr, the letter proved counterproductive for Shamir's purposes because Bush also stated that he fully endorsed Secretary Baker's May 22 statement.

28. "Bush Fights Language to Curb PLO Contacts," *Washington Post,* July 20, 1989; "Senate Kills Strict Curb on PLO Contacts . . . ," *Washington Post,* July 21, 1989.

29. "End the PLO Dialogue?" *Washington Post,* July 19, 1989.

30. Robert Pear, "Senator's Criticism of Israel Leads to Party Dispute," *New York Times*, August 6, 1989.

31. Don Oberdorfer, "Relations Withstand Buffeting, But Policy Specialists See More Questioning of Israel in US" *Washington Post*, August 2, 1989.

32. The text of the Baker five-point plan was eventually published in a US State Department press release on December 6, 1989. In it, the US "understands" (1) " . . . that there is agreement that an Israeli delegation should conduct a dialogue with a Palestinian delegation in Cairo"; (2) that Egypt cannot substitute itself for the Palestinians and that it will consult with Palestinians on all aspects of the dialogue, as well as with Israel and the US; (3) " . . . that Israel will attend the dialogue only after a satisfactory list of Palestinians has been worked out"; (4) that Israel will come to the dialogue on the basis of its May 14 initiative; Palestinians will come "prepared to discuss elections and the negotiating process in accordance with Israel's initiative," and "therefore, that Palestinians would be free to raise issues that relate to their opinions on how to make elections and the negotiating process succeed"; and (5) that the foreign ministers of Israel, Egypt, and the US meet in Washington within two weeks.

33. Quoted in David B. Ottaway, "Baker Plan for Middle East Dialogue Near Impasse," *Washington Post*, November 29, 1989.

34. See John M. Goshko, "Baker Expresses Impatience Over Stalemate on Mideast Talks," *Washington Post*, January 11, 1990; and Thomas L. Friedman, "Senator Dole's Jackpot Question on Foreign Aid Stirs Up Congress," *New York Times*, January 21, 1990. According to Friedman, Secretary Baker "hit the ceiling" after reading comments attributed to a Shamir aide suggesting that Baker was not serious about the Middle East process.

35. A 1988 Los Angeles survey reported that 40% of a non-Jewish sample thought press coverage of the *intifada* was fair, while 11% thought that it made the Palestinians look better and 13% thought that it made them look worse than they really are. But the majority of the Jewish sample thought that the press had made the Palestinians look better than they really are, and a wide margin was upset by television pictures of Israeli soldiers using physical force against Palestinians. Data cited by Fouad Moughrabi, "American Public Opinion and the Question of Palestine," ADC Issue Paper No. 22 (Washington, D.C.: American-Arab Anti-Discrimination Committee Research Institute, 1988), pp. 16, 22.

36. In a seminar at Tel Aviv University in Spring 1989, Mary Curtius of *The Boston Globe* and Martin Fletcher of NBC News both attested to the relegation of the *intifada* to secondary status in print and television news. Cited in the *Bulletin* of the Moshe Dayan Center for Middle Eastern and African Studies, Tel Aviv University (# 10, Fall 1989).

37. Fouad Moughrabi, "American Public Opinion and the Question of Palestine," *ADC Issue Paper*, No. 22 (Washington, D.C.: American-Arab Anti-Discrimination Committee Research Institute, 1988), p. 8.

38. Eytan Gilboa, "The Palestinian Uprising: Has it Turned American Public Opinion?" *Orbis*, 33,1 (Winter 1989), pp. 21-37; p. 26. The 51% sympathy score is from the *Los Angeles Times* survey in early April 1988. Gilboa also cites a Marttila and Kiley survey of April 18-24 that gave Israel a 61% sympathy score.

39. Gilboa, *op. cit.*, p. 36. See also Mark J. Penn and Douglas E. Schoen, "American Attitudes Toward the Middle East," *Public Opinion*, May-June 1988, pp. 45-48, for a similar conclusion.

40. Moughrabi, *op. cit.*, p. 3, citing a *Chicago Tribune* poll, reported on April 26, 1988.

41. Moughrabi, *op. cit.*, p. 11, citing *Los Angeles Times* poll results, published April 12 and 13, 1988.

42. Gilboa, *op. cit.*, p. 35.

43. Gilboa, *op. cit.*, p. 24; cf. also, "In a Poll, Americans Appear to Lose Sympathy for Israel," *New York Times*, July 8, 1988.

44. "Little Hope on the Mideast," *New York Times*, January 18, 1989. See also Fouad Moughrabi, "The *Intifada*: A Key Factor in Changing American Public Opinion," *The Return*, July 1989, pp. 20-21.

45. Penn and Schoen, *op. cit.*, p. 46.

46. Gilboa, *op. cit.*, pp. 28-29.

47. "Americans Polled Urge Israeli-PLO Talks," *Washington Post*, April 7, 1989.

48. Gilboa, *op. cit.*, p. 34.

49. "The *Washington Post*-ABC News Poll," *Washington Post*, August 5, 1989.

50. Michael W. Suleiman, *The Arabs in the Mind of America* (Brattleboro, Vermont: Amana Books, 1988), p. 153.

51. Suleiman, *op. cit.*, p. 155.

52. *The Economist*, February 6, 1988, p. 25, citing a poll taken by the Long Island newspaper *Newsday*.

53. Quoted in Linda Feldmann, "US Jews in Turmoil over Violence in Israel," *Christian Science Monitor*, March 4, 1988.

54. Cited in Edward Tivnan, "American Jews Break Ranks," *The Nation*, December 12, 1988, p. 649.

55. Dennis Hevesi, "Signers of Ad on Arab-Israeli Conflict Report Phone Threats," *New York Times*, June 25, 1988.

56. *The Economist*, February 6, 1988.

57. *Christian Science Monitor*, March 4, 1988.

58. Richard L. Strout, "Israel: the 'Sea Change' in US Opinion," *Christian Science Monitor*, September 28, 1979.

59. Edward Tivnan, *The Lobby: Jewish Political Power and American Foreign Policy* (New York: Simon and Schuster, 1987), p. 206.

60. E.J. Dionne, Jr., "Poll Shows Jews and Non-Jews Differ on Pollard," *New York Times*, April 12, 1987, reporting a *New York Times*/CBS News poll. Interestingly, 82 percent of the non-Jewish respondents did not know that it was Israel that Pollard had spied for. The main difference between Jewish and non-Jewish respondents was that 40 percent of Jewish respondents thought Pollard's sentence was too harsh, compared to 22 percent of non-Jews.

61. For a participant's account see Rita E. Hauser, "Behind Our Breakthrough with the PLO," *Washington Post* (Outlook Section), December 18, 1988.

62. Michael Lerner, "Who Speaks for American Jews?" *New York Times*, February 24, 1989.

63. On these developments, see Howard Kurtz, "A Critical Generation of US Jews," *Washington Post*, February 4, 1989.

64. The letter, dated November 16, 1989, states in part: "Yet just as public opinion is sharply divided among Israeli citizens on how peace and security can most constructively be pursued, so American Jews too hold diverse views. We have differed on how best to move toward implementation of your government's proposal for elections in the West Bank and Gaza. More basically, profound differences exist with respect to the principle of land for peace with secure borders, a principle that some reject outright, but, we believe, most American Jews do not reject." See also the account in the *New York Times*, November 17, 1989.

65. An address by Dr. Michael Neiditch, Director of Programs for B'nai B'rith International Affairs, at the Center for Strategic and International Studies, Washington, D.C., December 7, 1989.

66. Edward W. Said, "Sanctum of the Strong," *The Nation*, July 10, 1989, pp. 48-50.

7 THE SOVIET UNION, THE INTIFADA AND CHANGES IN PLO POLICY

I. P. Belyayev

Some people in both the West and the East translate the Arabic word *intifada* as "uprising." The *intifada* is more than that. It is a protest aimed at achieving a quite definite result—the cessation of the Israeli occupation of the West Bank of the Jordan River and the Gaza Strip and the realization of the national rights of the Palestinian Arab people, above all the right to self-determination. In particular, since the Palestine National Council proclaimed an independent Arab state of Palestine in November 1988, the *intifada* has had very specific objectives.

1. The Shape of the Palestinian State

I do not wish to rush into predictions about the time when the independent Palestinian Arab state will obtain a territory of its own, i.e., the West Bank and the Gaza Strip. It is perfectly clear, however, that the *intifada,* which has already been in progress for close to two years now, has brought forward this historic moment.

We in Moscow do not wish to be in a hurry to stress whether this implies an independent Palestinian Arab state as proclaimed in Algiers, or a confederation of an independent Arab state of Palestine with Jordan or Israel. It is quite obvious, however, that the Palestinians themselves take a clear-cut stand on this issue: first, an independent Arab state of Palestine should be established, and then the possibility will be considered of setting up a confederation with Jordan or Israel.

Usually, to mention the possibility of establishing a confederation of an independent Arab state of Palestine with Israel gives rise to doubts among an audience. These doubts normally boil down to the point that the Palestinian Arabs are not likely to agree to any kind of alliance with the Jewish state. As a general rule, the Palestinian Arabs' "irreconcilability" with Israel and, of course, Palestinian "terrorism" are then recalled. It is my strong conviction that such doubts are unnecessary. In particular, the establishment of a confederation of an independent Arab state of Palestine with Israel or, maybe, a tripartite confederation of an Arab state of Palestine with Jordan and Israel, will remove quite a few thorny problems that are now on the agenda of moves for a Middle East settlement. Prime among these is the highly complicated problem of the Holy City, East Jerusalem. The decision to annex occupied East Jerusalem to the Jewish state and proclaim the whole of Jerusalem the "one and indivisible" Israeli capital was unilateral, in that it was adopted by Israel alone. Even the United States, like almost all members of the international community maintaining diplomatic relations with Israel, has not yet recognized this action. Only two or three countries which do not play any substantial part in present-day international affairs are an exception in this respect.

The establishment of a confederation of an independent Arab state of Palestine with Israel could also help solve many other problems. One such problem would be that of disputed border territories. There would simply remain no grounds for such a dispute. Jerusalem could be proclaimed the capital of the confederation, alternately governed by specially appointed representatives of either party.

It might be argued that conclusions about such complicated Palestinian-Israeli and Arab-Israeli problems are easy to draw, but exceedingly difficult, if not impossible, to put into effect. I think that such reasoning leads us into a dead end, offering practically no means of settling the Palestine problem or other problems of the Middle East. It is hardly necessary for us to doom ourselves to such trials.

Yasser Arafat, who was recently elected president of the newly proclaimed independent Palestinian Arab state and who remains the leader of the Palestine Liberation Organization, has more than once affirmed the possibility of establishing a Jordanian-Palestinian or a Jordanian-Israeli or a tripartite confederation. These statements were made after the beginning of the *intifada* and testify to the Palestinian Arabs' willingness to work toward achieving a practical Middle East settlement. The main concern is to ensure that such a settlement should be really fair.

2. The Intifada

The world has witnessed a nearly 18-months-long active campaign of civil disobedience to the Israeli occupation troops, a campaign of refusal to become reconciled to the Israeli occupation, which has lasted for almost 21 years. The *intifada* is a military-political event. Its participants have the Israeli army as their principal opponent, even though they themselves do not bear arms. Note that in this particular case, one of the most advanced armies in the world, which has the most up-to-date means of warfare at its disposal, deals with or conducts military operations against unarmed teenagers, who at the worst resort to stone-throwing. That is precisely why the *intifada* has been dubbed a "revolution of stones."

The main force of the *intifada* is the young generation of Palestinian Arabs. Adolescents and young people between the ages of 14 and 18 have been and remain the nucleus of those who are acting against the Israeli invaders. They do not take up arms, being fully aware that they would immediately be accused of anti-Jewish terrorism in the occupied Arab territories if they did. In contrast, there exists a well-ramified system of Jewish settlements in these territories, whose inhabitants often fall upon the participants in the *intifada* with even greater violence than the Israeli soldiers do.

Israeli politicians and the owners of the Israeli mass media have made often successful efforts to convince public opinion that the Palestinian Arabs' struggle was a form of "terrorism." It must be admitted that, in the past, certain actions of the Palestinians, in particular against civilians and schoolchildren, were anything but humane. However, the Palestinian Arabs' actions against the Israeli troops can by no means be regarded as terrorism.

I do not favor referring to the *intifada* as a revolution. A revolution on the West Bank and in the Gaza Strip is still a long way off. One can only speak about it in the future tense. Yet the *intifada* reflects the general discontent of the Arab population of the Israeli-occupied Palestinian Arab territories with the outrages committed by the Israeli authorities for nearly 21 years.

The *intifada* is not an ordinary action of people dissatisfied with something or other. It is an organized civil campaign, which has a joint leadership. In my view, what is significant about it is that in the early months of the *intifada* the presence of the religious element was prominent, particularly in the Gaza Strip. A strong Muslim influence even showed itself in PLO documents. The religious factor is still present in the *intifada* and plays a noticeable part in it.

The *intifada* was a complete surprise to the Israeli military authorities, which seems rather strange. Was it really believed in Tel Aviv that the occupation of the Arab territories, referred to as "administered territories," would eventually lead to their smooth and painless annexation to the State of Israel? Such a belief would be extremely naive.

The *intifada* was no less unexpected by the Arab countries. In its early months, the Arab countries were the only ones in which no campaigns and demonstrations in support of the *intifada* were staged. Even in Damascus, the analysis of the nature and aims of the *intifada* took quite a long time.

The PLO leadership sized up the situation and established operative contacts with the local leaders of the *intifada* without delay. This is eloquently attested to by the fact that the participants in the *intifada* have pointed out time and again in their statements that the PLO has been and remains the sole legitimate representative of the Arab people of Palestine. The leaders of the *intifada* immediately gave their complete approval to the decisions of the 1988 Algiers session of the Palestine National Council on the proclamation of an independent Palestinian Arab state.

The *intifada* has become more than a response to the policy and actions of the Israeli occupation authorities. The powerful campaign of civil disobedience on the West Bank and Gaza Strip has grown into a strong national patriotic popular protest against Israeli attempts to perpetuate the occupation. In recent years, it was increasingly believed in Tel Aviv—at least, by the members of the "national unity" government—that the occupation as such had already become an integral part of life for the Palestinian Arabs, and that the Palestinian Arabs had already forgotten about all other things such as the full implementation of the well-known UN resolutions on the establishment of a Palestinian Arab state. But they had not forgotten.

Today, young Palestinian Arabs—adolescents and young people between the ages of 14 and 18—are a driving force in the *intifada*. They have not known the trials which their parents and relatives experienced under the yoke of the occupation, nor do they know the compromises to which people of the older generation might have agreed. They are fully resolved to win complete freedom in exercising inalienable Palestinian national rights, including the right to self-determination and the establishment of their own independent state—universal human rights which are guaranteed to them by Resolution 181 of the UN General Assembly of November 29, 1947.

Other UN resolutions have provided for the right of Palestinian refugees to return to their land and their homes. Those Palestinian refugees who cannot or do not wish to return must be paid a certain sum of money by way of compensation.

After the recognition by the Palestine National Council in Algiers in November 1988 of UN Security Council Resolution 242, there should clearly be an adequate response on the part of Israel to this recognition of Israel's right to existence. This should take place at an international conference on a Middle East settlement.

The *intifada* has already inflicted appreciable damage on the Israeli economy. The boycott of Israeli goods resulted in a drop in the goods turnover in the occupied territories by two thirds to reach 56 million dollars in 1988 as compared with 174 million dollars in 1987, and the downward trend continued in 1989, when there was a decrease in the volume of imports of goods and products from the West Bank and the Gaza Strip.

West European countries have changed their policies on Israeli products in response to the Israeli policy of suppressing the campaign of civil disobedience. The negative attitude of Western Europe toward Israel became so strong that Israeli Minister of Trade Ariel Sharon stated during a tour of a number of West European countries that "there is a trade boycott against Israel . . . Major West European countries abstain from any relations with Israel." Such things never happened in the past.

Late in 1988, West European countries launched a very interesting operation—the import of farming produce directly from Palestinian producers without Israeli middlemen. In response, Israel criticized the assistance rendered by the EC countries in carrying out a number of agricultural and industrial projects and developing the system of vocational education to strengthen the local Palestinian institutions. In this connection, the EC provided direct assistance to the occupied Arab territories, which amounted to 8 million European currency units ($8.88 million dollars) in 1987-1988.

The establishment by the EC member countries of direct contacts with representatives of Palestinian business circles living and operating on the West Bank and in the Gaza Strip in defiance of the wishes of the Israeli occupation authorities is an unprecedented phenomenon. It is a result of the *intifada* and evidence of its success.

The essence of the Israeli standpoint remains quite simple: Israel does not accept the idea of a Middle East settlement providing for Palestinian Arab rights. Regrettably, the military-political establishment of Israel is not ready either to discuss or to solve the Palestine problem. Israel today has no General de Gaulle of its own who could venture to assume full responsibility for taking a decisive step towards normalization of relations with the Arabs on the basis of the recently adopted decisions of the Palestine National Council. Instead, its proposals on issues such as autonomy seem designed to try to gain time to suppress the Palestinian Arab campaign of civil disobedience.

3. The Intifada and Soviet Policy

In what way has the *intifada* influenced the Soviet policy in the Middle East?

The *intifada* is a confirmation that the resolution of the Middle East (or Arab-Israeli) conflict has become even more necessary today than it was in the past. Assuming that the *intifada* will continue, we may become witnesses to a civil disobedience campaign growing into a real war. It is not to be ruled out that Israel, which is losing not only its nerve, but also its patience and its resources in its attempts to suppress the campaign of civil disobedience, may become the initiator of such a war.

The intensity of the struggle has already exceeded every possible level that is characteristic of a pre-crisis situation. That is why, in order to prevent still another crisis in the Middle East, efforts must be made to prompt the two sides—Israel and the Arab state of Palestine—to enter into negotiations. Such negotiations should be conducted on an equal footing, i.e., rule out *diktat* in any form whatsoever.

What is the essence of the Soviet stand on an independent Palestinian state?

The Soviet Union does not wish to force upon the Palestinians, the Arabs in general, or the Israelis, any particular definition of the future Palestinian Arab state, or any considerations of establishing or not establishing a confederation between the Arab State of Palestine and some other state. The recognition by the Soviet Union not only of the Palestinian right to self-determination, but also of the absolute Palestinian right to decide upon the path that the independent Palestinian Arab state will take, is the cornerstone of the Soviet policy in the Middle East. It is to be noted in this respect that Yasser Arafat, President of the proclaimed independent State of Palestine, has spoken for the establishment of a confederation with Israel. It is up to the Palestinians themselves to decide all their problems without any outside influence and without any intermediate stages.

During a recent stop in Cairo, Soviet Minister of Foreign Affairs Edward Shevardnadze met first with Moshe Arens and then with Yasser Arafat. This demonstrated that a businesslike political talk with the Israeli Foreign Minister was necessary and that a meeting with Arafat on an equal basis was no less necessary. It would be a good thing if the United States and Israel not only comprehended this, but took it into consideration in their day-to-day work during preparations for a Middle East settlement.

It is apparent that some US leaders are still reluctant to hold a dialogue with the Soviet Union about reaching a Middle East settlement on an equal basis. This attitude is at variance not only with the moment and the character of Soviet-American relations, but also with the interests of both our countries. The Soviet Union proceeds from the point that it must and shall respect US interests in the Middle East. No one in the Soviet Union is striving to infringe upon them or do any damage to them. It is to be hoped that the United States will act similarly with respect to the legitimate interests of the Soviet Union in the region, which are real and have existed for quite a few decades now.

Under such conditions, much could be achieved in responding to the *intifada,* while preparing for the solution of the Palestine problem and other issues involved in the settlement of the Middle East conflict. Israel is inclined to view every radical proposal on the Palestine problem as pressure or, even, as a threat. Yet the *intifada* has generated among Israelis a new attitude both to the participants in the civil disobedience campaign and to those who today represent the proclaimed independent Arab State of Palestine.

I believe that it is necessary to restore diplomatic relations between the Soviet Union and Israel. I am aware that Israel is more interested in this than the Soviet Union, though it still ventures to lay down quite a number of conditions. This, to my mind, reflects its inflexible approach to the policy of the Soviet Union—an approach that does not take into account the impact of the *intifada* on the Middle East and the world as a whole. In Cairo, the Soviet Minister of Foreign Affairs defined stages for the restoration of Soviet-Israeli diplomatic relations. I would view the problem somewhat differently. If there is a need to discuss with Israel the entire range of issues relating to the Middle East, then it would be better to do this systematically and without intermediaries. Today, even belligerent countries retain their embassies in each other's capitals, as was the case for five years during the Iran-Iraq war. New times have come. Today in Moscow the de-ideologization of international relations is strongly advocated. And I think that the restoration of diplomatic relations with Israel would be a right step in this right direction.

However, Israel should not consider that, having restored diplomatic relations with the Soviet Union, it could continue with its old irreconcilable and aggressive policy with respect to a Middle East settlement, in particular, with respect to the question of convening an international conference on the Middle East. As a result of the *intifada,* the convocation of such a conference now is in the interests of Israel, since the civil disobedience campaign on the West Bank and in the Gaza Strip may continue indefinitely. In the past, such campaigns resulted in the victory, for example, of those who stood for the independence of India and other countries. Today the settlement of the Middle East problem could remove tensions in the Middle East which may otherwise end in still another war between the Israelis and the Arabs. Israel does not need such a war today. That is why in Moscow the *intifada* is viewed as a kind of accelerator of a just settlement of all Middle East problems. It has presented a historic chance which Israel should not miss.

8 REFLECTIONS ON THE RECENT CHANGES IN THE CONFLICT

Yehoshafat Harkabi

The *intifada* has been an event of great historical importance, not only for the Palestinians but also for the Israeli Jews. It has made the Israelis more aware of the fact that the Palestinians constitute a national entity and are not only individuals subordinate to Israeli rule. More Israelis now understand that Israel will not be able to maintain for long its rule in the occupied territories, and that a Palestinian state is an historical inevitability. More Israelis have resigned themselves to the idea that Israel will have to negotiate with the PLO.

However, overplaying the importance of the *intifada* may distort the whole picture, as if the *intifada* is the only problem that needs to be remedied, and as if, had there been no *intifada,* all would have been fine. Paradoxically, such an approach may trivialize the Arab-Israeli conflict. Furthermore, criticism has been directed mainly against the Israeli means of quelling the uprising, as if only they have been wrong and not the political situation itself.

On the whole, the Israeli army has behaved with restraint. It could have employed much more drastic measures, following other Middle Eastern examples. The Israeli military high command has emphasized to the political leadership that the solution to the *intifada* is political and not military, and has not hesitated to announce this to the public, despite the explicit displeasure of the political leadership. The military command has withstood sharp criticism coming from political circles for its complacency. This is an extraordinary case, which should be appreciated, of the military being less bellicose than their political masters, and serving as a constraining factor on them. The *intifada* has drawn some international attention to the need to reach a settlement. However, its most important role has been internal, as a result of its great effect on the Palestinians as a nation-building force. Politically and historically, its greatest achievement has been the pressure it exerted on the PLO to moderate its positions and adopt a pragmatic policy. This was a paradoxical outcome, as the sufferings of the Palestinians under occupation from the measures of repression of the *intifada* could have had a radicalizing effect on them, increasing their acrimony and hatred.

In changing its long-held position and accepting a two-state settlement, the PLO has inaugurated a reversal of roles in the Arab-Israeli conflict which may have opened a new chapter in the annals of the conflict. Originally, the Zionist-Israeli side repeatedly expressed its readiness to accept partition schemes and thus endorsed a two-state settlement. By assuming a conciliatory stance, it won international support without which Zionism could not have succeeded. At the time the Arab position was adamant in advocating an Arab one-state solution. The change in the Palestinian posture tilts the international balance in favor of the Palestinians and against Israel.

I welcome the PLO's recent pronouncements of accepting a two-state settlement, but at the same time, as an Israeli, I view the change in the international balance of support with anguish. It is indeed folly to close our eyes to this new reality. If Israel makes the necessary policy changes, its lot will be incomparably better than if it eventually yields under duress. Unfortunately, Israel's present political leadership has not yet come to realize this.

There has been a basic disparity between the US and the Israeli position, which has only recently come to light. American rejection of the PLO was conditional and subject to reversal upon the PLO's acceptance of the three famous demands: recognition of Israel's right to exist, renunciation of and abstention from terrorism, and acceptance of UN Security Council resolutions 242 and 338. The conditional nature of the American rejection concealed the categorical nature of the Israeli rejection, which is not based on what the PLO *does,* but on what it *is,* namely, a national movement that claims that the Palestinians constitute a political entity, and that as such they deserve to have a state.

A settlement of the Arab-Israeli conflict can ensue from a negotiated peace agreement rather than from one dictated by the Israelis or by the Arabs. A dictated peace is hegemonic, namely, one side imposes its conditions on the other. A negotiated peace is, by nature, *egalitarian,* the outcome of a bargaining process. It does not mean equality in all details, but parallelism in status. The Palestinians cannot resign themselves to the idea that the Israelis deserve to have an independent state, while they themselves should be content with an autonomy under Israeli aegis. The Americans addressed the demand to the Palestinians to agree to the principle of a two-state formula and recognize Israel's right to exist as a precondition for their participation in the negotiation process, whereas a similar recognition by Israel of the Palestinians' right to have a state of their own is deferred, hopefully to be the outcome of the negotiations. This asymmetry in demands contradicts the egalitarian nature of a settlement. A preliminary mutual recognition of the two-state formula is a necessary prerequisite if there is to be real progress toward a settlement.

One important factor is overlooked by the advice offered to the Palestinians to accept Shamir's proposal of elections as good tactics to start negotiations which will enable them to move ahead toward the achievement of their national aspirations. The Palestinian difficulty with this proposal is not tactical, but strategic. The Palestinians remember Shamir's and the Likud's numerous declarations that Israel will never give up its control of the occupied territories, and that between the Mediterranean Sea and the Jordan River there will only be Israeli sovereignty. Thus, they are apprehensive that Shamir's proposal is only a means to ensure his goal and that elections, autonomy and Israeli sovereignty constitute one package deal.

Autonomy should not be compared to statehood in so far as a settlement that will usher in a Palestinian state may be part of a big international scheme to settle the Palestinian refugees and assist in the establishment of the new state. On the other hand, autonomy, considered as a partial and provisional step, may be accorded without the necessary preparatory arrangements, leaving the Palestinians to fend for themselves, encountering tremendous difficulties of all kinds. The whole venture may thus falter and end in chaos. The probational nature of the autonomy scheme may then be used as proof that the Palestinians do not deserve independence. Hence, the Palestinians should be interested in a gradual settlement, which will allow the molding of the institutions of statehood in an orderly and incremental fashion. They should prepare themselves not only for the blessings of achieving independence, but for its difficulties and disappointments. They should do this for their sake and for the sake of the stability of the settlement.

Palestinians may fear that the election and autonomy proposals are not the beginning of a road, but its end. An intimation, or even an assertion, by the Americans that this is not the intention and will not happen, cannot be convincing for them, unless it is embodied in an official undertaking. I do not represent the Palestinians, yet it seems to me that they will be reluctant to get on the train of negotiations unless they are apprised of the general destination. An important lesson can be drawn from the arms control negotiations, whereby the general principles are agreed upon by the parties prior to the commencement of the negotiations, which then deliberate on the details.

Nevertheless, if the Palestinians reject the elections proposal, a stalemate may ensue, and the Palestinian achievements that followed from the recent changes in the PLO's stature in the international arena after the PLO's acceptance of the American conditions, will ooze away rather quickly, especially if public opinion blames the PLO's inflexibility for bearing even partial responsibility for the stalemate. I do not consider that I should give the Palestinians advice. I am worried that a stalemate will be to the detriment of all parties. It is precisely a stalemate that may serve the extremists on both sides, and they may collaborate indirectly in bringing it about. For the Israeli and Palestinian extremists, the conflict is a race in competitive attrition in which they believe that their side will prevail, provided history's way is not blocked by a settlement, and that either Israel or an Arab Palestine (not necessarily a Palestinian Palestine) will eventually survive.

Charity begins at home and the brunt of my demands is directed at the Israelis and Israel. I have criticized Israeli policies copiously and, I dare think blatantly, in my recent book, *Israel's Fateful Hour*. I would like to use this opportunity to address some demands to Palestinians and Arabs as well.

The Arab and Palestinian position in the conflict is enmeshed in a basic difficulty to which attention should be drawn. Arabs have considered the establishment of Israel as a usurpation of land from its legal owners and, thus, illegitimate. Israel, according to this view, was born in sin, and therefore its existence has been congenitally flawed. From the illegitimacy of Israel, Arabs derived the conclusion that the situation is reversible and that they can bring about Israel's demise. Their recent acceptance of Israel's right to exist does not mean that its coming into being and Zionism are now legitimate, but only implies recognition that Israel is presently an accomplished fact, and that they have to resign themselves to its existence. In their internal debates, Arab moderates contend, somehow apologetically, that they have acceded to Israel's existence in deference to "international legitimacy" (*shar'iya duwaliya*). Thus, their recognition of Israel is an incomplete, even defective, recognition of something that exists, but that should not have existed and does not deserve to exist. I appreciate the difficulty. For Arabs, considering Zionism as legitimate could mean an admission that they have been living in the country illicitly, and have to surrender the land to the Jews, its allegedly rightful owners, now that they have come back. Such a claim is understandably unacceptable. Nonetheless, when Arab spokespersons recite a long litany of the evils of Zionism, as some renowned Palestinian academicians are fond of doing, and finally wrap it all up with a declaration of their recognition of coexistence with Israel, one cannot help but suspect that their recognition is very precarious and even dubious. The solution to this problem will be achieved pragmatically, with the passage of time, as bad memories and grievances are consigned to oblivion, and once the two adversaries cease to indulge in faulting and censuring each other.

I do not expect Arabs and Palestinians to become Zionists, but only to show some empathy toward Jews advocating Zionism. By the same token, Jews and Israelis should manifest empathy toward Palestinian suffering in the conflict, which even if not originally intended, was the outcome of the Zionist enterprise. Criminalizing Zionism or criminalizing the PLO, hailed by the Palestinians as their leadership and the embodiment of their national movement, is wrong both morally and politically.

Imputing attributes as if they were ontological facts: expansionism and racism to Zionism, terrorism to the PLO and previously unrelenting aggression to the Soviet Union, has proved to be a false approach, and should be expunged and banished from the political discourse of the Middle East. The greatness of the human race resides in the ability of people to transcend even those attributes which were justifiably ascribed to them. What is needed is not scoring points against our adversaries about the past, but finding tolerable solutions for the future.

The PLO's claim to be the sole legitimate representative of the Palestinians incurs responsibility for their actions and the need to impose discipline on recalcitrant Palestinian groups. *Noblesse oblige.* The PLO cannot be *al-mumathil al-shar'i al-wahid, ghair al-mas'ul—* "the sole legitimate representative, albeit irresponsible."

A worrisome occurrence is the contradictory messages that emanate from the PLO leadership. Some of its leaders sometimes express themselves differently when speaking to the Arab press, falling back on old bellicose themes, than in their statements to the western press which express moderation and brandish a desire for peace. It exposes them to the accusation that they speak with a forked tongue. This accusation may be exaggerated. No movement can impose absolute homogeneity and consistency of expression. However, the divergences are not ones of nuance; they are polar. They are used effectively by the Israeli proponents of the extreme line to impress upon the Israeli and Jewish publics that the changes in the PLO positions are not genuine, and that therefore Israelis have no other alternative but to continue the struggle—a struggle which is not about borders, or agreeing to a Palestinian state, but Israel's very existence. It helps to drive many Israelis to become "hawks out of despair." It makes a bad impression on world public opinion, as people start doubting the seriousness of the official Palestinian moderate pronouncements.

Many Israelis remember the PLO theory of "phases" (*marhaliya*), propounded in the 12th PNC's resolutions in June 1974, according to which a Palestinian state will serve as a springboard for additional demands and as a firm base for expansion. There are many declarations by PLO personalities to this effect. Thus, many Israelis are haunted by the possibility that no concession will satisfy the Palestinians, except the demise of Israel, and they can find many Palestinian pronouncements to this effect. Achieving peace is very much dependent on changing the Israeli political climate of opinion. Moderate Palestinians can make an important contribution to such a change by authoritative statements that peace will spell a finality to Palestinian demands and that the Palestinian search for peace is a strategic position and not a tactical one.

Palestinian moderates do not sufficiently appreciate the extent to which some of their pronouncements help Israeli extremists. Equivocal phrases which may hide a more extreme meaning, especially a "politicidal" one, should be avoided. No doubt there are Israeli pronouncements that assist the Palestinian extremists, but they come mostly from Israeli extremists, not from Israeli moderates.

It would be helpful if Palestinians in general become accustomed to distinguishing in their discourse between "the Land of Palestine" and "the State of Palestine," as the Israelis differentiate between "the Land of Israel" and "the State of Israel." So long as the Palestinians do not make this distinction and the term "Palestine" refers to all the territories west of the Jordan river, slogans like "the liberation of Palestine," which the Palestinians brandish to epitomize their goal, or "we shall continue the struggle until Palestine is liberated," may connote the aim to destroy Israel. Happily, the phrase "liberation of Palestine" does not appear either in the Final Statement of the 19th PNC or in the Declaration of Independence. However, when important PLO personalities flaunt it jubilantly in important conventions, a regression of sorts in the PLO position may have taken place.

The Palestinian "right of return" has to be qualified and limited to the Palestinian state. To Israeli ears, this claim sounds like the right to flood Israel with returnees. It also serves a trenchant argument that the Palestinians still adhere to their old positions. Let me stress that this argument is not only evoked by Israeli extremists, but also, for example, by respected Middle East scholars in the Hebrew University of Jerusalem. For many, the PLO's adherence to the right of return has become the measuring rod to evaluate how resigned it is to the existence of the State of Israel.

In the PLO's Declaration of Independence, the demand for a Palestinian state is based, as the declaration of the establishment of the state of Israel used to be, on UN General Assembly Resolution 181 of November 1947. Since previously the emphatic rejection of this resolution constituted a major cornerstone of PLO ideology, and was enshrined in the Palestinian Covenant, the change in position has to be acknowledged and explained. Otherwise, this inconsistency leaves one with a leery feeling. Introducing it cavalierly may give rise to suspicions of ulterior motives. A similar demand should be addressed to Prime Minister Shamir, who previously rejected the Camp David accords and has suddenly elevated them to be the centerpiece of his policy.

The PLO may consider it difficult to abrogate its Covenant in its entirety and prefer doing so in a piecemeal fashion. Here, too, a straightforward explanation would be very useful. The contradiction of the Covenant by the resolutions promulgated by the nineteenth PNC may have eroded the authority of the Covenant. However, only a special PNC session convened for the purpose of changing the Covenant can amend it, with the support of a special majority of two thirds of the total PNC membership. The PLO asserts the right of self-determination, but there is a great necessity to spell out clearly what it means, as it may veil ominous connotations. If it is simply a synonym for the right to statehood or the right to decide on the internal regime of a state, I do not see any objection. But if it means the right to determine unilaterally what areas will be included in this state, or where its borders will be, then it is very objectionable. In order to reinforce mutual confidence, terminology with equivocal catch-all expressions should be excluded.

The settlement of the conflict cannot be made by symmetrical compromises, with both parties offering commensurate concessions, because the situation is asymmetrical: Israel dominates areas thickly inhabited by Palestinians. Nevertheless, the onus of making concessions does not fall on Israel alone, and Arab contributions must not be limited to an august condescension to make peace with a Jewish state. The peace is as much for the sake of Arabs as for Jews. Palestinians and Arabs are not such a weak party to the negotiations that they can only receive concessions. The test of Arab peaceful intentions will be their readiness to meet Israel's security needs at the negotiation table. Israel's security sensitivities are not baseless.

Some circles on both sides of the conflict (and, Israelis may contend, perhaps justifiably, more among Palestinians) will continue to harbor vicious intentions toward each other, even after the conclusion of peace. The longer the strife, the stronger the urge for vengeance. The longer the absence of an agreement, the stronger vicious intentions become. Such dangers can be foiled only by a political settlement. The possibility of vicious intentions undermining the settlement is no excuse for not reaching a settlement; it calls instead for the settlement to be robust enough to withstand them. The negotiations should be protracted and the agreements very detailed, to prevent misunderstandings and divergences which may degenerate into serious disputes. Their wording should be concrete and clear, garnished with no so-called "constructive ambiguities," which are prone to prove destructive. International safeguards will be needed to rivet the agreements, nail down the parties' obligations and certify the finality of the respective demands.

It should be impressed on both Palestinians and Israelis that nothing is more blinding than self-righteousness, and particularly the self-righteousness of those who consider themselves wronged and oppressed. Let both understand that there is no just solution to the conflict, only a practical compromise. This will itself be a moral feat, precisely because it spares both parties from sufferings and calamities. To endeavor to be a realist is an ethical precept. The Jews may claim that it is historical justice that the Jews have a state of their own. The Palestinians claim that it is only justice that they should not pay for the wrongs history has wrought against the Jews. Let both beware of orators who, with great artistic talent, give their audiences the gratifying feelings of ebullience, of how just their cause is and how depraved and even ludicrous is the cause of the adversary. What we all need is not intoxicating frenzy, but the ability to transcend our emotions and achieve maturity of judgement. The choice facing us is not between good and bad, but the excruciating choice between bad and worse.

Mankind learns the hard way, rectifying its ways and changing wrong directions under the impact of calamities and tribulations. Eventually, the Arab-Israeli conflict will be settled and peace achieved.

The problem is how to spare both sides unnecessary sufferings on the road to peace.

The only settlement I envisage possible is that of two states within one homeland. One cannot persuade a Palestinian that Haifa or Jaffa are not Palestine; one cannot persuade an Israeli Jew that Judea and Samaria are not Eretz Yisrael. Both Palestinians and Israelis will continue to entertain sentimental allegiances to their common homeland (their *watan* or *moledet*), while they will exercise political rights only in their respective states (their *dawla* or *medina*). The situation is not symmetrical. For the Palestinians, the Palestinian homeland is only, as they call it, *al-watan al-khass* (the special homeland), as alongside it they have *al-watan al-'am* (the general homeland, i.e., the Arab world).

Having a common homeland may induce the Palestinians and the Israelis toward collaborative economic and perhaps political arrangements. However, slogans like "Benelux" are too early. It is hardly thinkable that one can jump from hostility to the intimacy of a common venture, and more so, even before arriving at mutual recognition and statehood. Nevertheless, such slogans may have the merit of allaying apprehensions that a settlement would entail complete disengagement between Israel and its neighbors, and even kindle some hope that the peace achieved may be more than negative in its nature, meaning merely the absence of violence.

Resignation to the final verdict of having only small states will be difficult and painful for all concerned. The diasporas of both the Palestinians and the Israelis are not helpful in this regard. Since the State of Israel and the hope for a Palestinian state are important components in the identity of Jewish and Palestinian Americans, both seem reluctant to resign themselves to the idea of a smaller homeland. They may not be conscious of this factor in their positions, which are often more hawkish than those of many Israelis and Palestinians in the occupied territories and in the PLO's establishment.

The State of Palestine and State of Israel will include as residents only part of the Palestinians and Jews. Both will have diasporas larger than their own populations. Both will need to develop a fertile relationship of mutual reinforcement with their diasporas. However, the situation is not symmetrical. Most Jews living abroad consider their residence as permanent, constituting a "final" diaspora, and they do not plan migrating to Israel, even if they like to leave such a possibility open to themselves. Many Palestinians, especially those living in Arab countries that did not grant them citizenship, used to consider their sojourn as a "transient" diaspora. A paradoxical outcome of the *intifada* is that it has highlighted to many of these Palestinians that the possible Palestinian state will be a small one, with only a limited absorption capacity. Such a realization, even if it was not completely new, constituted a shock that the *intifada* and its aftermath, including the changes in PLO's outlook, administered to the Palestinian diaspora. A settlement of the conflict will entail a process of conversion of transient Palestinian diasporas into final ones.

Both Palestinians and Israelis have to learn to view the conflict from the wide perspective of the exigencies of world order. Seeing their predicaments in the narrow confines of ethnocentric provincialism is a main source of deformation of judgement. No nation gets what it desires, or what it considers that it is rightfully entitled to. What we get is not what we wish, but only what is tolerable to the other political actors.

The trends toward world order include the improvement of relations between the United States and the Soviet Union; the internal changes in the Soviet Union; the extraction of the superpowers from the kind of involvement which structures and bolsters regional conflicts; the putative trend of international wars to become less frequent; and the growing hesitations statesmen may have in deciding to embark upon war. All these trends support the achievement of a settlement of the Arab-Israeli conflict and may help the moderates in their debates with the extremists.

The extremists of both adversaries enjoy one big advantage over the moderates, as their position is autonomous and is not dependent on a favorable response from the other side. The strongest argument of the Arab extremists against their moderates is that eventually the moderates will be disillusioned with the possibility of concluding peace with Israel, once it becomes clear that Israel refuses to meet even their minimal demands, and thus by default they will be impelled to join the radicals, even if only as "hawks out of despair." Such a development may be very detrimental to the cause of peace. Israelis should do their best to prevent this.

The Israeli moderates can maintain their ground for a long time. Encouragingly, it seems that the PLO's leadership understands that getting a positive response to its initiative of moderating its positions is a long haul. The extremist wings, inside and outside the PLO, are waiting eagerly for the efforts of the moderates to falter. How long the Palestinian moderates can wait is an open question. This feature of the conflict lends some urgency to the need for progress toward a settlement. Let all the parties concerned, Palestinians, Israelis and Americans, take this factor into consideration and exert themselves in producing some movement forward, even if the conditions are not fully clear and are not completely satisfactory. An improved version of elections may perhaps serve as such a starting point. Both the Palestinians and the Israelis are destined to have small states. However, both are gifted peoples, whose talents have been sharpened by their sufferings. Both should exert themselves in developing their states on the vertical dimension of excellence as model states, compensating for size by quality. Only thus will their states thrive and become a subject of pride to themselves and to their respective diasporas.

9 THE MEANING OF THE INTIFADA FOR JORDAN

As'ad Abdul-Rahman and Riad al-Khouri

1. Introduction

The Palestinian *intifada* is a response to national and political problems exacerbated by economic factors in a situation where democratic and less violent forms of expression have been curtailed and denied. This kind of popular resistance has major implications for the Arab world at every level, from life at the grass roots to diplomacy and power politics.

Among the *intifada*'s positive implications for the Arab world[1] have been:

1. The establishment of new options for the Palestinians and the Arab world vis-à-vis Israel.

2. Its successful achievement of direct political expression by the Palestinians, free of the restrictions which normally surround the PLO. It could prove contagious in the Arab world.

3. Its challenge and embarrassment to Arab governments.

4. Its boost to Arab morale after decades of setbacks and defeats. It also holds out hope for a Palestinian state and a return of Palestinian refugees or at least an improvement of Palestinian conditions. The *intifada* has raised hopes for a beginning of the end of the occupation and its attendant pressures, exploitation and humiliation. In the words of British Foreign Office Minister William Waldegrave in the Jabaliya refugee camp, Gaza, in March 1989, "coming here. . . reinforces the impression of the utter impossibility of continuing this military occupation."[2]

5. Its blow to Israeli claims strongly promoted in the West of maintaining a "liberal occupation" or an inexpensive or beneficial occupation.

6. Its enhancement of the international reputation of the Palestinian people.

7. Its example of grassroots struggle using limited means. It has integrated a variety of different political tendencies, as reflected in the inclusion under the national banner, for the first time since 1948, of exclusively Islamic parties, newly established and otherwise.

138

Counterbalancing these advantages for the Arab world have been:

1. An Arab and Palestinian retreat in the face of the international and regional balance of power. By accepting one fifth of the territory of mandated Palestine as the area of a Palestinian state, the Arab world has acknowledged a major historical setback at Zionist hands.

2. Further repression of the Arab peoples by regimes afraid of popular movements and concerned with the possibility of the spread of the *intifada*.

3. The frustration felt by ordinary people in the Arab countries unable to take part in or meaningfully support the uprising.

4. Habituation to daily news of people being killed and wounded.

5. Last but not least, the emergence of expressions of religious fanaticism as a reaction to Zionist political and religious extremism.

2. Jordan and Palestine

Because Jordan's links to Palestine are obvious, the meaning of the *intifada* for the country is powerful and immediate. Jordan is a conduit between Palestine and the Arab world. An overall study of the *intifada* and the Arab world must therefore begin in Jordan and examine the ways in which it is twinned with Palestine:[3]

1. With the arguable exception of Gaza's links to Egypt, Jordan is the only country in the Arab world which has had (and to some extent still has) political and administrative ties with Palestine since the Ottoman era.

2. Even during the Ottoman and other periods, administrative divisions were "horizontal," i.e., between the Palestinian coast and the hinterland, thus creating special links on many levels among areas on both banks of the River Jordan (e.g., Nazareth, Nablus and Salt; Karak and Hebron, etc.).

3. This, in turn, led to a great deal of social interaction and fusion in the form of commercial transactions, migration, emigration and marriage, etc. Thus, it is not uncommon to find Jordanian families which were originally Palestinian and vice versa.

4. The full practical unity which prevailed in the years 1948-67-88 greatly and comprehensively reinforced these ties.

5. In addition to all the above factors, Jordan's is the longest border with Israel. This has made the country's links with the people of Palestine special, irrespective of whether relations between the two societies and their leaders were warm or otherwise. Whatever

the percentage of Palestinians in Jordan was or is becomes less relevant if we remember that we are talking about twin lands and peoples.

6. If Palestinian/Jordanian unity is a sensitive and crucial issue, then so is the July 31, 1988 break or "disengagement" between the East and West Banks. To unravel the fabric of unity becomes virtually impossible in the face of joint socio-economic interests straddling the River Jordan.

7. Finally, the envisioning by the Israelis and Americans of a federal or confederal link between Palestine and Jordan as part of an overall Middle East settlement (and the acceptance of the idea of some such arrangement in a number of Arab and non-Arab quarters, including some Palestinian ones) makes the unity of the two banks a factor in the policies of the superpowers as well as regional actors.

3. Palestinian Politics after 1982

The summer of 1982 marked a turning point in the history of the struggle of the Palestinian people. The Israeli invasion of Lebanon in June of that year and the PLO's departure a few months later dealt a severe blow to the Palestinian people. This was felt on many levels: in the media, militarily, politically and psychologically. The short-term feelings of pride in the resistance that were visible during the "siege of Beirut" were soon dissipated.[4]

The departure of Yasser Arafat to Athens from Beirut symbolized a deepening rift between the PLO and Damascus.[5] Instead of heading for Syria, Arafat expressed his opposition to and disappointment with Damascus by establishing the PLO headquarters in Tunis. This was followed by mutual accusations and media campaigns. After the split in Fatah in 1983, the fighting in the Bekaa, the expulsion of Arafat from Damascus by the Syrian government, the fighting in Palestinian camps in the Tripoli region of north Lebanon, and the subsequent second expulsion of Arafat and his forces, Arafat looked to Egypt and then Jordan. This led to the development of a bilateral relationship between the PLO and Jordan, as embodied in the convening and decisions of the Palestine National Council (PNC) in Amman in November 1984 and the Jordanian-Palestinian Accord of January 1985.

These were years of deepening inter-Palestinian splits, the failure of the June 1985 Aden/Algiers Accords to achieve national unity, the setting up of the Damascus-based "National Salvation Front," and the "Camps' War" in Lebanon during 1985-88.

Jordanian relations with the PLO, however, quickly deteriorated and those with Syria improved. In February 1986, King Hussein declared an end or suspension of dialogue with the PLO, and this was followed by a further chill. The Amman Arab Summit of November 1987 witnessed a political and protocol crisis, as attempts were made to bypass the PLO. This was quickly accompanied by demonstrations in the occupied territories and then followed by the *intifada*.

4. Jordan and the Intifada[6]

The stones of the *intifada*, once thrown, made many ripples. Whether in the Arab world in general or in Jordan in particular, the responses covered the different colors of the ideological and political spectrum.

Reactions varied from one state to another. In the beginning, Jordanians, like other Arabs, were fascinated and captivated by the unprecedented popular, "spontaneous" and comprehensive uprising in the Palestinian occupied territories. Arab governments and political organizations hailed the *intifada*.

While some Arab governments and some popular political trends wavered later in their attitudes vis-à-vis the *intifada*, most official and popular Arab circles increased their financial and political support. The latter committed themselves to the *intifada* regardless of its avowed political program and positions, and irrespective of its interaction with the PLO. Two main factors influenced the attitudes of Arab governments and political movements to the PLO: first their "historical" position vis-à-vis the PLO, and second, their historical political or ideological commitments. All Arab forces that competed with or contradicted the PLO either because of vested interests or because of ideological-political differences suffered from a discreet change of heart toward the *intifada*. More specifically, the ultra-Arab nationalist and ultra-Islamic forces have been exhibiting a growing uneasiness about the "moderation process" which both the PLO and the *intifada* are jointly undergoing.[7]

Jordan's response to the PLO and the *intifada* since its eruption can be divided into three consecutive and overlapping stages: first, December 1987-March 1988; second, March-December 1988; and third, December 1988 until the present.

At its start, the *intifada* appeared to the Jordanian authorities and others as anti-PLO and an isolated, spontaneous, popular uprising.[8] But within a month or so, the independent nature of the eruption of the *intifada* notwithstanding, its PLO connections and affiliation became evident. This caused disappointment and even bitterness in some influential official circles in Amman where it was finally realized that previous efforts to cultivate the Palestinians had come to naught. The PLO was seen as the victor in the battle for the hearts and minds of the Palestinians and there were even reports of anxiety about an East Bank "*intifada*" or at least "troubles" inspired by the example of the occupied territories. This led to arrests on New Year's Eve, 1987, of several dozen activists from the Popular Front for the Liberation of Palestine, and subsequent arrests of others with political leanings which the government found dangerous at that particular phase of the *intifada*. General Yusuf Gharaybih, Chief of Amman Police and Deputy Chief of General Security, later revealed that there had been 114 demonstrations or attempted demonstrations during this period.[9]

During this phase, however, the Jordanian government allowed certain pro-*intifada* steps to be taken. Notable among these was the formation on February 25, 1988 of a "Popular Committee for Support of the *Intifada*." The Committee collected 1,250,000 Jordanian dinars in tax-free contributions in 1988 and even more in 1989.[10] The Jordanian government, following an example set by King Hussein himself, also awarded money to the families of those killed in the *intifada*. In addition, the government permitted various lectures and other semi-public utterances in solidarity with the *intifada*. The official media were generous in their coverage of events on the West Bank and Gaza, until late December 1988, when television reports began to be censored. The semi-controlled press, though privately owned, was also allowed to publish news and analyses favorable to the *intifada* throughout this period. The government even permitted some articles that made reference to both the PLO leaders and the role of the PLO and its growing relations with the *intifada*.

The second stage in this relationship began in March 1988 and was clearly evident during Land Day celebrations. During this period, there were disturbances in Palestinian camps and in the Jordanian universities during rallies, lectures and other occasions, as a number of Palestinian and Jordanian groups were given leeway to carry out activities that gave the appearance of an intra-Palestinian split and also fomented some Jordanian-Palestinian animosity. Parallel to this, there were continued press restrictions.

The Arab Summit of June 1988 gave unified support to the *intifada*. King Hussein's "separation" of the East and West Banks on July 31 finally made it official that "Jordan is not Palestine." However, initial shock, disbelief, rumors and counterrumors greeted the practical measures taken after this step (the dissolution of Parliament, the cancellation of West Bankers' citizenship and the downgrading of their passports, the cutting off of salaries of government employees on the West Bank, abolition of the Ministry of Occupied Territories, and cancelling of the West Bank development plan, etc.). Regardless of "who started it first," hardliners on both banks indulged their enmity in an unhealthy atmosphere which culminated in clashes on the university campuses during celebrations of the *intifada*'s first anniversary in early December 1988.

Incidents such as the explosion of two tiny bombs on April 9 and 16, 1988 were given extensive television coverage and helped to arouse the passions of various groups. More significant were the steps taken against several local and foreign journalists, starting in April, restricting and in some cases banning their professional activities. This culminated on August 31 in the dissolution of the boards of directors of the country's three Arabic dailies, as well as replacement of their senior staff. The Committee for Economic Security, operating under the Extraordinary Martial Law, ordered the dissolution "to safeguard the interests of the shareholders" in these dailies.[11]

The third and present stage in Jordanian-Palestinian relations coincided with the deepening of the economic crisis and marked a relaxation of tension between the two banks. There were Jordanian-Palestinian summits when Arafat visited Jordan on November 19, 1989 and April 15, 1989, and again in August 1989. There were also Jordanian-Palestinian-Egyptian summits in Aqaba in October 1988 and in Ismailiya in March 1989. These events and the emergence of a moderate Palestinian position were accompanied by a release of political prisoners in Jordan.

There were some incidents in the Spring of 1989, centered around the University of Jordan and certain refugee camps (especially during Land Day celebrations in late March 1989). The first effective pro-*intifada* play was also suspended because "it dangerously agitated the masses." However, the anti-government demonstrations in mid-April 1989 in areas in the southern part of Jordan that were considered solidly pro-government showed that the critical decisions confronting

Jordan could not be reduced to the issue of relations between Palestinians and Jordanians. As the year progressed, Jordanian-Palestinian relations took a healthier turn, reflecting the positive aspects of the probably temporary "break" between the East and West Banks. On the occasion of Arafat's visit to Jordan in August, 1989, the joint Jordanian-Palestinian Committee resumed its meetings and the Palestine National Fund's office in Amman was reopened. Some measures easing economic problems in the West Bank arising from Jordanian disengagement were subsequently taken. The Palestinian-Jordanian dialogue and coordination continued at the highest level.

5. The Economic Crisis in Jordan[12]

King Hussein's decision to cut Jordan's administrative and legal ties with the Israeli-occupied West Bank compelled the PLO to take full and exclusive responsibility for the Palestinians' destiny. It reflected a realization that unilateral Jordanian diplomatic efforts, which had been aimed at securing the convening of an international conference on the Arab-Israeli question, had come to naught. This realization was driven home by the *intifada,* which strengthened Palestinian support for the PLO. But Jordan was also disillusioned by its failure to win Arab backing, to influence American policy, or to entice Israeli Labor Party leader Shimon Peres to take a bolder position in support of peace moves. By the spring of 1988, King Hussein had finally concluded that a role for Jordan as the prime mover in promoting Arab-Israeli peace talks was too ambitious for a country which lacked clout even in dealing with the PLO. Jordan now set its sights more realistically. It remains an active player in regional peace efforts, but no longer seeks a leading role.

Meanwhile, in the spring of 1988, the interaction of a regional slump and local factors triggered a foreign exchange crisis in Jordan. The dinar's fall was met with measures which failed to restore full or substantial confidence and even accelerated the capital outflow. The country's role as a player in regional politics changed and its formal links to the West Bank were abandoned at the same time as the financial crisis was deepening. The flight of capital then became acute, with a lot of West Bank money being pulled out and a very small amount coming in to replace it.

The Jordanian dinar declined in value against the US dollar in the summer and early autumn of 1988. Faced with a severe shortage of foreign exchange and with debt repayment problems, the government introduced measures to cut imports, boost exports and curb consumer demand. The autumn's economic measures provided a mirror image of the earlier political steps. The economy, like Jordan's ambitious diplomacy, had overstretched itself. Ever since 1982, the government had maintained expansionary budgets even though Arab aid transfers were dropping, private remittances from Jordanians and Palestinians abroad were sagging, and domestic revenues were failing to offset the fall in foreign income.

The government borrowed to fill the gap; total government debt reached at least $6.5 billion. As the Central Bank's cash foreign exchange holdings were finally depleted (though its gold remained untouched), it could no longer meet the market's import-linked needs for foreign exchange. Faced with these pressures, the authorities allowed the dinar in effect to float. Almost immediately, the currency lost a further 15 percent of its value. The government banned some imports, floated interest rates, liberalized private sector registration of new companies, reformed investment incentives and enhanced export incentives. These measures were designed to increase exports and cut imports and thus redress the payments imbalance, reduce the trade deficit and ease the foreign currency shortfall. However, it was expected to take some time for overall benefits to materialize. Meanwhile, after a year of an acute balance of payments crisis, Jordan practically faced penury and attendant loss of control over policy.

Prime Minister Zaid Rifai had announced that the government would adopt an austerity budget for 1989, cutting infrastructural and other project spending. But there was little scope for a squeeze as approximately 60 percent of the budget is accounted for by salaries, pensions, defense and internal security, which are regarded as sacrosanct items.

The budget announced on December 31, 1988 projected a growing deficit. (This was blamed by the Finance Minister on the failure of Arab countries, except for Saudi Arabia, to honor their financial commitments under the decade-old Baghdad summit resolution.) This only added to the feeling of crisis. Jordan defaulted on its first scheduled debt payment of 1989. This caused concern in local, Arab and foreign financial circles, as did the way in which the default was handled. The dinar then resumed its fall. After panic dealing in early February, the government closed down the money-changers and once again attempted to set a stable rate for the dinar. Thus, the crisis left the Jordanian system at an even lower ebb of economic credibility.

The situation was somewhat alleviated in the summer of 1989, when Saudi Arabia and other Gulf states came to Jordan's aid. In August 1989, following King Hussein's visit to Saudi Arabia, the latter extended $200 million in financial aid. During the summer, Jordan also made agreements with other creditor countries and instititions to reschedule its debts due to be paid in 1989-90.

Yet the underlying reality was that, without much fanfare, Jordan had become another Third World debtor unable to meet its financial commitments. Things being what they are, it is unlikely that there will be any major restructuring of the economy in the manner usually associated with IMF proposals. The Jordanian system is not ready for the kind of change which an international lender would like to see. Loans from Middle East countries are more palatable to Jordan, but until oil prices climb to a new plateau, OAPEC states will remain reticent. Inflation is also likely to become a headache, though remittances, currently at their lowest level for a very long time, might pick up slightly. The dinar will clearly face very strong pressures.

In return for the economic sacrifices demanded by the government, Jordanians and Palestinians began to call for a greater say in the decisions that affect their daily lives and to seek the accountability of public officials. The lower house of Parliament, a sounding board for grievances, was dissolved in July 1988.[13] Accusations of a news blackout vis-à-vis the *intifada* also emerged. The troubles on the East Bank in 1989 underscored the demands. People were now openly calling for change, whether it be political or economic. Whatever the other motives behind these outbursts might be, such a public articulation of grievances had not been seen in Jordan for some time. In an attempt to deal with these rising pressures, the government held elections in November 1989, for which candidates representing a wide variety of different political and ideological tendencies were allowed to stand and in which a strong showing was made by candidates committed to the principle of an Islamic state.

6. The Intifada and the Crisis[14]

The current Jordanian crisis is not a mere economic recession. The roots of the crisis lie in the country's need to find a new role for itself politically and economically. For years, Jordan has attempted to play an important role in the region, with some success. The *intifada* has put an end to this particular phase of the country's history. As Palestine "ascends," Jordan's role appears to be diminishing politically, at least temporarily.

The November 1987 Arab summit held in the Jordanian capital was seen as marginalizing the PLO. Less than a month later, the outbreak of the *intifada* put the Palestinians back on the map, in some ways at the expense of a Jordan which was in danger of becoming "marginalized" itself, at least temporarily. But any reduction in the regional importance of Jordan is more likely to occur within the context of major economic changes. The *intifada* has had important effects on Jordan and its economy (just as Jordanian moves and developments have exerted a great deal of influence on events in the occupied territories).

In general, money has flowed out of the country and little has flowed in to replace it. In a regional slump, this would have been the case anyway, with or without the *intifada*. But events in the West Bank and in Gaza exacerbated the situation in Jordan, especially after the legal and administrative disengagement of July 31, 1988.

One of the immediate causes (as opposed to deeper, longer-term underlying factors) of this break with the occupied territories involved Jordan's straitened financial position. The cutting off of salaries and other forms of payment to the West Bank meant a not unimportant saving for a state with heavy internal and external deficits and (in July 1988) very low reserves.[15] The political/legal/administrative break having occurred, economic measures were then taken. These were ostensibly to demonstrate the seriousness of the disengagement and protect the crisis-ridden East Bank economy. But some felt that the cutting off of salaries, as well as the banning of certain imports from the West Bank and Gaza Strip, was designed to squeeze both the "disloyal" government employees and the *intifada*.

The case of the West Bank's olive oil exports[16] is an interesting example of this process. On December 8, 1988 (the first anniversary of the *intifada*) it was reported that Jordan had decided not to buy olive oil from the West Bank because, according to the Agriculture Minister, the East Bank's bumper crop covered domestic needs. On the purely practical level, olives, their extracts and byproducts are an important source of livelihood in the Levant in general and in Palestine in particular. At the time of the ban's imposition, Jordanian and West Bank sources said that it was part of an apparent power struggle involving the PLO. But Jordan's Agriculture Minister was quoted as saying "in view of the excellent season we have had, a decision has been taken not to import olive oil or olives from outside Jordan. Our production meets local demand and will be used."[17]

Before 1988, as a means of supporting the occupied territories, Jordan bought around 50 percent of the West Bank's agricultural production. But after the July 31 break with the occupied territories, the Jordanian government decided to treat West Bank goods like those from any Arab country. Replying to reports that Jordan might block all farm exports from the West Bank until the PLO negotiated trade agreements with Jordan, Jordan's Minister of Agriculture said "this is untrue . . . there is nothing political in our move."

Whatever the motives for the olive oil ban, it was another complicating factor in Jordanian-Palestinian relations. Meanwhile, the olive oil itself had to be sold elsewhere. Some of it went to Italy, as the European Community (EC) appeared to be stepping in to replace Jordan as a market for Palestinian agricultural products.

Palestinian citrus exports to Holland were another case of a change in the direction of trade of the West Bank and Gaza. In October 1988, Israel issued the first permits for direct fruit exports by Palestinian growers from the Gaza Strip to the EC. Israel's decision to implement an accord with the EC to let Palestinian farmers export their produce independently cleared the way for the European parliament to move on long-delayed trade protocols with Israel. As a result of protest at Israel's repressive handling of the *intifada,* the parliament had not previously been able to raise the necessary majority to endorse the tariff-cutting agreements. Previously, Palestinian produce had to be exported via Jordan or sold to Israel's state marketing boards for export under Israeli brand names. Israel mended fences with the EC, though the citrus exports turned out to be a commercial failure.

With the development of Jordan's own citrus industry, Palestinian exports would have had to find a new outlet anyway. But the *intifada* and the atmosphere of "divorce" between the two banks pushed the Palestinians to look for new markets. And the EC was willing and able to apply pressure on Israel to let the Palestinians export directly.

Meanwhile the "olive issue" took another turn when it was announced in March 1989 that Jordan was once again allowing imports of oil from the West Bank because the East Bank crop had been sold. From March 25 to May 24, 1989, 2,450 tons of West Bank olive oil and 616 tons of pickled olives were allowed into Jordan. This was to be permitted as "family gifts" but in practice could be distributed in the local market. Previously, Jordan had allowed visitors from the

West Bank to bring only two 16-kilogram cans of oil across the river as gifts to relatives. These rights were now to be assigned to commercial shippers. Khaled Qutob, secretary of the West Bank Agricultural Union, was quoted as saying: "In previous years, the Jordanian government bought our olive oil for official and military consumption. Now it will be sold on the private market."

Extraordinary measures are being taken to deal with the economic crisis on the West Bank and in Jordan. But in the atmosphere of the *intifada,* economic and financial developments can become part of the general crisis in Palestine and may be seen in strategic and not economic terms. After disengaging from the West Bank in July 1988, Jordan said it would import goods from the occupied territories "only if it needs them," a move which aroused resentment there at the time. Jordan continued to allow West Bank goods across the river bridges for re-export, and a Jordanian official said about 3,000 tons of West Bank olive oil had been exported to Saudi Arabia and other Gulf states via Jordan between mid-December 1988 and the beginning of April 1989.

In the meantime, Israeli government measures continued to have a terrible effect on the Palestinian economy. Among the deadliest of tools in Israel's economic armory is the refusal of permits to export West Bank agricultural produce to Jordan, particularly major items such as melons, vegetables and grapes (although the list also includes other products such as building stones). It would be a mistake to highlight Jordanian government measures in a way that diminished the importance of Israeli actions. Obviously, in the wake of July 31, 1988, a shock was felt by the people of Jordan and Palestine. The short-term effects were sometimes confusing and discomfiting; with time, these will diminish and be replaced by a more rational approach to integration and unity between people on both banks.

It suited certain groups on both banks, in the region and internationally, to talk about tension or confrontation between Palestine and Jordan. Coming in the throes of an economic crisis, there arose varying waves of ill-feeling on the East and West Banks. This, in turn, had the short-term effect of further eroding confidence in Jordan and its economy, and deepened the crisis. Nevertheless, the overwhelming majority of Palestinians living in the East Bank did not suffer in some kind of melodramatic fashion after July 31, 1988. And the terrible and continuing economic problems are hitting the population as a whole irrespective of origin or affiliation.

The disengagement between Jordan and Palestine can now be seen as a form of "distance for the sake of proximity," just as a married couple might engage in a separation to create a more friendly atmosphere later. In this context, the *intifada* becomes a positive factor in the framework of a new (possibly confederal) relationship between the two banks. As a common denominator among the USA, USSR, many Arabs, Jordanians, Palestinians, and an important segment of Israeli society, such a confederal link might be significant in an overall settlement.

Notes

1. See, for example, As'ad Abdul-Rahman and Nawwaf al-Zaru, *Al-Intifada: al-Juthur, al-Massar, al-Natai'j* (The Intifadah: Roots, Process and Results), Beirut: Muassasat al-Abhath al-Arabiya, 1989; Khalid Aayid, *Al-Intifada al-Thawriya fi Filastin: Al-Aba'ad al-Dakhiliya* (The Revolutionary Uprising in Palestine: The Internal Dimensions), Amman: Dar al-Shuruq, 1988, pp. 105-129; Abdul-Wahab al-Messiri, *Al-Intifada al-Filastiniya wa al-Azma al-Sahyuniya* (The Palestinian Uprising and the Zionist Crisis), Cairo, 1989, pp. 193-200.

2. Quoted in *The Jordan Times,* March 5, 1989.

3. See, for example, a Palestinian and a Jordanian view respectively: Khalid Al-Hassan, *Al-Itifaq al-Urduni al-Filastini lil-Taharuk al-Mushtarak* (The Jordanian-Palestinian Accord for Common Action), Amman: Dar al-Jalil, 1985; and Sa'id al-Tal, *al-Urdun wa Filastin: Wujhat Nazar 'Arabiya* (Jordan and Palestine: An Arab Point of View), Amman: Dar al-Jalil, 1984.

4. Among the many studies dealing with this period, see, for example, Michael Jansen, *The Battle of Beirut: Why Israel Invaded Lebanon* (London: Zed Press, 1982); Ze'ev Schiff and Ehud Yaari, *Israel's Lebanon War* (New York: Simon and Schuster, 1984), particularly Chapter 2; John Laffin, *The War of Lebanon: 1982-85* (London: Osprey, 1985); E. C. Hagopian, *Amal and the Palestinians: Understanding the Battle* (Belmont: Arab American University Graduates, 1985); As'ad Abdul-Rahman (ed.), *Munazamat al-Tahrir al-Filastiniya: Juthuruha, Ta'sisuha, Masaratuha* (The PLO: Roots, Establishment and Processes), Cyprus: Palestine Research Center, 1987, Chapter 21.

5. For further details on the various developments between 1982-1988, see the relevant issues of *Keesing's Contemporary Archives* and the monthly reports in the journal *Shu'un Filastiniya* (Palestine Affairs), published by the Palestine Research Center in Beirut and Cyprus.

6. Unless otherwise stated, the information in this section is based on the archive being compiled by Dar Al-Jalil Publishers (Amman), as well as several individuals who prefer to remain anonymous.

7. On this, see the various communiques issued over the past year by several Arab political groups as compiled by, among others, the Abdul-Hamid Shuman Public Library in Amman.

8. See, e.g., various issues of Jordanian newspapers during the first few weeks of the *intifada.*

9. General Gharaybih provided this information in a recorded public lecture at the Abdul-Hamid Shuman Scientific Cultural Center in Amman on August 27, 1988.

10. Information regarding this Committee was obtained from special access by the authors to its files.

11. For an elaboration of this point, see, for example, the various press reports on the proceedings of the Palestine Central Council held in Baghdad from July 30-August 2, 1988; an unpublished paper by Council member As'ad Abdul-Rahman on "The Meeting

of July-August 1988 of the Palestine Central Council" (in Arabic); Sa'id al-Tal, "The Hashemite Kingdom of Jordan and the Palestinian National Identity" (in Arabic) in the daily *Al-Dustour* (Amman, October 4, 1988), pp. 12-13. Finally, for a West Bank perspective, see Mahdi F. Abdul-Hadi, "The Jordanian Disengagement: Causes and Effects" (Jerusalem: Palestinian Academic Society for the Study of International Affairs, September 1988).

12. Events during this stage have been amply recorded in the Arabic and foreign press. For details, see the reference file prepared on this subject by the authors as well as *Keesing's Archives,* Vol. XXXIV, pp. 35858 and 36121.

13. Reviving it would entail a constitutional amendment. Half its seats were allocated to deputies from the West Bank, but as part of the King's diplomatic and political moves in August 1988, West Bank Palestinians were no longer to be considered Jordanian citizens. Therefore a future Jordanian parliament would be a purely East Bank affair.

14. Economic and related data in this section are contained in the reference file cited above. For other information, see footnote 7.

15. Unless otherwise stated, information in this section is derived from the reference file.

16. For those unfamiliar with the Levant, olives and olive oil are not merely staples, but part of a complicated symbolism centered around the olive tree (as in the adoption by Birzeit University, among other institutions, of the olive oil tree as a symbol). The olive and its branches represent peace, steadfastness, persistence and constant, long-term renewal.

17. Jordan produced 10,000 tons of olive oil in 1988 and retained 5,000 in stock; the West Bank harvested a big crop of about 35,000 tons, of which 20,000 was surplus.

PART 3: IMAGINING THE PALESTINIAN STATE

10 A LOOK AHEAD: THE FUTURE STATE OF PALESTINE

Hisham Sharabi

Shortly after the Palestine National Council passed its resolutions recognizing Israel and calling for a two-state solution of the Palestinian-Israeli conflict, Jewish fundamentalists opposed to the establishment of the State of Israel were very much disturbed by the turn of events. Representatives of Neturei Karta, the group most opposed to Zionism and an Israeli state, threatened Arafat that they would stop their support of the PLO if its recognition of Israel was not withdrawn. According to the Israeli daily *Hadashot* (Jan. 3, 1989), " . . . the Orthodox demand[ed] that Arafat promise that the Orthodox neighborhoods in Jerusalem will be part of the Palestinian state. They insist[ed] that he publicly declare his commitment to retain this neighborhood. Orthodox sources in New York [said] that the PLO tried to calm their anger with the explanation that their recognition of Israel is only a maneuver. Neturei Karta thinks that, even as a maneuver, [the PLO] should not recognize Israel."

Mr. Shamir and his colleagues may well be justified in thinking that it is just a maneuver. Indeed many rejectionists among the Palestinians think (or hope) it is. For the kind of solution now before us, if examined carefully, hardly satisfies the minimum demands of either side; it answers neither all of Israel's security needs nor the Palestinians' full claim to justice.

It is only the so-called moderates on both sides who today support the idea of a two-state solution and seek to make what seems unacceptable acceptable. Who are these moderates and is their moderation likely to achieve anything?

In itself, moderation is often a mystifying word and has meaning only when placed in a concrete context. But the problem in the present situation is that when we put the moderation of Palestinian and Israeli moderates in context, we discover a subtle but profound discrepancy between the two positions. This appears most clearly in their frequently contradictory expectations and in the largely insubstantial results of their discussions, which usually begin with great interpersonal warmth but often end, as a result of lack of meaningful progress, in feelings of frustration, mistrust, and even hostility. One reason for this is the desire of the Palestinian side to remember and the desire of the Israeli side to forget.

I know moderation through direct experience. For like many Palestinians in the United States, I had to be "moderate" to be heard, that is, to be allowed to tell our side of the story. Our American friends showed us by example the language we needed to speak, and how to be reasonable and credible. This meant, above all, restricting our discourse to the practicalities of the present and always refraining from dredging up the past. What was the point in talking about 1948, about the dispossession, expulsion, exile, and suffering of the Palestinians, when Jews could talk about the Holocaust? I was so "moderate" in those years that the copy-editor of a book I was then writing complained that the section on the Palestinians lacked proper historical background. I had to rewrite that section by dipping less cautiously into the forbidden past, and to tell how the Jewish minority in Palestine, composed mostly of recent immigrants, drove out the majority of Palestinians from their homes and land and forcibly prevented their return after the war, despite the appeals of the international community and repeated resolutions by the United Nations. Only now, with the coming of the *intifada,* has talking about the past become possible. The Palestinians, like feminists and blacks and gays, can talk about themselves without fear or self-imposed censorship, largely because they too have found the right way to rebel against injustice.

In the last few years, our moderation has been sorely tested by the way terrorism has been used against the Palestinians as an ideological weapon. Ironically, we found ourselves in the situation where, in Franz Werfel's words (used to describe the persecution of Jews decades ago): "the victim, not the murderers, [was] guilty." Suddenly experts on terrorism sprung up everywhere, writing articles and books on terrorism, and treated by the media and the intellectual establishment as serious academic experts. Conferences on terrorism were held at which members of the Reagan Administration, such as former Secretary of State Shultz and Ms. Kirkpatrick, not only attended but passionately participated. In retrospect, it becomes clear that what Henry Kissinger, and later Shultz and other government officials, had aimed at by developing the terrorism theme was to delegitimate the Palestine Liberation Organization, the only political expression of Palestinian national rights. The Palestine problem could then be dealt with, not as a national problem but one of local refugees to be settled by agreement with the Arab states.

For most Third World intellectuals, racism remains largely abstract until it touches their life directly. This happened in our confrontation with the terrorism problem. It was difficult at first to understand how responsible public figures and mainstream media could use language which implicitly linked a whole people to terrorism.

But there was another reason for our moderate orientation besides wanting our voices to be heard: realism. We now were convinced that the time was past when Palestinian rights could be retrieved by force, even if the Arab states were able to radically change the balance of power and willing to take on Israel in a full-scale war. If it was possible in the 1950s, or even in 1967, to reconquer the ancestral land taken from us by force, it was no longer so after the 1967 war. The world, including the Soviet Union, would from then on not allow a return to the status quo ante. After four decades of Israeli domination, Palestine had become as much home to a new generation of Israelis as it had been to Palestinians inside and outside Palestine. Nearly 60 percent of Israelis knew no other homeland besides Israel/ Palestine. Only a political solution based on partition was now possible. Such a solution has now been made legitimate by the *intifada,* which converted the dream of a Palestinian revolution into reality in December 1987 by transforming "armed struggle" from the outside into genuine internal resistance. Like similar uprisings of the colonial era, the *intifada* has been able, by devising its own methods of resistance, to blunt the occupier's military superiority and to reduce the balance of forces to a test of wills, the political outcome of which the next few years will reveal.

Let us recall that today the number of Palestinians living in historic Palestine (Israel, the West Bank and Gaza) is fast approaching the 3 million figure, or half the total Palestinian population inside and outside historic Palestine. The number of Israeli Jews is about 3.5 million. At the present rate of Palestinian births, assuming that Jewish immigration and Jewish emigration balance each other, the ratio will eventually be close to 40 percent to 60 percent in favor of the Palestinians—that is, unless mass expulsion of Palestinians is carried out, in the manner of expulsion of Jews from Germany in the 1930s before the concentration camps and the gas chambers. But the idea of forcing the Palestinians across the border is not new. As an article by Israel Shahak in the *Journal of Palestine Studies* (Spring 1989) shows, the idea of "transfer" has a long history in Zionist circles and is today openly discussed as one effective way of solving the so-called demographic problem. Another possibility, discussed less openly, is "mass killings." This chilling possibility was brought to the Knesset floor by Mapam MK Yair Tsaban (*The Other Front* [Jerusalem, Jan. 26, 1989]), who put it this way:

> I don't sleep well at night because of my worry that if we let things go on at this pace—political hardening and brutalization, repression, and escalation of the *intifada*—it follows that we will find ourselves in more and more difficult situations, and we may very soon see developments which will end in mass killings, and it is necessary to say this from this platform. We have already seen things in the world, and if this happens—the tears among us will go right down to the root. Israeli society will be torn [apart] . . .

Expulsion and more killing of Palestinians loom as possible eventualities if the present inflexible "live and let die" policy continues. Some Israeli writers have compared the present situation in Palestine to that of the Jews in Germany between 1933 and 1940, with similar implications for the future. The following quotation is from an interview carried by the Israeli daily *Haaretz* (Dec. 9, 1988) with Professor Amos Funkenstein, Chairman of the Department of Philosophy at the University of Tel Aviv, who describes himself as a "zealous Zionist." Professor Funkenstein compares the German government's attitude toward the Jews to that of the Israeli government toward the Palestinians.

> [B]etween 1933 and 1937, up to the *Kristallnacht,* the situation of Jews in Germany was in some respect better than that of the Arabs in the territories. In other respects, their condition was worse, but overall, the resemblance is remarkable. In the first place, both Jews in Germany and the Palestinians in the territories were "subjects" denied citizenship. Still, the Jews of Germany had at that time more lawful options they could pursue than the inhabitants of the territories. A Jew there in 1936 did not feel totally outlawed. Only in 1938 did the Nazis break into their homes and stage pogroms on the scale resembling ours. Generally, it was harder than here to subvert the legal order in Germany. The Nazis had to contend with the legacy of the Weimar Republic, and it took several years to destroy it. It is true that Germany in the end exterminated the Jews. But this became an actual policy only in 1940, under the seemingly apocalyptic conditions of "total war." It is also true that the Jews of Germany never resisted and never

started civil revolt. They were peaceful citizens, well-integrated into German society. Their "problem" existed only in anti-Semitic minds . . . It occurred to nobody that elderly Arabs ordered to remove the roadblocks from the streets are like the Jews of Vienna, whom the Nazis right after entering the city forced to sweep the snow . . . .
[Israel] is a society that feels threatened and develops paranoias. Here the analogy with German society after Versailles is striking. The talk about "the whole world [being] against us" or about "being stabbed in the back" was customary there.

Another leading Israeli intellectual, Professor Yeshayahu Lebowitz, sees the situation as having already reached a turning point. He maintains that Israel must now decide which way it will go. In his own words: "The result of any stand-off will be the absolutely certain destruction of the State of Israel, because the Arab world can't be destroyed. Israel can. Today we have power: tomorrow we won't." (*American-Arab Affairs*, 26 [Fall, 1988], p. 77).

So what is the way out? The formula for peace has been outlined, and the whole world seems agreed on it, if only the two sides would bring themselves to accept a solution based on partial, not comprehensive, justice, and to put their hidden agendas aside. Professor Y. Harkabi's statement in the Israeli daily *Haaretz,* approvingly published in Arabic in the PLO weekly, *Sawt al-Bilad,* on February 13, 1989, spells this out quite clearly:

The main feature of the Israeli-Palestinian conflict is that one cannot convince the Palestinians that Haifa and Jaffa are not part of Palestine, and one cannot persuade the Jews that Judea and Samaria are not part of Greater Israel . . . The Palestinians believe that the Israelis do not need a state, and the Israelis are convinced that the Palestinians should be satisfied with autonomy . . .

So the question becomes, how can peace based on partition be achieved?
Harkabi's answer is: By making a clear distinction between political reality and ideology. On the political level, the Palestinians as well as the Israelis will have to accept a truncated homeland—or as the Palestinian Israeli writer Anton Shammas has put it, "to trade the homeland of the mind for a narrow state underfoot" (*Harper's Magazine,* March 1989, p. 60). They will still cherish the idea of a

single homeland on the ideological-emotional level. If this could be done would it, then, be inconceivable that in some future time some kind of political arrangement might be reached whereby Jews could live in Ramallah or Hebron and Palestinians in Haifa or Jaffa without bitterness or hostility?

This vision clearly outstrips current reality—Israel's refusal to acknowledge Palestinian nationhood and the Palestinians' insistence on an independent, sovereign state—but it nevertheless lights up possibilities for the future to which we, mired in present brutality, are often not very sensitive. I here use the term vision to underscore the distance separating a realistic settlement from the unattainable dreams of expansion or liberation, the Israeli dream of a Greater Israel, more or less empty of Palestinians, and the Palestinian dream of restoring an undiminished Palestine.

One can say that while the Palestinians have now begun to move away from this dream, the majority of Israelis have not. Early in 1989, Salah Khalaf, a leading PLO figure, in a dramatic videotaped address to an Israeli-Arab symposium in Jerusalem, put the new Palestinian position this way:

> In the past we believed that this land is ours alone, and we did not believe the idea of coexistence between two states . . . .[Today] I address you and say to you that the Algiers resolutions, and Arafat's statements at the press conference in Geneva, reflect the heartfelt convictions of every Palestinian . . . .Some people wonder whether this coexistence is only a first step. We answer, no. We want a definitive settlement. But a definitive settlement will only come if peace is first . . . .The important thing is that the two peoples, the Palestinian and the Israeli, come to believe in the necessity of coexistence between two states.

So, for the Palestinians now the position is: If Palestine cannot be repossessed perhaps it can be recreated in a new form. This, in my view, is the import of the historic resolutions of the nineteenth Palestine National Council: trading the dream of total liberation for the palpable reality of a narrow state. That this radical change in PLO policy will induce a similar change in the Israeli position is, unfortunately, by no means certain.

Moving toward peace calls for an enormous effort. War often seems so much simpler. Recall that when, in 1973, perhaps the greatest opportunity for a comprehensive Middle East peace since

1948 presented itself, it was destroyed by Henry Kissinger's policy of dividing the Arabs by sponsoring partial agreements between Israel and some Arab neighbors resolving the easier issues, while leaving the major issue of the Palestinians untouched. This was made possible because Kissinger, as American Secretary of State, enjoyed the full backing of the American Jewish leadership and its allies in Congress. The same could happen again, in perhaps a somewhat different manner, under the Bush Administration. Since Kissinger, except for a fleeting moment during the Carter administration, the United States has, in Arab eyes, appeared to be more part of the problem than part of the solution.

It is noteworthy that even before Shamir's visit to Washington in April 1989, Yitzhak Rabin, the Defense Minister, told a group of visitors, according to the Tel Aviv daily *Yedioth Ahronoth* (February 24, 1989), that "the Americans are well content now, they do not look for any solution in the Middle East, and they will leave us quiet, at least for a year. The inhabitants of the territories are under a heavy military and political pressure . . . At the end they will be broken, and will themselves put pressure on Arafat to enable them to negotiate by themselves with Israel."

Already the euphoria created by the Algiers resolutions and the American-Palestinian dialogue seems to be dissipating. The Bush Administration, exhibiting little desire to build on the recent break-throughs, seems more inclined to pursue a policy of wait-and-see. But the practical effect of such a policy is shelving the idea of an international conference, around which there already exists virtual world consensus, and favoring what Rabin sees as leaving Israel alone, "at least for a year." Thus the peace process, instead of leaping ahead under the new administration, is now bogged down by the question of elections in the West Bank and Gaza. It would be justifiable to think therefore that by accepting Shamir's proposal the Bush Administration seems to have implicitly agreed to give Israel a little more time to contain the uprising and thus to recreate the kind of framework best suited to the kind of solution deemed acceptable by the present Israeli leadership, namely, some form of local autonomy for the West Bank and Gaza.

However, there are two things, in my view, of which we can be reasonably certain concerning the immediate future. The first is that, so long as Israel is ruled by the present right-wing leadership, there seems little likelihood of an early move toward a settlement of the Palestinian question. Mr. Shamir and his colleagues will continue to find ways to deflect any genuine attempt at reaching a peace agreement so long as he and his collaborators feel secure that the United States will not seriously oppose what they do, provided that it is done successfully. But, secondly, Israel's occupation of the West Bank and Gaza Strip cannot go on forever. Palestinian popular resistance will continue, and Israel's occupation will end. The only question is when and how the occupation will be terminated, and at what price to the Palestinian community in lives and further suffering.

The Palestinians have it in their power, if they consciously so decide, to build a true democracy in the Arab world. They have learned, particularly since the *intifada,* that liberation is not something to be won all at once at the end of a struggle. They know that it is achieved gradually in the course of struggle, and that it takes root slowly in the everyday relations between people before it is embodied in the formal structures and institutions of the state.

Ironically, this is the same kind of dream cherished by the early Zionists not so long ago! But the difference is that while the Zionist dream has remained largely a dream, the Palestinian dream seems already half realized. Few communities in similar circumstances have what the Palestinians already enjoy. They are engaged in a successful national struggle, one which is unique both in the extent to which it has mobilized practically every single member of the society, including women and children, and in the original, highly effective, non-lethal weapon it has now invented to achieve its independence.

Today the Palestinians enjoy the warm support of almost all the peoples and governments of the world. They have a homogeneous community on the ground. They have to displace no one in order to build their state, only to free themselves. The Palestinian community is, furthermore, unified in its cultural traditions and deeply rooted in its ancestral land. As a people the Palestinians form a cohesive society in which the power of the former landed families has disintegrated in the process of national struggle. Today there are relatively few class differences among Palestinians in the West Bank and Gaza, where over the past twenty years the gap between rich and poor has greatly narrowed, and most farmers own their land.

Palestinians also enjoy one of the highest levels of literacy in the Third World. There are more Palestinian university graduates per capita than there are Israeli university graduates. Under the occupation the Palestinians have succeeded in building their own independent institutions, despite limited material resources and relentless Israeli suppression. This includes, in the educational field, several universities and colleges, vocational centers, research institutes and elementary and high schools; in health care, a health system with several hospitals, clinics and emergency service stations in camps and villages; and, in the field of self-help organizations, workers and farm cooperatives, and several unions of workers, women and students. All this will contribute to the enrichment of Palestinian civil society and the development of organizations and institutions that will be independent of the state and its direct control. During the last forty-odd years Palestinian cultural life has also flourished, particularly in the plastic arts, drama, and the theater. Perhaps more importantly, Palestine today is the only territory in the Arab world where women can be said to have achieved a large degree of liberation—not through men's action but by their own struggle.

Thus all the makings for an exemplary free and democratic state are there. On day one of independence the Palestinians could inaugurate a society well on the road to modernity, a state that could be a living example to a part of the world where fundamentalism and patriarchy now threaten to bury the future in new forms of despotic structure. Here, sober development, based on agriculture and light industry, propelled by the intelligence and skills of a highly educated people, would displace the consumerist, mindless model of waste and ecological destructiveness characteristic of most of the surrounding countries.

In the last two decades, progressive thinking in the Arab world has shifted from the revolutionary model to the model of democracy. As in many post-colonial countries, the goal of revolution is no longer viable, for wherever revolution has occurred it has led not to freedom but to authoritarianism and neopatriarchy. As the goal of political struggle, democracy is now seen in three concrete objectives: human rights, civil rights, and self-determination. The Palestinian uprising, in embodying these objectives, foreshadows the shape of the future Arab struggle. If human rights, civil rights, and democratic liberties can be realized in the Palestinian state, what will prevent their realization across the Arab world?

But even dreams with strong roots in reality can founder. This can happen in Palestine unless the opportunity to make ready from now the proper conditions for the implementation of this dream is seized and consciously acted upon. Clearly the time for building Palestinian democracy is right now, by making conscious and articulate the values and goals of the new society, by preparing the ground for their incorporation in the structures of an eventual state. Hence the need for the existing apparatuses of the Palestine Liberation Organization to take from now the necessary measures to implement those reforms that will enable the Palestinians to start building their democratic state. This would seal the triumph of the *intifada*. But for the uprising to be genuinely reflected in the external administration of Palestinian affairs, there is no alternative to the radical transformation of the existing bureaucratic and political structures. Even if only minimum reform, not a full *intifada,* is carried out outside, a major step will have been taken toward securing a basis in democracy for the future Palestinian state.

Palestinian intellectuals at home and abroad have a special role to play in preventing the kind of post-independence disaster that we have seen happening in many Third World countries after independence. In this phase, they form the group best equipped to do what is most needed: To provide the true image of what a Palestinian state would look like, and to work out the means for its transformation into reality. Their duty would be to maintain a critical stance vis-à-vis the Arab and Palestinian status quo and to uphold the values of freedom and democracy in the face of regressive currents and movements. In the end, what is to be gained from creating a Palestine in which a combination of poverty and repression would only lead to a fundamentalist withdrawal? If intellectuals accept the role of apologists and propagandists they will contribute little to the ongoing struggle and will only strengthen the hand of the forces of reaction. As responsible critics and specialists in their various fields, on the other hand, they can be a material force protecting the achievements of the people's struggle and paving the ground for the flowering one day of a functioning democracy in Palestine.

11 A TWO-STATE SOLUTION: SECURITY, STABILITY AND THE SUPERPOWERS

Valerie Yorke

One result of the *intifada* and King Hussein's break with the West Bank of July 1988 has been to focus attention on the concept of a two-state solution to the Palestinian issue. The fact is that a negotiated Israeli-Palestinian peace treaty embracing two states on the land of former Palestine, one which exists (Israel) and one which would come into being (Palestine), is the only option currently available which could pave the way to a solution of the Arab-Israeli conflict. It is also the only option which the international community has not yet collectively pressed for. Official Israel refuses to negotiate with the PLO or contemplate an independent Palestinian state. But the Israeli body politic is divided on the issue. For those who reject full withdrawal on the grounds that the West Bank and Gaza Strip constitute *Eretz Israel,* the reasons for opposing a Palestinian state are clear. For those who favor withdrawal from the occupied territories in exchange for peace, the understandable fear is that a new Palestine, by virtue of the political intentions of its inhabitants, its inherent instability or its proximity would constitute an unacceptable danger to Israel.

This study seeks to challenge that conventional wisdom. It sets out a group of interrelated conditions which might form the basis of a negotiated, lasting and stable overall peace involving a Palestinian state. It examines the political ingredients of such a two-state solution, paying particular attention to the kinds of concessions that both parties might make to ensure that the solution serves the political interests of Israel and Palestine, and to minimize the risks of instability or subsequent breakdown. Acknowledging that fear and suspicion are not easily dissipated, and that geography makes it genuinely difficult for Israel to withdraw from the West Bank without endangering its security, I shall argue that a superpower role will be indispensable in bringing the parties to an agreement.[1] An assessment is made of how superpower backing for, and physical participation in, a network of security arrangements and guarantees would provide local and international actors with a crucial stake in maintaining the peace, and minimizing the dangers to the security of Israel and Palestine in the event of the peace coming under challenge.

1. A Two-State Solution: Stability and Security

Undoubtedly, local and international actors share an interest in avoiding devastating conflict and moving toward a lasting overall Middle East peace. But that shared interest does not extend to turning a commitment to peace into a concerted attempt to move from the current state of "no war, no peace" to a solution, let alone a two-state solution that might be stable and durable.

This is because the local and international actors involved in the conflict have divergent interests at stake. While the local actors may want peace they are subject to complex domestic inhibitions, requirements and aspirations militating against peace. While the US is officially committed to peace, the pressures of the Israel lobby prevent it from saying publicly that Israel cannot continue to rely on self-maintaining defense. In short, it has become taboo to spell out how the United States might provide the security assurances necessary to persuade Israel to withdraw.

It follows that a durable solution to the Palestinian issue based on two states can only come about when all the parties involved decide simultaneously that (1) the advantages of peace outweigh the advantages of a continuation of the status quo; (2) they have a stake in keeping the peace; (3) the risks of peace are fewer than those in the status quo. I shall argue that to achieve that shared interest among the parties the following minimum set of prerequisites would have to form the basis of a negotiated solution to the Palestinian problem. Each may not be necessary for the conclusion of peace, but in combination they constitute a set of interrelated conditions, which would minimize the risk of breakdown and maximize protection for the parties should infringements occur. A lasting durable peace would depend on them.

A. *Superpowers As Guarantors*

Superpower involvement in a final settlement is the key prerequisite on which the fulfillment of most other prerequisites would depend. A stable two-state solution in the context of a comprehensive Arab-Israeli peace would require the participation of both superpowers in a co-guarantor role. This is because the Middle East war has been waged with arms used and diplomatic support given by the superpowers. One result of this has been that the local parties can start wars, but the superpowers have influenced the eventual outcome through the exercise of restraint and deterrent power. It has thus become impossible for local parties to be decisively defeated. And there is no good reason why undefeated combatant states, left to themselves, should make major concessions that affect their security. It seems likely, therefore, that the fundamental Palestinian issue left unresolved by the stalemated war will only be brought to a settlement by the inducements and pressures of the superpowers who created the stalemate in the first place. Israel would certainly only be induced to give up the "strategic depth" afforded by control of the West Bank in exchange for a US practical commitment on the ground and the deterrent value this would provide.[2] And since the price of Soviet support for a settlement will be a co-equal role for itself, a joint and visible superpower presence will be necessary. After all, this war has been permeated by superpower rivalry, and the only stable peace can be one that both powers accept. Eventually, Soviet cooperation in agreeing to the maintenance of a military balance at a lower level in the Middle East will be as crucial to the preservation of any settlement as Soviet diplomatic cooperation in bringing it about.

B. *The Need For A Comprehensive Peace*

If it is to be stable, an Israeli-Palestinian peace must be part of an overall Arab-Israeli settlement. Unless the conflict between Israel and its other Arab neighbors is resolved, the Arab world will not endorse the Israeli-Palestinian peace and could seek to undermine it. Israel would have withdrawn from the occupied territories without winning the necessary commitment to peace from the Arabs, and it would face the danger of at least limited war and of terrorism.[3] Syria could be expected to support the terrorist actions of those extremists hostile to the settlement and seeking to destabilize the Palestinian entity.

The *quid pro quo,* therefore, for the necessary Arab endorsement of an Israeli-Palestinian peace will be the conclusion of Syrian and Jordanian peace treaties with Israel. Such treaties would provide for the withdrawal of Israeli forces from the Golan and the demilitarization of the evacuated areas, for the resolution of the territorial dispute along the Jordanian-Israeli border and for a demilitarized strip of Jordanian territory along the Jordan River. All this would pave the way for collective Arab and Islamic guarantees of the overall settlement and the new Palestine, and for undertakings by the appropriate Arab countries to provide crucial economic aid for an international fund in support of the peace settlement and to help resettle those refugees not wanting or not able to return to the new Palestine.

However, the *quid pro quo* for Arab cooperation may be more than this. In this author's view, it will also have to include some compensation for the loss of funds that the Arab negotiating parties will incur as they abandon their status as confrontation states, in order to tide them over the lean years to come.

C. *Reconciling Minimum Demands*

If a two-state solution to the Palestinian problem is to be accepted by the parties concerned it must accommodate the minimum Israeli requirement for full peace and security, and the minimum Palestinian requirement for an independent state. It must be negotiated by their authoritative leaders, for only PLO endorsement can lead to the pan-Arab support necessary to make the settlement stick. If it is to be stable and durable, it must also provide as many Israelis and Palestinians as possible with a stake in its maintenance. Such a solution would greatly reduce the numbers of those who might wish to join forces with residual rejectionists on both sides who, condemning their respective leaderships for having sold out, will seek to undermine it.

A stable and durable settlement, therefore, requires that the local parties show flexibility in order to close the gap between their irreconcilable demands. Neither side can expect to achieve all its demands and win a lasting peace. This is partly because the authority of the other negotiating party would then be undermined, and a loss of control to alternative, more demanding leaders could be expected. A settlement in which Israel's definition of security in the form of the maintenance of military control over the new Palestine was satisfied at the expense of Palestinian political rights, or in which the Palestinians achieved an independent state under conditions which posed a direct threat to Israel, would lack the necessary balance of interests.

The challenge, therefore, is to devise a "package deal" made up of reciprocal, albeit asymmetrical concessions which, when supplemented with outside inducements, would reconcile Israeli security needs with a full expression of Palestinian political rights.

D. *Treatment of All Outstanding Issues*

A peace settlement must deal with the full gamut of issues which concern Israelis and Palestinians (right of return, compensation issues, economic aid, water and Jerusalem) in order to minimize outstanding grievances once it has been concluded. In particular, a peace formula will need to accommodate the strong attachments of Palestinians and Israelis to the territory of the *whole* of former Palestine west of the Jordan River, without infringing upon the sovereignty of Israel or of the new Palestine, or endangering the security of those two states.

E. *Timing*

In order to promote the confidence necessary for both sides to move toward a peace settlement, ways must be found to accommodate Israeli and Palestinian anxieties *before* negotiations begin.[4] A long pre-negotiating period (two or three years) would provide time for the local parties to explore the kinds of negotiated tradeoffs that will have to be made and to prepare their publics to accept the necessary conditions listed above for a stable peace; and for key international actors to work out the details of their involvement in the peace settlement and prepare their own domestic publics for the inevitable security and financial commitments to be made. In particular, Washington should discard the orthodoxy that security guarantees should *supplement* a negotiated settlement and spell out the form that safeguards and guarantees might take before negotiations. In this regard, difficulties with the Congress should not be underestimated.

2. Political and Security Components of a Two-State Solution

The following paragraphs examine the main components of a negotiated settlement of the Palestinian issue based on a two-state solution along approximately the 1967 borders.[5] An assessment is made of the kinds of negotiated and mutually agreed tradeoffs across the range of political and security issues that might be included to maximize the durability and stability of the peace and minimize any damaging consequences that would follow from infringements of the peace treaty.[6] Particular attention is paid to the degree of outside support and participation that will be required both to bring about the necessary concessions for peace and to guarantee the settlement that might be expected to ensue.

The purpose of this exercise in imagination is three-fold, namely to demonstrate that (1) nothing less than a two-state solution can provide the basis for a stable peace; (2) provided the above prerequisites are fulfilled, there is no inherent reason why a Palestinian state should be unstable or endanger Israel; (3) the extensive outside involvement necessary to reconcile security and sovereignty issues would need to take untried and unprecedented forms because of the geography and short distances involved. These exclude any duplication of the Sinai system of early warning.

A. *Sovereignty*

A solution based on the creation of a sovereign, independent Palestinian state has the advantage of meeting most closely the national aspirations of the majority of Palestinians in the West Bank and Gaza, as well as in the Diaspora. Palestinians believe they have a right to self-determination in a state of their own in the territory of former Palestine, and they point to UN General Assembly Resolution 181, which enshrines the principle of two states in Palestine, as a source of international legitimacy. Palestinians collectively agree that the only acceptable peace is one which recognizes this right and provides for its implementation: nothing less will do. For the Palestinians, a sovereign state would end the indignity and suffering of Israeli occupation, and fulfill the psychological need for a territorial identity. It would provide a flag, citizenship and physical security.

This solution would be endorsed by the PLO and thus, in turn, win the approval of most Arab states, including Egypt, with whom it is vital for Israel to maintain its peace. Only a Palestinian state would conform with the PLO's Declaration of Independence of November 1988 based on UN Partition Resolution 181. Given the degree of international backing for the Palestinian state—more than 90 states have extended recognition—the PLO has no incentive to settle for less. Indeed, it would not risk accepting the political autonomy or Jordanian options as the basis for a final peace, since these are totally unacceptable to Palestinians and to wider Arab opinion.

Only the creation of a Palestinian state would put the legitimate Palestinian nationalist struggle on the side of a solution. No other solution would be perceived by Palestinians and Arabs as just or adequate compensation for the loss of their historic rights in Palestine. In short, only the acquisition of *full* Palestinian sovereignty would address the Palestinian problem in a substantive way and create the necessary conditions for a comprehensive Arab-Israel settlement. Full sovereignty is a *sine qua non* for a durable and stable peace.

From Israel's point of view, then, only the creation of a Palestinian state could pave the way to the full peace and security it requires. Israeli security ultimately depends on a peace acceptable to, and freely entered into, by the Palestinians and Arab states rather than on Israel's continued occupation of Arab territory. Even if Israel were somehow to achieve an agreement with Jordan, it would have to face the political and security consequences of having bypassed the PLO and suppressed Palestinian nationalist aspirations. The risk for Israel would be that instability on the West Bank and Gaza and in Jordan might ultimately lead to the creation of a Palestinian state on the West Bank, and perhaps on both Banks, but that neither the new Palestine nor the majority of the Arab states would have undertaken formal commitments to peace with Israel.

It must be assumed, however, that any Israeli government would only agree to a two-state solution as the basis of a negotiated peace treaty if it were satisfied that it had secured in the process an authoritative Palestinian commitment not only to a full peace but also to extensive security arrangements and guarantees.

Palestinians see no contradiction between the exercise of Palestinian sovereignty and negotiated political and security provisions to meet Israel's legitimate security fears.[7] Provided a settlement is based on the two issues of sovereignty and peace and reflects a balance of Israeli, Palestinian and Arab interests, Palestinians concede that the trade-offs in the peace agreements need not be symmetrical. They should, however, be reciprocal.

B. *Frontiers*

The Palestinian state would be defined by the 1967 border (with minor and reciprocal adjustments). The two parts of the state comprising the West Bank and East Jerusalem, on one hand, and the Gaza Strip on the other would be linked by an overland connecting route. The route would come under the authority of a new international Middle East Control Commission (see below), with freedom of access to the route and along it guaranteed by an international guarantor force with American and Soviet observers. Israeli and Palestinian citizens would be permitted to move freely across the other borders at specified, internationally controlled crossing points.

The advantages of a two-state solution based on the 1967 border would rest in a number of factors working for stability:

First, only this border running between the two states would be rooted in international legitimacy. This is because UN Resolutions 242 and 338 still remain the only internationally-accepted framework for Middle East negotiations on frontiers. Resolution 242 recognized the "inadmissibility of the acquisition of territory by war" and calls for "withdrawal of Israeli armed forces from territories occupied in the recent conflict." It also notes the right of every state in the area to live within "secure and recognized boundaries."

Second, the Palestinian leadership could negotiate these borders with collective Palestinian and Arab support. Palestinians and Arabs long ago abandoned their preference for the borders of the 1947 partition plan as unrealistic. By November 1978, Arab opinion had moved sufficiently on the border issue for 21 members of the Arab League, including the PLO, to agree for the first time at the Baghdad Summit to seek a negotiated peace on the basis of Israel's withdrawal to the 1967 borders and the right of the Palestinians to their own independent state. The 1982 Fez statement specifically mentioned the 1967 borders. And at its PNC meeting in November 1988, the PLO formally accepted UN Security Council Resolution 242, thereby joining the ranks of Syria, Egypt and Jordan. In short, the 1967 border would conform to the Palestinian concept of a just settlement.

Third, only the 1967 border and no other set of boundaries could win full peace and security for Israel. A growing number of Israelis argue that security and political considerations cannot be separated; that the only secure boundaries will be those freely accepted and recognized by the Arab world as a whole. According to this school of thought, the maintenance of "defensible borders" involving continued Israeli military control of parts of the West Bank would preclude a Palestinian solution and a comprehensive peace, and carry an unacceptably high price in terms of Israel's internal stability, self-confidence and international standing.[8]

Fourth, since the international community regards the approximate 1967 border as the only one rooted in international legitimacy, a peace settlement based on this border would be the only settlement that outside powers would be prepared to guarantee: the only one for which the United States might be prepared to offer Israel the crucial guarantee of last resort—a Mutual Defense Pact.[9] This is because the international community is unlikely to agree that Israel's definition of secure borders be accepted at the expense of the security needs and sovereignty of its neighbors. This would run counter to UN Resolution 242, which affirms the necessity for international security measures to protect the territorial inviolability and independence of all states in the area. Major modifications to the armistice lines would also be an infringement of the Preamble to UN Resolution 242. In addition, for Israel to behave at the expense of its neighbors as if it is the only state in the area with a security problem is contrary to a principle implicit in the UN Charter—namely, that a nation should not be permitted to expand its territories through conquest.

Fifth, Israel's withdrawal to a permanent border approximating the 1967 border could accommodate a distinction between the "legal" border and a mutually agreed security line beyond it, along which international forces, DMZs and monitoring stations might be located.[10] It is not inconceivable that Israel might have access to this security system for observation purposes.

Sixth, Israel's withdrawal to the approximate 1967 border could pave the way for the negotiating parties to agree on reciprocal border rectifications. These would be devised to enhance Israeli security needs and Palestinian political requirements, thereby increasing the stability of the settlement. One possible trade-off might be Israeli retention of the Latrun road to Tel Aviv with some of its surrounding land now under Israeli control, in exchange for the return to Palestine of Litfa or the Israeli part of the divided Arab village of Beit Safafa. The Palestinians might consider the acquisition of villages around Tulkarm and Qalqilya as appropriate candidates.[11]

C. *Population, Palestinian Refugees and Israeli Settlements*

Palestine's population would comprise the West Bank and Gaza Strip populations, Palestinian refugees returning to the new state and Palestinians living abroad who chose to opt for Palestinian citizenship. But how could agreement be reached on the controversial Palestinian refugee issue? How many refugees would be permitted to return and where would they go?

It is unlikely that this complex problem would prevent an Israeli-Palestinian peace once negotiations began. Hardline positions could be expected to give way to some flexibility, once hostility between the protagonists gave way to the desire to reach a peace on the basis of a two-state solution. However, a negotiated formula would need to take account of, and reflect in some way the following realities and minimum demands.

Israel's preference (and minimum demand at the outset) would be to make its withdrawal to approximately the 1967 borders and the creation of a Palestinian state conditional on an unequivocal renunciation of all Palestinian claims on Israel. In addition to territorial claims, this renunciation would apply to property and repatriation claims. Some Israelis say they would even exclude compensation claims because payment would be an acknowledgement of the Palestinian right of return. Nor can Israelis contemplate an unlimited flow of refugees to the West Bank and Gaza, which they maintain would merely strengthen the desire of Palestinians to return to Israel proper and aggravate Israel's demographic problem. For Israel, peace based on a two-state solution would have to include a resolution of the refugee problem with an agreement by the Arab states, in particular Syria and Jordan, to resettle refugees.

For their part, the Palestinians regard the right of every refugee to return to his place of origin, including Israel, as a sacred principle. It is a principle enshrined in UN resolutions and one which they cannot easily concede. After all, they argue, the Palestinian problem did not originate with Israel's occupation of 1967, but in the 1948 war. A West Bank and Gaza Strip state would not, therefore, supply sufficient redress for the grievances of a sizeable element of the Palestinian refugee community. Moreover, any imposed limitation on a return to the new Palestine would be regarded as an intolerable and unjust limit on Palestinian sovereignty.

By contrast, many Palestinians in private concede that in the context of a two-state solution some compromise could be reached on this issue which would go a long way toward meeting Israel's understandable security fears. Concessions, these Palestinians say, would have to be negotiated on the basis of reciprocity. However, the concessions envisaged fall far short of what any Israeli is prepared currently to contemplate.

Pre-settlement negotiations would reveal the scope for greater flexibility, but the following approach, based on reciprocal trade-offs between the Palestinian refugee and Israeli settlement issues, might be taken.

The Peace Treaty would distinguish between two mutually exclusive

Israeli and Palestinian states with sovereignty resting in the state on the one hand, and a shared "homeland" embracing the whole area of former Palestine west of the Jordan River on the other. It would also distinguish between (a) those Palestinians and Jews who had rights in pre-1967 Israel, and the West Bank and Gaza, respectively, prior to 1948, and (b) those Palestinians who left the West Bank and Gaza and those Israelis who settled in the occupied territories after 1967.

Within this framework the negotiating parties would agree on a number of practical measures to be implemented in mutually agreed stages during and after the transitional period.

1. A limited number of 1948 Palestinian refugees, say between 50,000 and 100,000, would return to Israel proper in a family reunification scheme in mutually agreed phases, and would be subject to Israel's rule of law. Israel would draw on an International Fund for financial help.

2. Palestinians would return to the new Palestine over a five-year period in numbers set by Palestine and mutually agreed by parties to the Peace Treaty.

3. The Jewish settlements which existed in the areas of the occupied territories in 1948 would stay in the Palestinian state under Palestinian sovereignty with special links to Israel. The IDF would be responsible for the evacuation of all other settlements by the end of the transitional period, but these would not be dismantled.

4. Palestinians returning to Israel proper and Jews living in Palestine would enjoy the right of residency but exercise their political rights in their own states.

5. An International Fund would be set up by outside powers as part of the peace treaty. Arab states would pay contributions equivalent to the value of Jewish property confiscated or, alternatively, according to their means. Israel and Palestine would also contribute. The Fund would be used to compensate all Palestinian refugees not returning to Palestine or Israel, Israelis evacuating settlements in the occupied territories and Jews formerly resident in Arab countries.

6. Arab countries signing peace treaties with Israel would endorse these provisions, including an agreement to absorb mutually agreed numbers of Palestinian refugees into their own states. Access to financial aid from the International Fund would be the *quid pro quo*.

7. The signatories to all the peace treaties would agree that these provisions amounted to a resolution of the Palestinian refugee problem and fulfillment of all UN resolutions on this subject. The United Nations Relief and Works Agency (UNRWA) would cease to exist as

far as its services were concerned, though its personnel and data base would be made available to the Palestine authorities. Israel would declare the renunciation of its claims on Arab countries.

8. The negotiating parties would agree to discuss from time to time during and after the implementation of a settlement the possibility of reciprocal arrangements on issues such as unrestricted tourism, and an annual right of residency for small numbers of Israelis and Palestinians (as mutually agreed) wishing to reside in the neighboring state.

The advantages of this formula would rest in a number of factors working for stability. It would have the merit of providing symbolic practical measures which would go some way toward accommodating deeply-held feelings on both sides for the whole of the land of Palestine, while also reflecting the practical realities on the ground. For Palestinians, the sense of injustice resulting from total exclusion from pre-1948 Palestine would be avoided. For Israelis, religious ties with parts of the West Bank would have been acknowledged. The settlement would meet the Palestinian demand that the principle of reciprocity be respected wherever possible. It would incorporate the principle of the Palestinians' right of return. And it would provide for a resolution of the refugee problem. Moreover, in a peaceful post-settlement environment these extra Palestinians inside Israel would not ostensibly pose a grievous threat. The same would be the case with the Israeli settlers in Palestine.

Only such a formula, which involved elaborate trade-offs reflecting a balance of Israeli, Palestinian and Arab interests, could win the support of the PLO and the majority of Palestinian, Arab and Israeli opinion. Only such a formula, which took some account of deep attachments of Palestinians and Israelis to the homeland of the whole of Palestine, would stand a chance of bringing all Israeli and Palestinian elements to accept the peace treaty as final and an end to making claims over the territories of each other's states. These results could not be achieved if Israel insisted on a renunciation of the Palestinian right of return and the maintenance of all settlements established after 1967. Nor could they be achieved if the PLO were to insist on the full implementation of the right of return and the evacuation of every settlement. Were the Israeli and Palestinian leaderships to negotiate conditions under which Palestinian nationalism or Israeli religious sentiment became overly constrained, or which embodied perceived or actual security risks, they would become vulnerable to the criticisms of would-be challengers. The stability and durability of the overall peace would in due course be undermined.

Admittedly, Israeli and Palestinian negotiators would find it difficult to negotiate a compromise formula such as this which inevitably contains a degree of risk, at least in the short term. Israeli negotiators would be reluctant to endorse the return of even a limited number of Palestinians, because of the security, danger and aggravation of tensions among Israel's Arab community. Palestinian negotiators would fear that the continued presence of settlers inside their sovereign state would become a target of terrorism. The new state's limited absorptive capacity would pose another constraint. But these potential dangers could be alleviated by other provisions in the peace treaty: a more flexible Israeli policy toward Arabs in Israel; generous compensation for Palestinians choosing not to take up residence in the new state; and flexible attitudes on the part of Arab states where Palestinians now reside. The economic policies chosen by the new Palestine government, combined with the willingness of Palestinians in the Diaspora to invest in Palestine, would also play a part in increasing the new state's absorptive capacity.

The implementation of this part of the agreement would be complex, with difficulties arising over which Palestinians would return to Israel and Palestine and where they would live, and how settlers are to be evacuated. A joint Israeli-Palestinian team could be set up, and any disagreement could go to the Control Commission's supervisory committee for arbitration.

D. *Palestine's Foreign and Defense Policy*

Palestine's foreign policy orientation and defense posture will be crucial in the pre-negotiation discussions leading to a peace treaty. Policy preferences will not necessarily coincide with alternative options available and eventually chosen. Choices will be circumscribed by the requirement for policies consistent with Palestinian sovereignty, the need to convince Israel that Palestine would not be a threat, the need for cooperative relations with its neighbors and the need to avoid political entanglements which could drag the Palestinians into unwanted conflict. Most importantly, Palestine's defense and foreign policy choices would need to accommodate the elaborate security arrangements on the ground, as well as international guarantees which will themselves be the *sine qua non* of Israeli withdrawal and the creation of the Palestinian state.

Any Israeli government confronted with the prospect that a Palestinian state might one day not be under Israeli military control would say it needed protection against four types of threat: a surprise Arab conventional attack from the East, the risk that the West Bank would become a Soviet base, the infiltration of heavy weapons, particularly artillery pieces, into the area; and terrorist raids by Palestinians in and outside the new Palestine trying to undermine the settlement.

Correspondingly, the Palestinian government would want protection from government-sponsored Israeli intervention or Arab armed intervention resulting from changes of government; from Israeli reprisals, however precipitated; from Israeli elements, acting independently of their government, who were dissatisfied with the peace treaty and would be prepared to engage in terrorism across the border to try to undermine it; from the danger of becoming the battleground for external warring states; and perhaps from the infiltration of Palestinian irredentists who regarded an independent state as a sellout and no more than a territorial base from which to continue military action against Israel.

What kind of foreign policy would be consistent with these requirements? Let us consider a non-aligned posture for Palestine. The security fears of Israel and Jordan combined with their vastly superior military power suggest that a new Palestine's interests would be best served by maintaining the non-aligned status *vis-à-vis* the superpowers set out in the Palestinian Declaration of Independence.[12] In this context, Palestine would undertake not to adhere to military alliances or permit foreign troops to be stationed on, or pass through, its territory. It is not inconceivable that in the context of the peace treaty, Palestine would go further and voluntarily declare military neutrality.[13]

The advantages of such a posture are the following. Nonalignment and military neutrality would be consistent with the maintenance of a defense capability for the new state, as set out below. It would be compatible with membership of the United Nations and the Arab League (except for its Defense Council and Security Pact). Most importantly, non-alignment could pave the way to international and regional importance and prestige—Palestine could, for example, become the headquarters for a variety of regional organizations. And here I have a suggestion: Palestine could volunteer East Jerusalem, its capital, as a site for a sub-center of the United Nations Disaster Relief Organization (UNDRO) and a disaster relief stockpile center.[14]

Jerusalem is geographically well-placed in relation to the earthquake belt and to the Horn of Africa. And UNDRO needs a complement to Pisa in Italy from which emergency aid is currently dispatched.

E. *Palestine: Demilitarization or "Limitation of Armaments"*

There is a broad international consensus that a Palestinian state would have to be virtually demilitarized, whatever its future constitutional arrangements: and that token strips of Israeli and Jordanian territory should also be demilitarized. One suggestion made by a former American official is that the PLO should offer to demilitarize the Palestinian state as an inducement to Israel to take the risks involved in negotiations. It is too early to say whether such a condition would be acceptable to Palestinians, although the pre-negotiating phase is likely to reveal some Palestinian flexibility on this issue.

It is my contention that full demilitarization would not be conducive to stability. Understandably, Israel, having withdrawn behind 1967 borders, would want the Palestinian state demilitarized except for a lightly armed internal police force. But demilitarization of the state would be regarded as an intolerable limit on their sovereignty by the PLO and by more moderate Palestinians as well. No Palestinian will accept the indignity of being a citizen of an unarmed state. And no Palestinian transitional regime or subsequent government could afford to be deprived, for symbolic and security reasons, of the essential element of sovereignty and key to its authority—an army. Nor could any PLO leader undertake prior to negotiations to demilitarize a future Palestinian state. To do so would be to forfeit his political credentials with the Palestinian fighters in Lebanon. They require sophisticated arms to confront Israelis, Syrians and Lebanese and are not, therefore, psychologically prepared for discussions relating to the demilitarization of Palestine.

The PLO position would also be motivated by considerations of security and longer-term stability. Once the state was created, the Palestinian government would be confronted with a major internal policing task as well as the need for a minimal deterrent. Most importantly, the Palestine military forces could play an important role in integrating the sizeable body of ex-fighters accustomed to a military way of life. Army duties would help channel energies away from troublemaking, and towards the task of state-building: an important factor working for stability.

Many Palestinians and PLO officials close to Arafat in private reiterate the view, first expressed more than ten years ago, that a full-fledged army would not be conducive to stability either. They maintain that a "limitation of armaments" would be consistent with their new state's needs and open to consideration, once the Israeli occupation is ended and negotiations for a comprehensive peace begin. They recognize that a Palestinian army could never compete with Israeli and Jordanian armed strength and would be considered provocative. Palestinians could not rely on self-defense and would need to depend on collective Arab guarantees and non-Arab external forces to protect their territory from Israeli reoccupation or Arab intervention. Besides, the new state could not spare financial resources, badly needed for development, for the purchase of modern weapons systems.

The PLO's views on demilitarized zones and guarantor forces are equally long-standing: in January 1978, Arafat publicly proposed that borders of an independent Palestinian state should be policed by an international peace-keeping force with demilitarized areas on both sides of the border.[15] This position remains unchanged apart from two recent refinements: the PLO would agree to the placement of an international guarantor force on the Palestinian side of the border only; and it would accept a multinational force outside the United Nations.[16]

As for the Soviet view, Soviet academics see no difficulty in maintaining what would amount to a quasi-demilitarized status of Palestinian territory, provided the Palestinians agree. With a satisfactory settlement on the Golan and in Lebanon, it is not inconceivable that Syria and the other Arab states might accept that it is in their interest, too, for the Palestinians to accept this limit on their sovereignty. It seems, therefore, that a strict limitation of forces on their territory may be the price that Palestinians are prepared and obliged to pay in return for a state and for outside protection.

Nonetheless, Palestinians would not like the loss of sovereignty that a "limitation of armaments" and international military control would entail. By way of compensation, the Palestinians would wish to achieve full sovereignty in a state of their own as quickly as possible, and regain their part of Jerusalem. Whether or not to confederate with Jordan after independence would be for the Palestinians to decide.

The aim would be to satisfy the aspirations of the majority of Palestinians, thereby preventing rejectionists from gaining support for irredentist claims on Israel during or after the implementation of the settlement. What would be required therefore would be as short a transitional phase as practicably possible.

If Israel's objections to a West Bank settlement are truly security-based there is a strong argument that, provided Israel receives security assurances beforehand, it should agree to withdraw fully by the end of a transitional period during which security arrangements would be established.

F. *Palestine's Defense Posture*

If a limitation on Palestine's force levels was agreed as part of a peace treaty, the following approach might be taken.

The Palestine Army (PA) would be limited in size, with manpower levels only high enough to absorb the bulk of the Palestinian regular armed forces. Three brigades, or 9000 men, have been suggested as an appropriate force. In addition, an army corps, conceived to play the role of fulfilling essential state-building tasks, would be established, comprising 10,000 men.

The categories and numbers of weapons that the PA would acquire should be determined by two considerations: first, the minimum number of conventional-type weapons to enable what would in practice be an internal policing force to be credibly called the Palestine Army, and second, the weapons needed for internal policing tasks. The first requirement could be met by any configuration of numbers and types as long as this did not threaten Israel. The second requirement would be dictated by the capabilities required to fulfill a number of missions. Among these would be the task of the Palestinian authorities of containing tensions following Israel's withdrawal, helping to resettle returning refugees, quelling inter-factional disputes, patrolling borders and preventing armed raids by extremists across the frontier with Israel. Further down the road, the Palestinian state will become a significant center of tourism and pilgrimage, service industries and a busy transit route. The flow of humanity to the east and west will necessitate efficient security and intelligence operations if the Palestinian government's obligation to prevent the use of violence against its neighbors is to be fulfilled.

To allay Israeli fears, the PA could be configured so as to be defensive in nature. Offensive weapons systems or forces that could be used offensively, such as transport aircraft, helicopters, strike aircraft and tanks would be permitted only at minimum symbolic levels. Heavy artillery would be excluded. Defensive weapons such as anti-tank and anti-aircraft missiles, APCs with 20 mm. cannons and reconnaissance vehicles, would be kept at specified levels no higher than necessary for playing the limited deterrent role and reforming the internal security missions outlined above. Mortars, rifles and machine guns would be unlimited.

The Palestinian navy, based in Gaza, would be equipped with the light patrol craft necessary for coastguard and search and rescue tasks. The airforce, which would support the PA in its internal policing task, would comprise light reconnaissance aircraft and helicopters. The aircraft could be based at Qalandiya airport.

Limitations on force levels of this sort would fall short of the preference expressed by some Palestinians for national armed forces of greater strength, say one-third the strength of the Jordanian Army.[17] But the armed forces visualized here would have minimal aggressive capacity, and their obvious inferiority in the face of Israeli and Jordanian strength would minimize suspicions and the risk of preemptive action against them. Palestine's interest may also lie in self-imposed limitations, partly to facilitate the government's monopoly over armaments in the early years and partly to ensure that economic resources are devoted to building the state. Furthermore, force levels of the sort described would reduce the temptation for outsiders to break restrictions on arms supplies to the region in general.

These force levels would also be consistent with the nonaligned status or neutrality (which under international law permits a defensive capability) of the new Palestine. Furthermore, they would be sufficient to permit Palestine to offer troops to UN peace-keeping missions (in areas other than the Middle East) and thus assume responsibilities in the international arena. Were Jerusalem to become a regional center and stockpile for UNDRO (as suggested above) then Palestine's army could provide (1) standing teams of medics and communications experts to be flown to disaster areas and (2) engineers and maintenance experts to service items in the UNDRO hardware stockpile.

G. *The Palestinian State and Israeli Security*

Would and could an independent Palestinian state with these sorts of manpower and weapons levels constitute a security threat to Israel?

Would they be compatible with a stable relationship between Israel and Palestine?

The potential challenge of a Palestinian state armed to this degree would depend on the likelihood of its weapons being deployed offensively against Israel and the danger they would pose if they were used. As discussed earlier, this would be dramatically reduced by the terms of the peace treaty and its overall regional and international context. Under the treaty, Palestine and Israel would have undertaken binding reciprocal commitments to respect the sovereignty, political independence and territorial integrity of the other, to refrain from the use of force and to end hostile propaganda, economic blockades and boycotts. The conclusion of bilateral peace treaties between Israel and Syria, Jordan, Iraq and Lebanon would have removed the specific grievances of these states against each other. Arab ratification of the Israeli-Palestinian peace based on the creation of a Palestinian state would have neutralized pan-Arab irredentism against Israel and paved the way to an Arab League guarantee of Palestine. The superpowers would have recognized the non-aligned status of Palestine and would themselves have a stake in the success of the overall settlement which they had in cooperation helped to bring about.

In short, this combination would have involved Arab and outside powers in an interrelated set of obligations reflecting their collective interests and self-interest, as well as providing financial assistance for Palestine and guarantees for the settlement as a whole. Against this background, Palestinians would have to consider what conceivable benefit would result from abrogating the treaty or challenging the peace, and whether they would wish to risk losing the advantages of statehood for which the majority had struggled for over forty years.

In this analysis, the new Palestine would appear to have no interest in challenging the peace. This does not of itself provide a guarantee that it would not do so. However, could the force levels outlined above threaten Israel?

Let us consider some of the threats most frequently cited.

It is argued that a Palestinian state would remain hostile. So deep is the Palestinian irredentist urge, the argument goes, that Palestinians would before long turn their attention to Israel proper. But a Palestinian state, with the arms levels discussed above, could not on its own conceivably present a credible military threat to Israel's security or survival in the foreseeable future. With its lack of warning time, its single airstrip, its single access to the sea at Gaza running through Israeli territory, its land crossings to Jordan by way of two bridges,

Palestine would be totally vulnerable to Israel's overwhelming military might. The levels of weapons suggested here could do little more than deter Israel from taking retaliatory action after lesser Palestinian irredentist operations that escaped the PA's detection: and they might also marginally lessen the impact of any raids that Israel did undertake.

Israel might argue that, with its forces withdrawn behind the "green line," it lacked "usable warning time" against an Arab conventional threat through Jordan in which Palestine would play a vanguard role. With Arab military preponderance of 9:1 and with Israel's population centers three minutes flying time from Iraq, withdrawal would imply, according to this school of thought, an unacceptable security risk.[18] But how credible would the threat be? Whether or not a Palestinian government chose to confederate with Jordan, the negotiated "limitation of armaments" for the West Bank and Gaza would still apply, and any illegal build-up of arms supplied through Jordan would not go undetected. The situation would be one in which Israeli and Jordanian forces were separated, since the peace treaty with Jordan would have provided for a demilitarized strip on Jordanian soil, and Jordan could be expected to keep its armed forces at a distance from the Jordan River as in the past. There would be the early warning in time and space that strict security arrangements separating the armies in the Sinai, on the Golan and on the Lebanon border would provide. Israel's own aerial oblique sensors would be capable of picking up troop and aircraft movements at a distance of at least 200 miles. Combined with the intelligence that Israel's commercial and diplomatic presence in Arab countries would provide, the threat of a surprise, coordinated Arab attack against Israel, either on all three fronts or through Jordan, would be unlikely.[19]

Nor is there reason to suppose that the Palestinian government would wish to invite Jordan to intervene militarily, thereby risking a devastating Israeli attack on its own territory and possible re-occupation. For its part, Jordan would be unlikely to try and reassert its control over the West Bank, partly because the King would find no East Bank constituency to support this policy, and partly because he would not want to risk domestic unrest on the scale of the *intifada*, which would have an unacceptable destabilizing impact on the East Bank.

The uncertainty of Jordan's future poses another potential danger. A Palestinian takeover cannot be ruled out. Less dramatic would be the evolution of a Palestinian-Jordanian confederation with the Palestinians exerting more control through their influence in Jordan's government. Neither development would pose a challenge to Israel unless they involved the movement of Syrian or Iraqi forces into Jordan (not formally excluded in the Jordan-Israel peace treaty). This possibility means that without firm outside security guarantees to compensate for its loss of strategic depth, Israel would reserve the right in a future treaty to reoccupy the West Bank and Gaza Strip if another Arab state began to move into Palestine, or if Arab armed forces moved in significant numbers into Jordan.

What of the terrorist threat? Israel would undoubtedly argue that the majority of Palestinians would still hanker after the liberation of the whole of Palestine after the creation of their state. According to this view, the danger is that Palestine's government would be unable or unwilling to abide by treaty obligations. The PA's arms could fall into the hands of rejectionists, or revolutionaries could acquire portable missiles elsewhere. The PA would not, or could not stop commando operations across the border, and might even condone them. Extremists would, the argument continues, draw on the support of discontented 1948 refugees living in camps in neighboring countries and those Palestinians returning to the new state who found their expectations disappointed.

The counter-argument is that with the creation of a Palestinian state, the collective Palestinian motivation to regain all the land would diminish. Certainly, Palestine's government, whose majority would inevitably consist of West Bank and Fatah moderates, would turn its efforts to state-building tasks and fulfilling treaty obligations. Backed by, and dependent upon, Arab and other aid donors who want stability, such a government could be expected to punish offenders. In the context of an overall peace, which contained provisions to phase out the camps and resettle refugees, residual, ideologically-motivated irredentists would find it increasingly unrealistic to aim at seizing power. Others would be likely, in the interest of the new state and out of respect for Palestinian institutions and law, to renounce the use of force.[20]

Could Israel cope with terrorist incidents originating in the new state? The answer is an unequivocal "yes." Terrorism would not pose a strategic threat to Israel. Admittedly, remaining Israeli settlers would be more exposed. Furthermore, following Palestine's independence, Israel would have to rely on a reduced intelligence capability, and on cooperation with what would inevitably be only an embryonic Palestinian intelligence network and an inexperienced internal security force. But, if it were faced with less than full cooperation, Israel would be well-placed to retaliate in a uniquely effective way by squeezing communications between the two parts of the new Palestine, by blocking its access to the open seas, or by closing its borders. Whether or not a Palestinian state might become a Soviet base would depend on the Palestinian and Soviet wish for the close political and military ties that this would involve. But, mindful of Israeli security fears, the new Palestine is likely to pursue the non-aligned status set out for itself in its Declaration of Independence. The Soviet Union, as a party to the settlement agreed by the Palestinians and other Arabs, and as joint-guarantor of the settlement with the US and other UN powers, would have a considerable stake in the maintenance of peace. The idea should be ruled out that Palestine or the Soviet Union would wish to take the one step—military alignment—that would invite Israeli retaliation, undermine peace and threaten US-Soviet relations or make the Soviet Union undertake the unenviable task of protecting a vulnerable client-state, sandwiched between Israel and Jordan.

Nevertheless, few Israelis would have confidence that the peace treaty would ensure their security, and most would be impervious to the above political and military arguments that a Palestinian state would not pose a serious security threat. And while the non-aligned status and the limitation of arms suggested here would leave Palestine precariously exposed, this would be insufficient security assurance for Israelis, who are wary of any Palestinian offers. Equally important, PLO leaders recognize that a Palestinian army could never defend a vulnerable Palestinian state and its inhabitants against all threats. In particular, they fear that a change in Israel's government could lead to re-occupation, or that the new Palestine would become entangled in a wider Israeli-Arab conflict.

It seems overly optimistic to suggest that after years of bitter struggle, a political settlement in itself would produce neighborly Israeli-Palestinian relations. Accidents would be bound to occur. One possibility is that remaining Israeli settlers or extremist Palestinians might set off a dangerous cycle of violence. And Israel, which would have surely reserved the right (along the lines of the 1974 Israeli-Syrian Disengagement Agreement) to retaliate against the Palestinian state if it became a significant terrorist base, could then be expected to intervene. This would not only upset the Israeli-Palestinian settlement but could also threaten the wider Middle East peace.

The essential requirement, therefore, would be for security arrangements that would combine Palestine's non-alignment and limitation of arms with firm and indefinite international guarantees in order to convince Israel that the new state would not threaten its security, and to compensate Israel for its loss of strategic depth. Similarly, Palestinians must be reassured that neither Israel nor Arab states would intervene in their sovereign territory. What is therefore required is a bold innovative security plan—one which would subordinate local party guarantees to outside military protection for a mutually agreed period of time, with the superpowers playing a crucial symbolic role. Who would perform this enforcement task and how?

3. An International Security System

At the outset of an Israeli-Palestinian peace settlement, the local parties must be induced to cooperate by the visible implementation of their basic demands. Since their sovereignty will be circumscribed by some limitation of armaments, the Palestinians should not be asked to accept *any* form of continued Israeli presence on their soil after Independence Day. A phased withdrawal of Israeli troops could take place prior to Independence, during a transitional period as agreed at Geneva. Steps in an Israeli withdrawal, which would give time for Israel to make readjustments of defense arrangements and for an international guarantor force to take over, should be matched with a phased introduction of moves towards peace.

A. *An International Guarantor Force*

With the withdrawal of its military presence and the majority of its settlements, and the prospect of the emergence of a PLO-led independent state after a relatively short transitional period agreed at Geneva, Israel should receive the proper and visible protection on which it insists from the start of its withdrawal. An International Guarantor Force (IGF) should therefore be stationed in demilitarized token strips astride the Israeli-Palestinian frontier (or on the Palestinian side only, if agreed), along the connecting corridor, and astride the River Jordan, staying indefinitely regardless of the new Palestine's constitutional relationship with Jordan.

The key tasks of the IGF on the West Bank and Gaza Strip and along the connecting corridor between them would be to maintain the limitation of armaments that would have been negotiated for those areas at an all-party conference at Geneva, or elsewhere, and the demilitarized status of token strips in Jordan, Palestine and possibly Israel as well. This it would do by denying access to Israeli and Arab forces, by preventing terrorist raids and reprisals wherever possible, and by stopping the entry into the West Bank and Gaza of weapons unauthorized by the Israeli-Palestinian treaty, and confiscating those that escaped detection at the frontier.

Relations between the IGF and the Palestinian internal security force would inevitably be sensitive. The IGF and PA should cooperate in investigating alleged breaches of the peace agreements on Palestinian territory. If the Palestinian authority reduced its involvement (for whatever reason), the IGF would carry out the necessary inspection on its own. The IGF would be empowered to apprehend and disarm any offender. But, in order to preserve good relations with both Israeli and Palestinian authorities, it would hand over those apprehended to their respective political authorities.

To fulfill these tasks, the IGF would need contingents that are (1) militarily capable of fulfilling the tasks; and (2) recruited from states that are both politically willing for their men to fight and suffer casualties, and politically acceptable to Israel, Palestine and Jordan. National contingents could not come from (a) any Middle Eastern states; (b) the United States or Soviet Union, for the reasons discussed above; or (c) from states unacceptable to Israel, Jordan or Palestine. There would have to be an equitable geographic representation requiring equal contributions from NATO and the Warsaw Pact, as well as a non-aligned representation. France and Britain have both indicated their willingness to participate in international forces established in a final settlement. These countries and other willing EC countries might offer trained personnel.

The IGF would be stationed astride Israeli-Palestinian borders and along the Jordan River in demilitarized frontier strips (over which it would have jurisdiction), up to 1,000 meters wide on each side and demarcated by sensor lines. The local parties would cede to the international authority the right to use these zones and any areas needed for airstrips, but the width of the zones would permit operations to be carried out from one side of the frontier if any party withdrew its cooperation. However, both the Israeli and Palestinian authorities could be expected to cooperate with a force whose duty it was to protect them.

Military experts maintain that the technical feasibility of such operations is not in doubt. The force, they say, should consist of up to 10,000 men armed with anti-aircraft and anti-tank missiles, APCs, heavy mortars and helicopters for rapid reaction and reconnaissance. It could be logistically maintained from Cyprus. If an airfield there (possibly the Royal Air Force base at Akrotiri) was made available, large aircraft could bring in supplies and reinforcements. Thereafter, light aircraft would transport them to air strips in the frontier zones. Sufficient financing and supplies would need to be made available and the international authority's members could help by earmarking manpower and logistical support for the use of the IGF.

B. *Monitoring and Verification*

The second component of the proposed security regime would be an efficient and impartial monitoring system.

1. Local party surveillance would serve as an important confidence building measure. Systems already used in the Sinai and on the Golan, suitably adapted for West Bank and Gaza conditions, provide precedents. Military experts maintain that airborne radar devices (in an airship, for example) over Israel proper would pick up aircraft movements in neighboring countries as far away as Iraq. But, if Israel were to insist after its withdrawal on the maintenance of a local early warning system on the escarpment overlooking the Jordan River, the Palestinians might be prepared to compromise—if this system were manned by Israeli civilian personnel ferried to and fro by the IGF's helicopters. Alternatively, such a facility could be manned by a third party, with Israel monitoring the situation from its own territory.

The organized exchange of intelligence between Israel and the new Palestine would supplement national intelligence gathering. In the style of the Helsinki accords, Israel and Jordan could announce planned military maneuvers in advance, and Palestine could keep the Israelis and Jordanians informed of any planned but non-routine movements of the PA.

Air reconnaissance conducted by Israel and Jordan over their own territories would supplement intelligence gathered from international surveillance stations. It is conceivable that the Palestinians might agree to Israeli overflights (which would presumably continue over the whole area of Palestinian territory during the transitional period) over the Jordan Valley after Independence for a mutually agreed period. Apart from providing early warning, high-definition aerial photography helps to confirm that local parties are adhering to agreements. Since aerial photography can be used to back up complaints, international inspectors could be requested to carry out additional inspections and furnish all three parties with their findings. Another innovation would be a joint photo-interpretation team to discuss data collected.

2. However, the military reliability and credibility of the IGF would depend on an efficient and impartial *third party* surveillance system to control borders and to monitor and verify military activities around the Israeli-Palestinian border and along the Jordan River.

(A) Border verification techniques would include: IGF checkpoints at the two bridges across the Jordan, at crossings on the Green Line and along the Gaza Strip's frontier, at either end of the connecting road; systematic and regular inspection of demilitarized zones which would take place at random rather than be pre-scheduled; ground patrols along the borders; and IGF control of routes into and out of demilitarized zones. Night Observation Devices (NODs), long-range NODs and helicopters would be needed for ground verification.

(B) As in the case of the Palestinian limitation of armaments and the stationing of the IGF, a monitoring system would be part of the *quid pro quo* for the creation of the Palestinian state and the full peace Israel seeks. This would comprise a mix of border and area verification techniques: unmanned sensors, watch stations and on-site inspection located in the frontier zones, and air reconnaissance.

(C) American aerial reconnaissance would be a key verification measure, not least because results of American missions would provide Israel, Jordan, Palestine and the IGF with additional surveillance data. Formalized Soviet air reconnaissance of Palestine's borders (as opposed to satellite reconnaissance, which presumably takes place anyway) should be part of a final agreement. It might provide a welcome second source of information for all parties, particularly Syria.

(D) Of fundamental importance would be the presence of American and Soviet personnel on this front (as on the others) in a strictly non-combatant role. They would be attached in a civilian capacity to the monitoring stations, but their personnel would not come under the Force Commander, nor could they play a role in instruction, except through the Control Commission. By their participation in monitoring and by providing air reconnaissance data, as well as financial and logistic support, the superpowers would demonstrate their identification with and commitment to the success of the IGF and the security regime. If superpower civilians were located in more vulnerable positions in the frontier strips, this would add considerably to their vital symbolic deterrent effect.

(E) This analysis assumes that by the end of a transitional period, Israel would have withdrawn completely from the West Bank and Gaza Strip and that international safeguards and guarantee forces would be in place. Under this scheme, there could be no open Israeli-Palestinian frontier. Instead, there would be electronic and unmanned sensors all along the borders, although the width of demilitarized zones could vary, as suggested above. The limited number of crossing points would permit free movement of labor and goods. Over time, however, the barriers could be lifted, but only as and when both parties agreed. Given the close economic relations between Israel and the West Bank and Gaza, Israel and Palestine would want to remove the inconvenience of these security precautions as soon as their confidence in each other grew.

Would the international force just described meet Israel's security needs? Admittedly, the force would not be equipped to engage in full-scale conventional battle but, as discussed above, the threat of a surprise attack against Israel from the eastern front seems unlikely. Once a comprehensive Middle East peace agreement was signed, the presence of an international guarantor force on the West Bank and Gaza Strip, linked to an effective monitoring and air reconnaissance system and visibly backed by both superpowers, would make it less so. Another problem would be the containment of raids by extremists from both sides. No guarantor force could, for example, provide cast-iron protection against infiltration or the use of mortars, rockets and small SAMs (which could be fired against planes flying in and out of Ben Gurion airport) but the aim of the guarantor force would be to contain these threats at a level acceptable to Israel and to make the international cost of retaliation by air attack too high for Israel to contemplate.

It is unlikely that the UN would undertake the tasks outlined above. Israel would, in any case, object to being made dependent on a body it regards as being both ineffectual and biased. Theoretically, the United Nations can use force to maintain or restore international peace and security. But, although the United Nations authorized the use of force (other than in self-defense) under the special circumstances of the Congo, that procedure generated a strong objection amongst most member states to a repetition. Certainly, the required majority of UN members might not be willing to create a fighting force, as suggested here, to police the borders of a Palestinian state. Some members would have to be convinced that deployment of such a force was not an unreasonable form of discrimination against Palestinians; others, sharing Israeli skepticism, would have to be satisfied that the force would act impartially, and they would argue that even if it were agreed to extend the "defensive capabilities" of the UN force, the use of the veto in the Security Council would prevent enforcement action. This degree of uncertainty would be critical to Israel.

Practical objections would compound these political difficulties. The experience of the UN force in Lebanon (UNIFIL) has illustrated the difficulty of persuading contributing states to allow their forces to suffer casualties over long periods, and its inability to make Israel comply. Also, it would be difficult for the Security Council to agree to an indefinite undertaking of, say, an initial mandate of fifteen years and then a review on how to improve operations as its membership changes every year. Although the incentives for success would be high, it is unlikely that the UN could conduct quasi-combatant operations effectively because of the problem of referring to the Security Council for decisions relating to unforeseen contingencies and the resulting delays. With the present UN procedures in force, a UN force would not cross the necessary threshold from peace-keeping to peace-enforcement.

C. *Middle East Control Commission*

The third component of the international security system would be an entirely new intergovernmental organization (Middle East Control Commission) set up under a Middle East peace treaty and registered with the UN. Its constitutional status would be comparable to that of other security organizations set up under treaties, e.g. NATO. Consisting of treaty signatories, the superpowers (as Co-Chairmen), West and East Europeans and others supporting the Middle East peace treaty and resulting agreements, this organization would authorize, recruit and administer the proposed guarantor force which would have the mandate to police Israeli-Palestinian frontiers and fight, if necessary, to repel minor interventions in either direction across them.

The MECC would have a politically-balanced representation, and its members would need to be supported by Israel, Palestine and the other Arab parties, and by both superpowers. It would be financed by its members according to their means: oil-consuming states (e.g., Japan) and oil-producing states, profiting from the peace, would be expected to play a supportive role.

The international community may be understandably reluctant to create a new security regime and international authority to administer this degree of military control outside the UN framework, but political difficulties should not prevent innovation when peace is at stake. The requirement is for a group of states to agree upon a guarantor force and administrative body along the lines suggested for the specific purpose of controlling the frontiers of Palestine. Crucial to the success of this innovatory security plan and to the durability of the settlement would be a system of guarantees and sanctions, and an accompanying suppliers' agreement on arms transfers to the region.

D. *Multilateral Guarantees and Sanctions*

The fourth component and backbone of the security regime would be the exercise of sanctions by the future external guarantors, in particular the superpowers. Sufficient superpower cooperation to permit *enforcement* of the settlement by diplomatic, economic and even military sanctions will be essential.

Once the Peace Treaty is implemented, minor, perhaps accidental, violations of the agreements by both sides should be expected. International personnel working with the Israeli, Palestinian and Jordanian security forces would help resolve disputes resulting from small incidents. As trust grew, disputes would be dealt with through the mechanisms supplied by normal state-to-state relations, or joint commissions could be established for the purpose.

The Treaty would have to contain provisions to cope with serious violations: repeated infringements, terrorism and officially supported reprisal raids. Major breaches of the settlement might include an attack on the IGF or a failure to control extremists raiding across the borders. Early warning stations might reveal preparations for an attack on any of the borders.

Potential guarantors would undoubtedly prefer to act under UN auspices. But there might be disagreement within the UN over the degree of delegation of authority to the Secretary General. Formal multilateral political guarantees would, therefore, be undertaken independently of the United Nations by the United States and the Soviet Union and by other powers, either together or separately, to guarantee both the DMZs and borders between Israel and neighboring states, including the new Palestine, as well as the other agreements reached under the Peace Treaty. Signatories would undertake to impose within "agreed ground rules" economic and military sanctions against violators, aimed at restoring the *status quo ante*. What might these be?

1. The chief economic backers and military suppliers—the US, the Soviet Union (and to a lesser extent Britain and France)—would take the necessary action along previously agreed lines. Sanctions would be negative in form, limited to those that could be accomplished externally to the area, and did not require active superpower cooperation on the spot. These might include: threats of delay or stoppages of economic aid to an aggressor, the blockade of ships carrying goods to an aggressor, or the boycott of goods originating in such a state. More seriously, the shipment of arms permitted under the agreement could be stopped.

2. The implementation of sanctions would come close to being an automatic mechanism: it would depend on the single principle that the superpowers could be expected to support their respective clients if the latter were threatened, but to desist from doing so if their clients sought to upset the status quo. If the superpowers could not, or were unwilling to cooperate to the degree necessary to implement such sanctions, it would mean a return to the uncertainties of the past.

3. A key prerequisite would be an understanding to cooperate in an emergency. Diplomats speculate that, once committed, the Soviets would be meticulous in observation of obligations. If the signatory powers of the formal Declaration of Guarantee failed to agree on a joint course of action, then each guarantor should be prepared to carry out its obligations according to its interpretation but within the "agreed ground rules." These would comprise a formalization of the *de facto* understanding between the superpowers to show restraint in their unilateral action and in their efforts to maintain a balance of forces between Israel and the confrontation states.

4. Any unilateral action taken that did not conform with the "agreed ground rules" would signal a serious breach of superpower understanding regarding support of the peace and would threaten the stability of the area. If Israel's ultimate security was at stake, an American guarantee of last resort for Israel might then be involved. Similarly, *de facto*, if not formal, guarantees for some Arab states by the Soviet

Union could be expected to come into play. But the Palestinian state would be an exception: its ultimate survival would depend on superpower agreement to respect its non-aligned status.

E. *The Importance of Arms Control Measures*

Middle East wars have been partly contained by superpower restraint in supplying arms; the key to an enduring peace would be a similar willingness to control arms supplies. This is because superpower support for arms control would be linked by the peace treaty agreements to visible superpower support of international forces and superpower guarantees of frontiers: any local state threatening another with force would be challenging its own material backer. The international guarantor force on the West Bank and Gaza would be designed to stop commando and reprisal raids, while DMZs and other safeguards would prevent minor infringements from escalating. They would also provide an early warning system in the event of a full-scale attack and deprive the Arabs and Israelis of opportunities to react to infringements with conventional arms. But it would be the superpowers, as the chief arms suppliers, who would simultaneously be the major deterrent and the enforcement force.

The survival of the Palestinian state and stability in the Middle East after a negotiated peace will depend on the military balance of forces, as well as the political relationships between the former confrontation states. It follows that a political settlement seeking to stabilize the area should aim to include arms control measures. These need not prevent Middle East states from maintaining forces and arsenals to meet certain security needs (though Palestine would be subject to special restrictions), but they must seek to stabilize the military balance.

Not only must the present arms levels eventually be lowered: a balance must also be kept in a complex of relationships. This would be an unprecedented enterprise requiring agreement on arms transfers to the region as a whole. Its chances of success would depend on an understanding between the superpowers that cooperation over arms control in this area was in their own self-interest.

The difficulties of controlling arms levels, even after a peace is negotiated, are not to be underestimated. The parties to the peace will want to shift resources to domestic tasks and outside powers will have a vested interest in underwriting the peace and lending credibility to their roles as guarantors by exercising restraint in arms transfers. But regulation of arms flows will be complicated by demands by Arab states for weapons to deal with potential inter-Arab disputes; Israel's desire for a qualitative edge; arms sales diplomacy on the part of the suppliers; and the sheer complexity of defining a military balance.

The instrument of control of exports of conventional arms and technology would be the Permanent Standing Arms Control Commission (PSACC).[21] It would be set up under the peace treaty, with the US and Soviet Union as Co-Chairmen. (The two superpowers supply roughly 32 percent and 31 percent respectively of total arms supplies to the Middle East.) Its membership, which would have to be agreed at the peace conference, would also need to include the secondary suppliers and the recipient states negotiating the peace.

The Committee's functions would be to establish what should no doubt be the varying level of arms of each Middle East state required for its security; to coordinate policies of the main arms suppliers and to regulate arms transfers accordingly; to check the implementation of arms transfer restrictions; and to exercise sanctions against states violating agreements and/or guarantees to act in support of a state under threat.

The PSACC, which would be linked by the peace treaty to the Middle East Control Commission, would decide on appropriate sanctions and guarantees. With the superpowers still the chief suppliers to the region, it would be their agreement to cooperate over arms control measures and enforcement action that would count. With their ultimate leverage over recipient states, it is the superpowers who would render sanctions effective. Thus, any local party challenging the force or the security measures connected to it would be challenging its own material backers and would trigger immediate implementation of sanctions agreed by the arms control committee. These might include the denial of vital weapons systems, components and spare parts permitted under arms transfer arrangements, or the withholding of economic aid.

The question is whether the superpowers are sufficiently committed to a Middle East peace and regional stability to cooperate to the extent required. Evidence suggests that they do potentially have the political will. They have exercised tacit restraint in the past to avoid being drawn into dangerous confrontation. Although without precedent, a superpower role in monitoring and enforcing control of the frontiers of a Palestinian state and maintaining an arms control system for the region would provide the basis for a two-state solution along the lines suggested in this paper, giving the Palestinians self-determination and protection and Israel the security assurances it needs. It would also reduce superpower military competition and the likelihood of confrontation, and would represent a major step towards detente in the Middle East.

Notes

1. This paper has drawn on points made in two earlier studies by the author on the same subject. For a full discussion of the importance of superpower participation in security guarantees and safeguards on the ground in a Middle East peace, see David Astor and Valerie Yorke, *Peace in the Middle East: Super Powers and Security Guarantees* (London: Corgi, 1978). See also Valerie Yorke, "Palestinian Self-Determination and Israel's Security," *Journal of Palestine Studies,* Vol. 8, No 3 (Spring 1979), pp. 3-26.

2. See Astor and Yorke, *op cit.*, pp. 62-77. In 1975, the Israelis called for an American presence in the buffer zones of Sinai.

3. For this point and for a discussion of alternative options for peace, see Mark Heller, *A Palestinian State: The Implications for Israel* (Cambridge: Harvard University Press, 1983). See also Heller, "A Palestinian State: Thinking the Unthinkable," *Moment* (September 1988), pp. 41-51.

4. Arab statesmen wonder why the US does not offer Israel a bilateral guarantee to encourage it to make peace. But US policymakers know how difficult it would be to persuade Congress to offer a US bilateral guarantee of Israel's frontiers until *after* a comprehensive settlement. The argument for spelling out the shape of guarantees *before* a settlement is rarely publicly made, and the difference in the two approaches rarely discussed.

5. A plethora of blueprints for peace were published during the 1970s. See *Toward Peace in the Middle East*, published by the Brookings Institution in Washington, December, 1975, which provided the basis for President Carter's subsequent proposals for a comprehensive peace. For a Palestinian view, see Walid Khalidi's important article, "Thinking the Unthinkable: A Sovereign Palestinian State," *Foreign Affairs*, Vol. 56, No. 4 (July 1978), pp. 695-713.

6. The author has drawn on views expressed publicly and privately by Israelis and Palestinians from a variety of backgrounds over the past twelve years. Interestingly, Palestinian officials have been consistent in private on the areas where the Palestinian side would be prepared to show flexibility.

7. Interviews by the author with advisors to Yasser Arafat in Beirut and Damascus in the spring of 1977. See the statement of the PLO's Deputy Chairman, Salah Khalaf (Abu Iyad), "All Security Arrangements and Guarantees Can Be Discussed," *International Herald Tribune*, March 10, 1989.

8. For the substance of the Allon Plan see Yigal Allon, "Israel: The Case for Defensible Borders," *Foreign Affairs*, Vol. 55, No. 1 (October 1976), pp.38-53.

9. For a discussion of US and Israeli attitudes toward such a formal bilateral alliance and the kinds of proviso that the Americans would wish ideally to attach to, say, a mutual defense pact, see Astor and Yorke, *op. cit.*, pp. 44-58.

10. President Carter himself made the distinction between permanent and sovereign borders along approximately the 1967 borders and "defense lines" beyond these for a period of time. *United States Information Service (USIS)* March 10, 1977.

11. See Avi Plascov, "A Palestinian State? Examining the Alternatives," *Adelphi Paper* No. 163 (Spring 1981), p. 23.

12. For the full text of the Declaration of November 15, 1988 see *Middle East International,* November 18, 1988, pp. 22-23.

13. For a discussion of the neutrality issue, see John Mroz, *Beyond Security* (New York: International Peace Academy, 1980), pp. 138-163.

14. Interview with Hugh Hanning, formerly affiliated with the International Peace Academy, New York, in April 1989. UNDRO is in need of an international zone for a stockpile center in the region.

15. *World Service News Bulletin,* January 13, 1978. See also *New York Times,* November 22, 1978.

16. Interviews by the author with a PLO official in London, February 1989.

17. Khalidi, *op cit.,* pp. 703-705.

18. In its detailed analysis of six options for the future of the occupied territories, the Jaffee Center for Strategic Studies sets out the security concerns involved in withdrawal from the West Bank. The Jaffee Center for Strategic Studies, *The West Bank and Gaza: Israel's Options for Peace* (Israel: Tel Aviv, 1989), pp. 161-183.

19. Interviews by the author with British officials specialized in military affairs, March 1989.

20. Interview by the author with PLO leader Salah Khalaf in Beirut in the spring of 1977.

21. See Astor and Yorke, *op. cit.,* pp. 144-149.

12 THE ECONOMIC VIABILITY OF A PALESTINIAN STATE

George T. Abed

1. Introduction and Background

The concept of "economic viability" is a surprisingly imprecise term. The term takes on different meanings depending on the context. The "economic viability" of a project (meaning returning a profit) is certainly different from the "economic viability" of a state, as states are not usually thought of as commercial undertakings required to show a profit.[1]

Another difficulty is that when the term is applied to states, questions of economics become hopelessly entangled with questions of politics. To the professional economist, the test of viability is thus no longer so clearcut. Indeed, on the very question of the viability of a state in Palestine, a fellow economist once tried to wrestle with the issue but found that:

> Economists have seldom been faced with the problem of appraising an individual country's capacity for survival and growth. True, analysts have frequently advised prospective investors as to the safety and profitability of specific foreign investments, adducing evidence from the state of the debtor economies as a whole. But the evaluation of an entire operating economy, not simply as an investment for outside capitalists, but in terms of whether it is a "going venture," and in an effort to ascertain what population it can eventually support without outside aid at given standards of living, this is a relatively novel problem.[2]

The author was the then young Alfred E. Kahn (who would later acquire public recognition as the deregulator of the airlines under President Carter). The time was 1944, and the country in question was the contemplated Jewish state in Palestine.

Indeed, for a long time prior to the establishment of the State of Israel, questions related to the viability of a state in Palestine constituted a dominant theme in the economic literature of the Zionist movement. And on this issue, the Zionist message was as simple as it was constant. A Jewish state in Palestine was economically viable and there were no assignable limits, *a priori,* to the capacity of Palestine to absorb additional immigrants.

It was of course not surprising that, given their motives, the Zionists would tend to put a gloss on the economic viability of their enterprise in Palestine and on the related issue of the absorptive capacity of the land. Walter Lowdermilk, then Assistant Chief of the US Soil Conservation Service, after completing an examination of soil and land conditions in Palestine and other Arab countries in 1939, concluded that to estimate the final absorptive capacity of Palestine "could be impossible, for the absorptive capacity of any country is a dynamic and expanding concept." He added that certain improvements in land and water utilization would " . . . in time make possible the absorption of at least four million Jewish refugees from Europe, in addition to the 1,800,000 Arabs and Jews already in Palestine and Trans-Jordan."[3] (He was apparently unconcerned by the fate of those Arabs who were constantly on the increase as well.) Lowdermilk even went as far as to quote approvingly an 1875 statement by Sir Charles Warren of the Palestine Exploration Fund to the effect that Palestine (as later defined by the Mandate) could support as many as 12 million people.[4]

This was also the line of argument taken by the Jewish Agency for Palestine in its statements before the Royal Commission in 1936, and before the Anglo-American Commission of Inquiry which began its deliberations in January 1946. In the Agency's submission to the latter, Chaim Weizmann dismissed any rigid notion of "economic absorptive capacity," stating flatly that "the economic absorptive capacity of a country is what its population makes of it."[5]

What can be said about the economic viability of a state in Palestine now, when in an ironic twist of history, the tables have been turned and the former believers have become the new skeptics? Antagonists of a Palestinian Arab state comprising the West Bank and Gaza Strip cast doubts about such a state's economic viability. It is argued that the land area is too small and poor in natural resources, the economy would remain underdeveloped and dependent, and the population pressures would be overwhelming. In short, unable to survive the internal and external pressures that would be brought upon it, such a state could, according to this view, become a source of instability in the region. Hence, argue the skeptics, the need for a solution via Jordan or some other approach not involving the establishment of an independent Palestinian state.

It is essential to underline a fundamental point. Arguments about the economic viability of a Palestinian state are about practical matters of *how* to manage the country's affairs after independence and not about whether or not the Palestinian people have a *right* to independence in the first place. The *right* of the Palestinian people to self-determination and to sovereignty on the land they have inhabited since time immemorial is embedded in the long and unbroken history of the Palestinian people's ties with the land and is enshrined in the principles on which the international community has conducted its affairs in modern times. Such a right does not require confirmation by arguments of economic viability, nor can it be reduced or abrogated by the alleged absence of such viability. Since World War II, over 120 countries have gained their independence. Whatever one's judgement may be of the eventual consequences of such a development, the right of these countries to sovereignty was hardly ever justified on grounds of economic viability nor was it ever denied on grounds of the absence of it.

The economy of a Palestinian state will, however, be conditioned by the final shape of the political settlement of the conflict in Palestine and of the wider Arab-Israeli impasse. The geopolitical framework for the contemplated Palestinian state carries with it specific, and in some aspects binding, economic implications.

2. Outlines of a Settlement: The Economic Implications

The outlines of a political settlement required for the analysis of the economic viability of a Palestinian state may be defined with reference to the emerging Palestinian consensus as expressed in the declaration of the Palestinian National Council (PNC) in Algiers in November 1988. It should be added that I am adopting this frame of reference in a strictly methodological and hence value-neutral sense. It is used to define the geopolitical framework needed for the analysis, without necessarily endorsing or rejecting any specific political views implied therein.

Nor do I necessarily make any assumptions about the early attainability of the terms and conditions implicit in the PNC's political program. Indeed I happen to believe that the road to Palestinian statehood is long and difficult, and will be especially painful for the Palestinians themselves. But given the broad support the PNC's program has received in the Palestinian and international communities, it seems reasonable to treat it as a suitable framework for the further analysis of the economics of a Palestinian Arab state.

A settlement embodying the establishment of a Palestinian state may therefore be presumed to be based on the following five substantive, as distinct from procedural, principles:

1. Complete withdrawal of the Israeli occupation forces from all lands conquered in the 1967 war, including Arab Jerusalem.

2. The early exercise in Palestine of the right of self-determination by the Palestinian people including the right to establish an independent and sovereign state in Palestine.

3. The reinstatement and early implementation of the Palestinian refugees' right of return and/or compensation.

4. The return to full Palestinian Arab control of all natural resources, specifically land and water, forcibly and illegally appropriated by Israel during the period of occupation.

5. All other issues outstanding between Palestine and Israel are to be resolved on the basis of equality of treatment and reciprocity of rights and obligations. This principle may encompass a number of issues such as arrangements for mutual security and for the protection of citizens of one state choosing to settle within the boundaries of the other, minor adjustments of boundaries, sharing of resources, openness of frontiers, normalization arrangements, and so on.

The formulation of a political settlement in these terms necessarily restricts the analysis to the Palestinian-Israeli dimension of the Arab-Israeli conflict. Although such a restriction may be justified for purposes of the analysis in this paper, I wish to emphasize that a resolution of the conflict in Palestine must be a part of a more comprehensive settlement of the Arab-Israeli conflict, including the withdrawal of Israeli occupation forces from Lebanon and from the Golan Heights, and the settlement of other outstanding issues with the Arab "confrontation states." A partial settlement based on a "local solution" in Palestine without a just and stable solution to other aspects of Israel's conflict with the other Arab states would not endure and does not therefore constitute a satisfactory framework for the analysis undertaken here.

In terms of its Palestinian implications, a settlement based on the above principles constitutes the minimum requirement for the provision of cohesion and integrity to the new Palestinian state and to the Palestinian Arab community that will reside in it. It would also pave the way for the reintegration of the new state into the larger Arab community, with all that entails in terms of strategic, political and economic arrangements. Such a settlement can, and I do not say will, afford the reconstituted Palestinian society the opportunity to grow and develop with at least as high a probability of success as any other state in the region.

The economic implications of a settlement, however, give rise to three substantial problems of adjustment in the post-settlement period. These essentially are problems of demography, of non-renewable resources, and of economic structure. Clearly the three are interrelated but I will discuss each of them separately before proceeding to propose an economic development program to deal with them.

A. Demography

There is at present a total of 1.7 million Palestinian Arabs living in the West Bank (including East Jerusalem) and the Gaza Strip.[6] Just under 4.3 million Israelis, including about 650,000 Arabs, live in Israel proper.[7] The establishment of a state and the opportunity for Palestinians to exercise their right of return are likely to lead to a considerable increase in the Arab population of Palestine. Although a large number of Palestinian refugees, especially those still living in camps outside Palestine (Jordan, Lebanon and Syria), will seek to return almost immediately, the process of absorption and reintegration of these and other Palestinians, including those now living in camps in the West Bank and the Gaza Strip, may be assumed to take 3-5 years.

However, I estimate that within the first two to three years of independence, nearly 700,000 Palestinians residing abroad will *seek* to return within the framework of a phased repatriation program. In addition, more than 340,000 refugees now living in camps in the West Bank and Gaza (not to speak of refugees living outside the camps in these areas)[8] will need to be included in the absorption and settlement program during the transitional period. Given the present and prospective constellation of powers in the Arab region and in the world at large, a political settlement of the Arab-Israeli conflict is likely to entail the repatriation of perhaps no more than between 50,000 and 100,000 to areas conquered by Israel in the 1948-49 war under a comprehensive agreement on refugees. Consequently, the vast majority of the Palestinians seeking to return will have to be repatriated or at least enfranchised in the new State of Palestine comprising the West Bank and Gaza.

With this additional influx, the population of the Palestinian state would rise almost immediately to about 2.4 million (using 1990 statistics). On the conservative assumption that no *net* migration takes place during this period (there could be flows in either direction but the assumption is that these flows will somehow balance out), the total population of the Palestinian state would increase further by almost one million, to about 3.3 million, by the year 2000.[9]

By then the population density for the whole state would be about 560 persons per square kilometer, a rather high figure. Gaza's population density, depending on whether or not economic developments there would induce outward movements over time, could exceed 2700 inhabitants per square kilometer. In order to put these figures in some international perspective, comparable measures may be cited for some of the more crowded countries at present: Israel 210, Belgium 325, Japan 325, the Netherlands 360, Taiwan 555, Hong Kong 1900, Singapore 4200.[10]

The demographic dimension may also be viewed from a wider perspective if we take into account likely developments in both Israel and the Palestinian state. By the year 2000, assuming no substantial net migration into Israel, the total population of historic Palestine (i.e., Arabs and Jews) would approach 8.0 million. By then the population density for all of historic Palestine would be about 300 inhabitants per square kilometer. It would admittedly be a crowded country, somewhat comparable to Belgium or Japan, but not unmanageably overpopulated.

Returning to the issue of absorptive capacity, it should be stated that there is no hard and fast rule about the ability of any country to support any given population. It depends very much on the resources available (land, water, climate, capital, technology), the character and dynamism of the population itself, the openness of the country to economic interchange with other countries, the organization of economic activity, and so on. None of these factors are in themselves decisive, as can be attested by the number of countries that have successfully overcome one or more such handicaps.

Chaim Weizmann's apt statement that "the absorptive capacity of any country is what the population makes of it" is by and large valid. This is not to say that the demographic factor does not matter; but while it must be taken into account in the design of a development program, it nevertheless should not alarm economic planners.

B. Natural Resources

The second major problem that must be tackled within the framework of a development program for the new Palestinian state is that of natural or non-renewable resources, primarily land and water. Let me first summarize the basic facts of the situation.

The land area of the West Bank is just under 5,600 square kilometers (sq. km.) while that of Gaza is about 360 sq. km. The two areas together constitute about 22 percent of the total area of mandatory Palestine.[11]

An essential fact about land in the occupied areas is that Israel has placed its control over about 50 percent of the area of the West Bank and 34 percent of that of the Gaza Strip.[12] It has also issued military orders or has promulgated land use plans to restrict Arab use of virtually all remaining lands. The occupation policies and practices have had the effect of generally directing all resource exploitation activities to the accommodation of Israel's geopolitical requirements. Israel has also built up a system of roads and infrastructural facilities which have substantially altered the potential use of much of the land and water resources of the area. Needless to say, a political settlement embodying the establishment of a Palestinian state would have to entail the return to Palestinian sovereignty of all land currently under Israeli control in the West Bank and Gaza Strip.

Of the total land area of the West Bank, about 36 percent is used for various forms of agriculture, about 7 percent for built-up areas and public infrastructure, while the remaining 57 percent is either unused (rocky, steep gradient, etc.) or used as grazing pastures. Of the total cultivable (and largely cultivated) area of about 2 million dunums (m dun.) only about 145,000 dunums are irrigated, of which about 40,000 dunums are cultivated by Jewish settlers.[13] The irrigated Arab land area in the West Bank has remained about the same since 1966 because of Israeli-imposed restrictions on the use of water by Arab farmers. It is estimated that irrigable land in the West Bank could be expanded to 535,000 dunums with the availability of water. This potential would represent the most promising opportunity for the expansion of agricultural production in the West Bank, if such an expansion were deemed to be cost-effective in the new constellation of costs and prices.

Of the total area of the Gaza Strip of 363,000 dunums, about 205,000 dunums (or 56 percent) are already under cultivation, of which 37,000 dunums have been allocated to Jewish settlements.[14] A substantial area of the Strip (more than 16 percent) is already built up. The expansion of cultivation is severely restricted by the lack of suitable land and even more so by crippling water constraints.

A cursory review of the water situation in the West Bank and Gaza also reveals divergences between conditions in the West Bank and those in Gaza. But above all, it shows the severity of the constraints placed by the Israeli occupation on water utilization by Palestinians.

The central fact about water resources in the West Bank is that the area's own natural supplies are potentially more than adequate to meet the needs of the present and future population (including returning refugees) well into the next century. The West Bank's potential annual output of water on a sustained yield basis is in excess of 700 million cubic meters (mcm).[15] However, Israel appropriates for its own use more than 60 percent of this total supply by tapping water supplies in deep aquifers largely underneath the surface of the West Bank. In addition, Jewish settlements are allocated 30 mcm-40 mcm per year. The total annual Arab consumption of water in the West Bank (consumption by more than 1 million inhabitants) is restricted to about 115 mcm. The overall annual consumption of water per capita in Israel is about 4 times that in the West Bank and household consumption is about 6 times.[16]

It cannot be overemphasized that the future economic wellbeing of the Palestinian state is critically dependent on the renewed availability of this resource. It is thus absolutely imperative that any political settlement should provide for the restoration of Palestinian rights to the water now used by Israel, an amount which constitutes about one quarter of that state's total annual water supply.

In any event, as regards the water requirements of the West Bank portion of the Palestinian state, there should be enough water to expand the area under irrigation nearly fourfold (and hence considerably improve the food balances of the new state), raise the level of water consumption for household use to reasonable standards, and accommodate the industrial demand for water without any damage to the natural replenishment process of water resources in the area.[17]

As for the Gaza Strip, current water use (about 120 mcm per year) is estimated to exceed natural supplies by about 60 mcm.[18] The widening deficit has led to a drop in the water table and to a marked increase in salinity with serious adverse effects on Arab agriculture. Although the restoration of water rights currently exploited by Jewish settlers, together with improvements in efficiency, would provide some relief for a period, water constraints in the Strip would soon set in and limit further economic development in the region. The only escape is through drastic reductions or perhaps even the gradual elimination of the agricultural sector (which consumes about 90 percent of available water supplies),[19] the construction of desalination plants in conjunction with power generation, or the transfer of fresh water from outside the area altogether.

To recapitulate, land and water resources for the new Palestinian state do not seem to pose insurmountable problems although serious crowdedness and rising water shortages in the Gaza Strip will continue to impose unavoidable constraints on the course of economic development there. This will remain the case even after the full restoration of Arab rights over water resources in the Strip. In the West Bank, on the other hand, the political settlement outlined earlier (incorporating the restoration of Arab rights over land and water), while increasing the intensity of land use, would nevertheless *improve* the resource balance, and hence the prospects for economic development in the area.

C. Economic Structure

Under the general heading of economic structure I will simply highlight a few of the key imbalances that will require immediate attention once the occupation has been removed and a state is established. There are essentially three overriding imbalances and a number of secondary problems of structure that fall in this category.

1. *External Orientation*

One of the most destructive economic effects of the prolonged occupation of the West Bank and Gaza has been the isolation of the occupied areas from their traditional, and by and large natural, Arab markets, and the forced reorientation of the Palestinian economy toward the specific requirements of Israeli hegemony.

External trade and capital movements between the occupied areas and the Arab countries (especially imports) have been severely restricted and replaced by unconstrained Israeli access to the Arab markets in the areas. Restrictions on Arab utilization of water and lack of access to external markets (including Israel) stunted agricultural growth while licensing authority and other administrative powers were used by Israel to suppress industrial development in the West Bank and Gaza. The obstruction of indigenous development created a crippling dependency relationship and reduced the occupied areas essentially to the roles of (1) an easy market for Israeli goods (on the eve of the *intifada* Israel's exports to the areas approached $1.0 billion and, for Israel, the occupied areas constituted the second largest single national export market after the US); and (2) a pool of cheap labor, especially for Israeli requirements in the construction, agriculture and lower-paying service sectors.[20]

It is clear therefore that any effort to renormalize the Palestinian economy's external economic relations will entail wrenching changes in its production base and in its relations with the outside world. These adjustments are likely to be costly and painful in the early phases of statehood.

2. *Manpower*

Another visible and critically important distortion arising from the prolonged occupation is the deformation that has beset the development and deployment of Palestinian manpower in the occupied areas.

In the first place, restrictions on economic development in the private sector and the stagnation or decline in the activity of the public sector (except perhaps for the growth of the Israeli security apparatus) narrowed considerably the employment opportunities for the professional, the highly skilled, and the entrepreneurial categories of manpower in the occupied territories. This led to substantial emigration by some of the potentially most productive elements of the labor force and deprived the areas of a key factor in their social and economic development.[21]

As a consequence of this massive expatriation, the absolute number of workers employed in indigenous activity in the West Bank and Gaza stagnated during the entire 22 years of occupation, remaining at around 155,000. Thus the entire increase in the size of the labor force during this period was forced in the direction of either emigration or employment in Israel, where the total number of workers approached 130,000 just before the *intifada*.[22] The direct effects of this expatriation were an absolute decline in employment in the commodity producing sectors, a high proportion of workers' income spent in Israel itself, and enormous human resource losses arising from long and costly transportation requirements, outright discrimination and monopsonistic exploitation of workers. Also important are more subtle effects such as those arising from the peculiar structure of Israel's demand for expatriate labor and its adverse implications for the educational orientation and skill development of the Palestinian work force itself. For example, about 14,000-15,000 Palestinian college graduates are unable to find work appropriate to their level of education, and it is common to find persons with a university degree working as taxi-drivers or as construction laborers in Israel.

The high demand for unskilled workers in Israel, combined with the security-related exclusion of non-Jewish workers from highly skilled and professional jobs, as well as discrimination and racism in allocating jobs, have served to channel Palestinian workers away from the need to acquire advanced education, professional training or higher skills. This deskilling of Palestinian manpower in the occupied territories has had a catastrophic effect on one of the most valuable and widely noted attributes of the Palestinian people in general, namely, their strong commitment to and attainment of relatively high standards of education and professional development.

The third and final point related to the question of manpower is the serious deterioration of the entire educational and manpower development infrastructure during the period of occupation. This is not to deny that through the Palestinians' own efforts, and in the face of persistent obstacles thrown in the way by the Israeli authorities, certain *quantitative* improvements in private education did take place (including the opening up of several institutions of post-secondary education). But the fundamental point is that educational standards declined, and vocational and technical training stagnated. In the case of agricultural manpower training, it was eliminated altogether when the Israeli authorities converted the Khaddouri Agricultural College on the West Bank into a community college which did not teach agriculture. Al-Najah University, which has been given the funds and the land for an agricultural school, has been denied permission by the authorities to establish the school. Al-Najah University has also been denied permission to establish a School of Science and Engineering.

Any reconstruction and development program in the new Palestinian state must therefore confront an enormous task in the development of the educational and skill development infrastructure. The problem will be far greater than the reorientation and reabsorption of workers now employed in Israel, and workers returning from exile. The entire skill and occupational structure of the presently active workforce, and the associated infrastructure, will have to be redirected toward the new and entirely different requirements of indigenous Palestinian development.

3. *Infrastructure*

The physical infrastructure in the occupied areas has deteriorated in general. Per capita measures of such facilities as paved roads, hospital beds, and the surface area of school rooms, have all declined during the 22 years of occupation.[23] Some improvements in communication systems and power delivery networks were introduced more to reinforce Israeli hegemony than to serve the needs of Arab localities. As Benvenisti and Khayat note: "Physical infrastructure is primarily planned to accommodate Israeli interests—especially settlement construction, Jewish agricultural development, and military needs."[24]

Even under Jordanian and Egyptian administration, the physical infrastructure in the West Bank and Gaza did not receive high priority in terms of public outlays, although it did not materially deteriorate during the period. Under Israeli occupation, housing shortages persisted despite the heavy investment by Palestinian families in private, single-family dwellings, financed largely by remittances from Palestinians abroad.

Social infrastructure, on the other hand, came increasingly under the control of the Palestinian communities themselves. It developed, and in some important respects improved, despite obstruction by the Israeli authorities. The private educational system expanded quantitatively, even if lack of resources limited the extent of qualitative improvements. Especially in the 1980s, local councils, charitable societies, professional associations, voluntary committees and production cooperatives, all sprang up and grew, in part to fill a widening gap in officially supplied services. An indigenous, locally run, grass-roots system providing a wide spectrum of services (health, education, social welfare, manpower training and medium-term agricultural and industrial development credit) began to take shape as an alternative to the alien and largely discredited system operated by the Israeli occupation authorities.

In sum, the deterioration of physical infrastructure under occupation would require massive investments not only to upgrade infrastructural facilities but also to restructure present facilities and networks toward the emerging development needs of the new Palestinian state. The investment program must also take into account the huge backlog of needs that have accumulated over a period of more than 40 years of underinvestment and repression.

The example of the development of social infrastructure affords the new state an opportunity represented by the immensely valuable grass-roots infrastructure that has developed under, and in many respects despite, the occupation. There are more than 400 local organizations, institutions, associations and committees operating in virtually all Palestinian towns, villages and refugee camps. This new "civil society" is based on institutions that are locally constituted and democratically based, and can therefore respond most efficiently to local needs.[25] In the absence of a sovereign national authority, most of these organizations have for many years served as quasi-governmental departments and agencies. Since the *intifada*, they have taken on additional tasks, and have been joined by many new ones (mainly the "popular committees") to provide an even wider spectrum of services in the new conditions. Any system of social, educational, health, cultural, and economic services to be instituted in the context of the new Palestinian state must therefore make use of this most valuable experience for establishing new governmental and quasi-governmental infrastructures.

3. The New Palestinian Economy: The Legacy and the Future

Even if it were to end soon, it is clear that Israel's occupation of the West Bank and Gaza would leave the emerging Palestinian economy burdened by colossal handicaps and distortions. The first order of business in the new state will therefore have to be how to tackle those problems.

Assuming that the political settlement will take the shape outlined earlier, the economic problems of the nascent state would stand out in sharp relief. In this new context, the issue of economic viability would be stripped of its ambiguity and take on the specificity of a testable hypothesis.

Can the new Palestinian state be economically viable?[26]

Yes it can, provided that, within a reasonably short period of time (say 5-7 years), it is able to overcome its inherited handicaps and proceed on a course of sustainable economic growth. The only means of ensuring such a course is through the articulation of a comprehensive reconstruction and development program and underpinning it by adequate resources—human, technical, and financial on the one hand, and by enlightened, predominantly liberal, growth-promoting policies on the other hand. Such a program would have to deal with three closely related tasks: the reorientation and restructuring of the economy, the absorption of substantial numbers of incoming refugees, and the laying of the infrastructural and institutional foundations of the new economy. I will now briefly examine the economic implications of each of these.

A. *Reorientation and Restructuring*

This would require essentially the dismantling of the crippling dependency relationship that has been imposed upon the Palestinian economy by the exigencies of the occupation. The disengagement from the Israeli economy would be most pronounced and most rapid in those areas where the dependency is the greatest—the export by the occupied territories of labor services, and the import by the occupied territories of Israeli goods.

As a corollary to this shift, the Palestinian economy would have to turn inwards, at least to some extent, in order to develop its own resources and to increase the production of its own requirements. This would have the effect of gradually rectifying the imbalances that have arisen over a period of more than twenty years. In addition, the Palestinian economy would be expected to draw closer to those of Jordan and the Arab countries and would thereby reestablish the economic and financial relationships that were abruptly severed, or at least severely constrained by the Israeli occupation. Finally the Palestinian economy would also establish largely free and open relationships of economic interchange with the rest of the world, although initially at least, some protection of some of its domestic industry may be required.

As to the Palestinian economy's relationship with Israel, it would depend almost entirely on the nature of the political settlement reached not only between Israel and the Palestinians but also between Israel and the Arab states as well. The closer this settlement comes to fulfilling the Palestinian and other Arab legitimate aspirations and requirements, the closer the economic and financial relations between Palestine and Israel are likely to be to what may be called "normal." If, however, the sovereignty of the Palestinian state were to be constrained by the terms of the settlement and the problems between Israel and the Arab countries were to remain unresolved or only partly resolved, economic relations between the new state and Israel would remain embryonic, and those that did develop would be strained and unstable.

It is perhaps not necessary to elaborate on the proposition that the new Palestinian state's economic relations with Jordan will flow from the special relationship that has governed the state of affairs between the two (Palestinian and Jordanian) communities over the past few decades. Suffice it to say that, from the standpoint of the economic viability of the Palestinian state, it is essential that the nascent state evolve its own system of political and economic organization, using as a guide the Palestinian people's own distinctive national experience both at home and in exile, *prior* to rushing into formal arrangements of confederalism or other forms of merger with Jordan, essential as these arrangements might be for both parties in the long run.

The sectoral origin of the economy's output would have to be restructured to allow for a considerable increase in the output of agriculture and industry and a great expansion and modernization of the services sector. Development in this sector would focus especially on tourism and financial services, in both of which areas the Palestinian economy could rapidly develop a comparative advantage. The share of industry in gross domestic product (GDP), which has stagnated in the range of 7-9 percent for the past 22 years, would have to be raised to a more "normal" 30-35 percent.[27] Agricultural output, especially of cash crops grown on the expanded area of irrigated land, would increase considerably, as would basic food supplies such as meat, poultry, dairy products and the like. Extensive agriculture for grain production will become increasingly unremunerative and the Palestinian state would have to continue to depend on grain imports.

The single most important feature of the development program (the restructuring) is to be the massive capital and technological deepening that will have to be incorporated into all sectors of the economy. For the Palestinian economy to transcend the inherent resource constraints and to avoid slipping into a state of permanent underdevelopment, it would have to invest enormous resources in the training and retraining of manpower, in basic and applied research, in the adaptation and development of new technologies, and in the introduction and operationalization of the most efficient production techniques. This would require that special attention be given to the development of highly-skilled professional and scientific manpower as well as extensive interaction with the most advanced industrial countries through education, research, joint ventures, purchase and adaptation of technology. Only by these means will the Palestinian economy be able to leap-frog current technology and prepare for the twenty-first century in the most expeditious and effective manner.

In other words, the Palestinian economy will have to lift itself from the state of subsistence and underdevelopment which has been imposed upon it during a period of more than four decades to a state of dynamic growth based on high-level manpower, technology and entrepreneurial and managerial talent. The new Palestinian state, being the homeland of more than five million Palestinians, will undoubtedly draw in some of the most dynamic elements of business, entrepreneurial, professional and scientific manpower currently prospering in their countries of residence. The repatriation of this high-level manpower would enable the new state to make use of a most valuable experience already acquired in the course of the Palestinians' participation in nation-building in other states.

B. *Absorption of Returnees*

As indicated earlier, it may be reasonably assumed that between 650,000 and 700,000 Palestinians now in exile will seek to return to the new state during the first 2-3 years of independence, although their repatriation, resettlement and absorption into the new society may take longer. (This, incidentally, may be contrasted with an almost equal number of Jews who arrived in the newly established state of Israel in the three years 1948-1951). Depending on the circumstances, the number could conceivably be larger. Although the absorption and reintegration of this additional number of people into the emerging Palestinian economy would present the authorities of the new state with complex and daunting challenges, three aspects deserve particular attention.

The first is, of course, the infrastructural requirements of such a task, primarily housing, schools (more on this later) and the need for intermediate facilities. The second aspect is the increase in the labor force contingent upon such an influx. On the conservative assumption that the labor force participation rate among returnees will be 20 percent (approximately the same as the present population of the occupied areas), an additional 140,000 jobs will have to be created simply to accommodate this segment of the population. There is an additional need to eventually create around 120,000 jobs to absorb workers now employed in Israel, although this particular task could be phased over a somewhat longer period. The third point is that aside from the small numbers that may be permitted to be repatriated to areas within Israel proper, almost the entire inflow of returnees will have to be accommodated in the West Bank, as the absorptive capacity of the Gaza Strip will have run up against its tolerable limits.

In addition, the resettlement and absorption program will have to address the problem of reintegrating an additional 340,000 refugees now living in camps in the West Bank (95,000) and the Gaza Strip (245,000) and possibly some portion of the nearly 500,000 refugees not living in camps (about 280,000 in the West Bank and 205,000 in the Gaza Strip) in those areas.[28]

C. *Building for Sustained Long-Term Growth*

All of these elements can be brought together in a comprehensive development program for the emerging Palestinian state. The program will have to concentrate initially on two basic tasks for which the bulk of investment resources would have to be allocated. The first is the physical, and to a lesser extent the social, infrastructure, while the other is manpower development. These two features of the plan will dominate the first phase, perhaps from 0-5 years, but their importance will gradually decline in relative terms, as investments in industry, in agriculture and in services, undertaken largely by the private sector, will come to dominate the later phases of the adjustment program.

One aspect of the requirement to accommodate a large influx of returnees both from abroad and from work in Israel is ameliorated somewhat by the proposed development strategy as large numbers of young adults will be absorbed into the massive training and re-training effort, while an even larger number will find employment in the extensive construction program required by infrastructural development.

Concerning manpower training, it would be necessary for about one third of all students enrolled in the last three years of secondary education (about 25,000-30,000 if returnees are included)[29] to be enrolled, as soon as practicable, in vocational and technical training institutes. In addition, no less than 20,000 adults initially, the number rising to 40,000 within a few years, will need to be continuously enrolled in training and retraining programs, some of which will be run and funded by the state while many will be managed by private industry with partial state support. The training programs will need to cover the full spectrum of the economy's requirements—from basic three-month courses in operating agricultural machinery to 12-year programs for neurosurgeons. Finally, local university education will need to be thoroughly overhauled and will have to be redirected toward the radically different requirements of the new economy and society. As a consequence, it may expand somewhat in size (from the current 14,000 students) but the most urgent requirement here will be the improvement in quality.

As to infrastructure, the development of which will dominate the first phase of the program and thus claim by far the largest share of its resources, it may be useful simply to outline the key components and indicate approximate, order-of-magnitude estimates of costs (all in 1990 prices). Such a program will have to be phased over a period of 10-15 years. The various components would also need to be articulated so as to ensure synchronization of expenditures as required by the forward and backward linkages of various components. In any event, the bulky components of the program (roads, airport, electrical generation capacity) will require between one and three years of planning and design, whereas other elements (e.g., housing) could start immediately.

The single most urgent and costly element in the physical infrastructure of the new state will be housing. In order to accommodate the housing needs of only the incoming population and of the refugees now living in camps in the West Bank and Gaza, approximately 200,000 housing units will have to be built during the adjustment period of, say, 10-15 years, at a total cost in 1990 prices of approximately US$4.5 billion. Such a construction program will employ an average of about 25,000 workers annually, and perhaps as many as 40,000 in the initial period if the program is "front-loaded."

Other elements of the physical infrastructure are shown in the accompanying table, along with approximate costs for the whole development program. The total cost of such a program in 1990 prices (including a contingency allocation of about 10 percent) would be about US$13 billion. The pattern of outlays over, say, a 12-year period will not be even, as the program requires a greater emphasis on infrastructure in the first phase, with probably about US$2.0 billion in the peak year declining to about US$0.5 billion in the terminal year. These figures do not include the normal capital expenditures that will be allocated annually from the state budget for the expansion, repair, and construction of other facilities. This aspect would add on average US$0.5-US$0.75 billion annually although the funds may not be required in these amounts in the early stages of the program.

Not all of the resources required for the infrastructural expenditure program would have to come from public funds, especially in the case of housing and educational facilities. Moreover, many of the infrastructural facilities could, once operational, generate the necessary revenues for maintenance and repair (through a system of fees and charges on the consumption of water, electricity, communication, health and recreation services, etc.).

Reconstruction and Development Program:
Estimated Infrastructural Costs[30]
(US$ million at 1990 prices)

Physical Infrastructure	**9,500**
1. Housing (200,000 units)	4,500
2. Roads (5000 km)	1,250
3. Irrigation, land reclamation and rural infrastructure	1,200
4. Power/electricity capacity and networks	750
5. Water and sewage facilities	600
6. Communications	400
7. Air and Seaport	350
8. Public buildings	300
9. Other facilities	150
Social Infrastructure	**2,450**
10. Hospitals & other health facilities	1,200
11. Educational facilities	600
12. Social institutions	300
13. Public facilities (parks, etc.)	150
14. Tourism facilities	100
15. Other facilities	100
Contingency (10%)	**1,200**
Total	**13,150**

Parallel to the development of the physical and social infrastructure, there will be both public and private sector investment in expanding the production of industrial and agricultural commodities and remunerative services (tourism, banking and insurance). Initially, this investment will be in smaller amounts, but it will rise steadily as the infrastructural facilities are gradually put in place. Thus if the industrial sector is to raise its share in the future GDP of the country to a target of, say, 30 percent, a net cumulative investment of more than US$7.5 billion will have to be made in this sector. In the agricultural sector, assuming that expanded irrigation for the production of high value crops proves cost-effective, approximately 1.5 billion will need to be invested in production facilities (aside from the investment in infrastructure). Finally, about US$0.75 billion will need to be invested in tourism and other services. Allowing for other capital expenditures, the total investment in productive capacity of the economy, mostly from private sources (although public lending may also be required) would be just under US$10.0 billion during the 10-15 year period.

Taking into account the interrelationships between the public and private sectors in terms of their respective shares in financing and combining the two streams of investments, one would arrive at an estimate for the total program of US$23.0 billion, of which the share of the public sector would be about US$12.0 billion.[31]

When the estimated figures are placed in proper perspective, they do not appear overwhelming. One may surmise that of the total public share of the costs of $12.0 billion spread over about 12 years, about $6.0 billion could come from the Arab countries, another $4.0 billion from official bilateral assistance, and $2.0 billion from international financial and development institutions. The private sector share of the program, just under $10.0 billion, will come largely from private Palestinian, Arab and international businessmen and entrepreneurs who could essentially channel their investments into remunerative projects in industry, agriculture and services. The above distribution of investment shares assumes that the public sector will underwrite a variety of indirect costs in the form of investment subsidies, concessionary loans, marketing and credit facilities and so on. These costs could also be borne in part by international agencies.

D. *Economic Organization and Development Policies*

One of the most critical issues that will face the political leadership of the new state is the set of principles on which the organization of the economy is to be based. These essentially turn on such fundamental questions as the delineation of roles for the public and private sectors, the use of the economic system to ensure a minimum level of social justice, property rights and their regulation in society, the extent of reliance on the price mechanism in decisions on production and distribution, and the degree of openness of the Palestinian economy to interaction with other economies in the region and elsewhere.

Derived from these issues is a set of economic policies that must be designed in light of the manner in which the above issues are ultimately resolved. For example, an economic system that affords the private sector wide latitude requires a set of economic policies (on taxation, foreign exchange, currency and banking regulation, etc.) that enables the private sector to fulfill its role as defined by such a system. These same policies must also be reflected in the management of the reconstruction and development outlined above. In other words, this program can only be conceived and articulated in light of the decisions the political leadership makes concerning the fundamental issues of economic organization in the new society.

The debate on these issues is likely to be rich and wide-ranging, and is bound to be influenced by the experience of the Palestinian people themselves, the experience of neighboring Arab countries and, unavoidably, that of Israel. It should also be placed in the context of the developments which have been unfolding with stunning rapidity in the socialist countries of Europe and Asia. Without prejudging the eventual outcome of this debate, one only needs to point out that all these factors point in the direction of an economic system that allows a dominant role for the private sector, where the price mechanism is the primary instrument for the allocation of resources, where fiscal and regulatory policies are designed to ensure adequate incentives while mitigating the excesses of the maldistribution of income and wealth, and where the exchange and trade system is virtually free of controls.

Certain policies implying a strong public sector role would inevitably be required, especially as regards land and water resources management, basic services (education, health, welfare, the environment) and facilities (transportation and communications). But even in such areas of quasi-economic activities, the system of independent public authorities (commissions), organized within the law but outside the direct influence of the state apparatus, may prove to be most appropriate. In any event, if the resources for the above development program are to be efficiently mobilized and if the development program itself is to have a chance of being implemented expeditiously and effectively, the required economic policies would have to rely heavily on the market forces and minimize state intervention in the management of the economy.

E. *Economic Impact of the Development Program*

To put these figures into some perspective, one may compare the expenditures on infrastructure for a population rising from 2.4 million in the initial year to 3.3 million 10 years later with the infrastructural outlays of the Jewish Agency, World Zionist Organization and the State of Israel for Jewish settlements in the West Bank and Gaza, which house about 67,000 inhabitants. Such outlays during the period 1968-1986 amounted to $2.4 billion.[32]

One may also compare the prospective average annual capital outlays of the Palestinian state of about $1.5-$2.5 billion to capital expenditures in other countries. Generally speaking, such outlays for a given country size are a function of the level of development as indicated by per capita GNP. For example, Arab oil countries with high GNP per capita tend to overspend (in relation to the norm) while poorer countries naturally underinvest. The State of Kuwait, for example, with a population of 1.8 million (about two-thirds of the prospective average population of the Palestinian state) and a per capita GNP of about $15,000 allocates about $3.5 billion annually to capital expenditures. In comparison to the future State of Palestine, Kuwait's basic infrastructure is fully developed, but resources are more ample and unit costs are probably higher. Jordan, on the other hand with a population of 3.8 million and per capita GNP of only $1,600, spends about $500 million (public sector only) annually on development.[33]

One of the most critical issues that will confront policy makers in the new state, assuming such an investment program has been formulated, is how to phase actual investment expenditures (which are unusually large in relation to the size of the emerging economy) so as to minimize their inflationary effects. Indeed, powerful inflationary forces arising from both the supply and demand side will dominate all economic policy concerns, at least during the early phases of the program. If these forces are not kept under strict control, the thrust of the program will be dissipated with little lasting effect. Although space does not permit a full treatment of the subject, certain precautionary remarks may be in order. In the first place, the program may have to start slow in order to allow for the construction and operation of certain key infrastructural facilities in order to permit the orderly shipment and distribution of key imports. Secondly, private and public consumption will have to be severely curtailed in order to permit the non-inflationary absorption of the relatively sizable investment expenditures implied by the program. Fiscal and monetary policies will have to be designed for the purpose. Thirdly, the external trade and exchange system will have to be completely free of controls in order to permit the release of mounting inflationary pressures into the external sector. Fourthly, the mobilization of domestic resources would have to go hand in hand with the receipt of external funding for the development program. In this respect, the excess supply of labor caused by the return of large numbers of refugees and by the repatriation of workers now employed in Israel will have the effect of easing somewhat the severity of domestic resource constraints.

Taking into account earlier remarks concerning manpower training, the infrastructural program could employ as many as 80,000 workers annually. If we include employment generation in the social infrastructure (including government) and in the services sectors that will be stimulated by the investment program, it can be estimated that, after an initial adjustment period of perhaps short duration, more than 120,000 job opportunities will be created on an annual basis. This would still leave the emerging Palestinian economy with the task of creating an additional 80,000-100,000 jobs (somewhat less than the number of persons now working in Israel), and this task will require the attention of the planners and the authorities to ensure that a phased plan for creating this number of jobs is formulated and incorporated into the overall development program.

The economic aim of this development program will be to gradually raise per capita GNP from the pre-*intifada* level of about $1200 for both the West Bank and Gaza to about $3500 (in 1990 prices) at the end of the program period. This would be comparable with the kind of growth rates achieved in postwar Europe during the years of Marshall Plan aid. Attaining these rates would require the capital obtained from the aid and investment described above, at an average annual capital/output ratio of about 5:1. It would be reasonable to assume capital/output ratios of about 3:1 in productive private investments, and about 7:1 or 8:1 in infrastructure. These ratios would permit the growth of per capita GNP at the desired rate.

At this level, average income in the Palestinian state would place the country in a reasonably favorable position among the developing economies. Of the 151 countries for which the World Bank has data on per capita GNP, a country with this level of GNP would have been placed at approximately number 51 in 1986 statistics.[34] Per capita

GNP at the end of the transition period would be comparable to that of, say, Greece now, but only about 60 percent of Israel's current per capita GNP.

Such a level of income would be in line with other socio-economic indicators of the Palestinian population. These indicators, such as literacy rates, life expectancy at birth, infant mortality rates, and school enrollment ratios, are at present somewhat more favorable in relation to the level of income in the occupied areas. As indicated earlier, the occupied areas have been subjected to repressive conditions which have stunted their economic growth, although the Palestinian people's own drive for social and individual improvements continues to be manifest.

4. Conclusion

This study has sought to examine questions related to the economics of Palestinian statehood in the context of a political settlement that would ensure a minimum level of protection of the integrity of the new state. In it, I have sought to identify the major issues that would confront such a state, while leaving many of the details to be worked out. While it is difficult to make some of the quantitative estimates, I believe that any errors in the estimates are not likely to materially alter the conclusions reached in the analysis. However, one point needs emphasizing. A number of assumptions used in the analysis may be valid only in a predominantly favorable environment. If any of the fundamental favorable conditions were to fail to materialize (e.g., reduced Palestinian sovereignty, less than full withdrawal of Israeli forces from *all* lands conquered in 1967, or inadequate material support from the Arab and the world community) the economic viability of the new Palestinian state would be commensurably compromised.

In conclusion, the answer to the query about the economic viability of a Palestinian state is that such a state, established within the framework of the political settlement outlined at the beginning of this paper, can indeed be viable, provided certain fundamental conditions are fulfilled. Moreover, and this is probably a more important point, the establishment of a Palestinian state as a homeland in which the majority of Palestinians may reside and to which all Palestinians may belong, would afford the Palestinians, with the help of the Arab states and the world community at large, a unique opportunity to build a modern, healthy and progressive society that would contribute materially to the future peace and prosperity of the entire region.

Notes

1. Various notions of "viability" have been applied to independent states, among them the ability of the country to meet the basic needs of its population and to develop without excessive or chronic dependence on external borrowing, the capacity of the country to develop according to expectations and/or in line with the progress of other states in the region, and, in the context of the current Third World debt crisis, the ability of the country to service its external debt. Although the first of these concepts is probably the most widely acceptable, all suffer from imprecision when subjected to operational tests.

2. Alfred E. Kahn, "Palestine: A Problem in Economic Evaluation," *American Economic Review,* Vol. 34 (September 1944), p. 538.

3. Walter Clay Lowdermilk, *Palestine: Land of Promise* (New York: Greenwood Press, 1968), a reprint of the 1944 work published by Harper and Row, p. 227.

4. *Ibid.,* p. 228.

5. The Jewish Agency for Palestine, *The Jewish Case Before the Anglo-American Committee of Inquiry on Palestine* (Jerusalem, 1947, also reprinted by the Hyperion Press, Westport, Connecticut, 1976), p. 495.

6. According to the latest estimates (1987) of the West Bank Data Base Project (WBDP), the "permanent population" (i.e., residents plus those out of the country for less than a year) of the West Bank was about 1,068,000 and that of the Gaza Strip 633,000. See Meron Benvenisti and Shlomo Khayat, *The West Bank and Gaza Atlas* (Jerusalem: WBDP and the *Jerusalem Post,* 1988), pp. 27-31 and p. 109. The figure for the West Bank exceeds the estimate of Israel's Central Bureau of Statistics (CBS) by about 210,000 persons. Both exclude the Arab population of Jerusalem of about 136,000. If we take a mean estimate for the West Bank and include Jerusalem in the calculation, the total Arab population of the West Bank and the Gaza Strip would be about 1.7 million.

7. Calculated from the State of Israel, Central Bureau of Statistics, *Statistical Abstract of Israel, 1988,* pp. 32-39. These figures exclude the Arab populations of occupied East Jerusalem (136,000) and of the Golan Heights (15,000).

8. The figure of 700,000 is calculated as follows: all the Palestinian refugees living in camps in Jordan, Lebanon and Syria (428,000 in 1987 according to UNRWA figures) plus an arbitrarily chosen ratio of 20 percent of refugees living outside camps in these countries (both figures augmented by 3.0 percent annually to arrive at a 1990 estimate), plus 30,000-50,000 from among Palestinians residing in other countries who for various reasons have residency difficulties and therefore may be included in the early phases of a repatriation program. For estimates of refugees, see United Nations Relief and Works Agency (UNRWA), *Maps of Operation: 30 June 1987* (Vienna: UNRWA Headquarters, 1987).

9. The projection implied in this figure is based on assumptions of moderate growth as calculated in the State of Israel, Central Bureau of Statistics (CBS), *Projections of Population in Judea, Samaria and Gaza Area up to 2002* (Jerusalem, 1987), after adjustment for an underestimation of the population in the base (1982) year, as pointed out in Benvenisti and Khayat, *op. cit.*

10. The population density of the future State of Palestine comprising the West Bank and the Gaza Strip (with, presumably, a land corridor connecting them) is based on an area of the former of 5,500 sq. km and of the latter of 365 sq. km as cited in Benvenisti and Khayat, *ibid.,* pp. 25, 113. Other population densities cited in the paragraph are derived from population and area statistics found in the World Bank, *World Development Report,*

1989, and *World Bank Atlas, 1988.*

11. The total surface area of mandatory Palestine is assumed to be 26,320 sq. km. See Anglo-American Committee of Inquiry, *A Survey of Palestine* (Government Printer, Palestine, 1946), Vol. I, p. 103.

12. Meron Benvenisti, *The West Bank Database Project: A Survey of Israeli Policies* (Washington, D.C.: American Enterprise Institute, 1984), pp. 20-21; and the *West Bank Data Project's 1986 Report* (Jerusalem: WBDP and the *Jerusalem Post*, 1986), p. 25.

13. One dunum equals 1000 square metres or .2471 acres. Figures in this paragraph are derived from Meron Benvenisti and Shlomo Khayat, *op. cit.*, p. 25.

14. *Ibid.*, p. 112.

15. The potential annual water supplies available to the West Bank are variously estimated at between 600 million cubic meters (mcm) and 800 mcm. See discussion in Benvenisti and Khayat, *op. cit.*, pp. 25-27; D. Kahan, *Agricultural and Water Resources in the West Bank and Gaza: 1967-1987* (Jerusalem: West Bank Data Base Project, 1987); and H. Awartani, *The Economy of the West Bank and Gaza* (Arabic), Chapters I and V (unpublished manuscript).

16. See the above sources as well as Uri Davis, "Arab Water Resources and Israeli Water Policies," in A. M. Farid and H. Sirriyeh, *Israel and Arab Water* (London: Arab Research Center, 1985) pp. 16-24; and the Arab Thought Forum's *Shu'un Tanmawiya* (Development Affairs), Jerusalem: Arab Thought Forum, March, 1988.

17. The irrigated area in the West Bank could be expanded to approach its maximum potential, to about 450,000 dunums (as compared with about 105,000 dunums now), thus consuming an additional 225 mcm; and household water consumption in the West Bank and Gaza could increase from the current estimated level of 15 cu.m to about 80 cu.m per capita, thus taking up an additional 160 mcm. Remaining uses could rise by an additional 20-30 mcm. All of these increases in water consumption would be approximately equal to, and according to some estimates even less than, the amounts of water currently appropriated by Israel from the water resources of the West Bank alone. It should be pointed out that whether or not irrigated agriculture in the West Bank *should be* expanded to the level indicated remains an economic question that must be decided on the merits of the case.

18. Benvenisti and Khayat, *op. cit.*, pp. 113-14, and Awartani, Chap. I.

19. This proposition is not in fact as radical as it may seem. Water-using, extensive citrus agriculture has been curtailed considerably and replaced by high-value, water-consuming, intensive agriculture. In Israel itself, and in spite of the local resistance of diehard Zionists, the present official policy is to reduce the cultivated areas because of mounting water constraints.

20. See Yusif Sayigh's "Dispossession and Pauperization: The Palestinian Economy Under Occupation," in G. T. Abed, *The Palestinian Economy: Studies in Development under Prolonged Occupation* (London: Routledge, 1988), for an analysis of the special character and development of the dependency relationship between the occupied areas and Israel. The data on trade are from Israel's *Statistical Abstract, 1988,* Table XXVII/12, p. 715.

For data and analysis of the role of Palestinian Arab labor from the West Bank and Gaza in the Israeli economy see Moshe Semyonov and Noah Lewin-Epstein, *Hewers of Wood and Drawers of Water: Non-citizen Arabs in the Israeli Labor Market* (Ithaca: Cornell University Press, 1987), especially Chapters 4 and 5.

21. The "brain drain" from the occupied areas is evident not only in the entrepreneurial and professional success of those Palestinians who left the areas for the Arab (especially oil-exporting) countries, but also in the "thinning out" of the age and occupational structures of the remaining labor force in precisely those categories that would normally be the most productive. For example, despite the fact that Palestinians abroad tend to be generally prominent in the medical sciences, the occupied areas in the early 1980s did not have a single specialist in pathology, anesthesiology, bio-engineering or in any number of other highly specialized occupations. The ratio of males in the West Bank in the age

groups 19-45 years was in general about 20 percent *below* its normal value on account of emigration. See Israel, Central Bureau of Statistics, *Statistical Abstract of Israel, 1988,* No. 39, p. 706 and Hani Makbul, *Al-Awda al-Dimugrafiya fi al-Difa al-Gharbiya* (Jerusalem: Arab Studies Society, 1987), pp. 271 and 277.

22. For labor force data see the *Statistical Abstract of Israel, 1988,* p. 732. Israeli official statistics do not include the 20,000-25,000 Palestinians who work in Israel without a work permit; they also exclude workers from East Jerusalem from West Bank statistics.

23. M. Benvenisti and S. Khayat, *op. cit.,* pp. 37-39.

24. M. Benvenisti and S. Khayat, *op. cit.,* p. 36.

25. It is interesting to note that efforts by Palestinians to organize responsive, self-help institutions to address local development needs and requirements were generally opposed and, in many instances, thwarted by the Israeli occupation authorities. See, for example, Mohammad K. Shadid, "Israeli Policy Towards Economic Development in the West Bank and Gaza" in G. T. Abed, *op. cit.,* pp. 121-138. Since the *intifada,* the occupation authorities have closed down a large number of medical, social and economic development institutions and have outlawed the "popular committees." See, e.g., the Welfare Association's *Tanmiya* (Geneva), Vol. 3, No. 4 (December 1988). It is still the case that a large and increasing number of grass-roots and largely voluntary development groups operate without official sanction.

The literature on the "civil society" that has developed under occupation is still sparse, in part because of the security risks to the voluntary, grass-roots organizations under existing conditions. Suffice it to say that those groups and organizations which had developed mainly before the *intifada* have expanded their role and scope of activity since then. For a brief discussion of this phenomenon, see David McDowall, *Palestine and Israel: the Uprising and Beyond* (London: I. B. Taurus, 1989), pp. 110-122. Also see Samir Hlaili, "Grass-Roots Organizations in the West Bank," Palestinian Association for the Study of International Affairs (PASIA), Jerusalem, August 1989 (unpublished paper), and *Shu'un Tanmawiya* (Development Affairs), Jerusalem, No. 1, 1988 and No. 3, 1989.

26. The economic viability of a Palestinian state cannot be said to have preoccupied professional economists. Only two studies on the subject may be cited to date—Elias Tuma and Haim Darin-Drabkin's *The Economic Case for Palestine* (London: Croom Helm, 1978) and the less substantial Vivian Bull, *The West Bank: Is It Viable?* (Lexington Books, 1976). Emile Nakhleh's *The West Bank and Gaza: Toward the Making of a Palestinian State* (Washington: American Enterprise Institute, 1979) only broaches the subject. The book edited by G. T. Abed, *The Palestinian Economy: Studies in Development Under Prolonged Occupation* (London and New York: Routledge and Chapman Hall, 1988), provides a comprehensive background, but seeks to formulate a strategy of dynamic survival under repressive conditions rather than development in the context of independence. Most other studies on Palestinian statehood deal primarily with the political and strategic issues, largely from an Israeli vantage point, and do not directly address the issue of economic viability. These include Mark A. Heller, *A Palestinian State: The Implications for Israel* (Cambridge: Harvard University Press, 1983) and the Jaffee Center for Strategic Studies' *West Bank and Gaza: Israel's Option for Peace* (Tel Aviv: Tel Aviv University, 1989).

27. For example, for a group of 13 upper-middle income countries with a range of per capita GNP of US$2020-US$5810 in 1987, the range in the shares of industry in GDP was 32 percent to 43 percent. This is the group to which Palestine would belong once its economy "matures" following an intensive reconstruction and development program. See World Bank, *World Development Report, 1989* (World Bank and Oxford University Press, 1989), Tables 1 and 3, pp. 165 and 169, respectively.

28. UNRWA, *op. cit.*

29. Figures for secondary school students for the West Bank and the Gaza Strip are taken from the *Statistical Abstract of Israel, 1988,* Table XXVII/48, p. 754, while the same enrollment ratio is assumed for the returning refugees. All figures are for 1987/88 and have

been augmented by 3.0 percent per year to 1990, the base year for estimates of the reconstruction and development program.

30. Most estimates are based on actual costs prevailing in the late 1980s in Israel or in Jordan, taking into account the ruggedness of the terrain and its impact, for example, on the cost of highway construction. The following details are given as an indication.

For *housing,* it is assumed that the 1.2 million additional persons will need 200,000 housing units on the basis of 6.0 persons per unit. Current (1987) occupancy rates are about 6.5 persons per unit, and this figure does not appear to have changed much in recent years (see Simcha Bahiri, *Construction and Housing in the West Bank and Gaza,* Jerusalem: WBDP, 1989), pp. 44-51. The average surface area per unit is assumed to be 90 sq.m (recently constructed units in the occupied territories have been larger) and the cost per square meter is assumed to be a conservative US$250 in 1990 prices. Employment figures are based on worker productivity of about 70 sq.m per year; actual figures have ranged between about 66 sq.m and 82 sq.m (see S. Bahiri, *ibid.,* p. 20, and E. Tuma and H. Darin-Drabkin, *The Economic Case for Palestine, op. cit.,* pp. 82-87).

The cost estimates for roads are based on raising the road length to population ratio to about 2.0 km/1000 pop. for both the West Bank and Gaza, with the ratio of the former assumed to be 2.5 and for the latter 1.0, the difference due to differences in spatial settlement. In 1966, the ratio for the West Bank was 2.3 and since then it has declined (largely as a result of population increases and near stagnation in road construction in *Arab* areas) to 1.8 km/1000 population (see Benvenisti and Khayat, *op. cit.,* p. 34). The total road length required by the end of the program period would be about 6700 km. Taking into account the total length of existing (1985) roads, about 1750 km, this would imply *new* construction during the entire period of reconstruction and development of about 5000 km. Assuming US$250,000/km as the cost of construction (1990 prices), the total cost of the new road network would be US$1.25 billion.

Other estimates are only indicative, although every effort has been made to utilize actual data and to apply them conservatively.

31. This assumes that the public sector will underwrite about 70 percent of the infrastructural costs and about 30 percent of the costs of investment in productive capacity.

32. Benvenisti and Khayat, *op. cit.,* Table 2, p. 32.

33. The data on per capita GNP are for 1987 and are from the World Bank, *World Development Report, 1989,* Statistical Appendix, Table 1, p. 166. The data on capital expenditures are from International Monetary Fund, *Government Finance Statistics Yearbook,* Vol. XII, (Washington, D.C., 1988), p. 443 (Kuwait) and p. 439 (Jordan).

34. The World Bank, *Atlas 1987* (Washington, D.C., 1987), pp. 16-17.

13 THE SHAPE OF THINGS TO COME: POLICY AND POLITICS IN THE PALESTINIAN STATE

Laurie A. Brand

Ila mata satusaffiruna, wa li-ayya hulumin . . .
  How long will you journey and toward what dream?
Wa idha raji'tum dhata yawmin
  And if you return one day
Fa li ayya manfan tarji'un, li ayya manfan tarji'un? . . .
  To which land of exile will you return, to which land of exile?
Laysa liya manfan li-aqula liya watanun
  I do not even have a land of exile so that I may say I have a
  homeland . . . [1]

So wrote Mahmoud Darwish in his famous *qasidah* about Beirut, capturing in it the essence of the psychological and political climate that prevailed among Palestinians following the death, destruction, and dispersal of the summer of 1982. Few, if any, could have imagined then that little more than six years later, a sustained, popular uprising among the Palestinians of the occupied territories would lead to the negation of the negation of 1982, the ultimate affirmation of national identity, the proclamation of a Palestinian state.

At a time when many are pondering the possibilities of the effective establishment of a Palestinian state as well as the many, serious obstacles that stand in the way, it is useful to bear in mind the despair of that period. Despite the November 15, 1988 Declaration of Independence by the Palestine National Council (PNC) and PLO chief Yasser Arafat's December 1988 Geneva Declaration (which opened the way for a US-PLO dialogue), as well as the obvious movement in certain quarters in Israel, most observers of and participants in the Palestinian national movement believe that the road to real independence is still long and uncertain. Recalling 1982 and 1983, therefore, is useful if only to remind all those concerned that the once unimaginable can indeed come to pass.

However, in order to fulfill the task of this study, to speculate regarding the shape of the future state, the most salient question—will a Palestinian state in fact be established on the ground?—must be assumed as a given. The most problematic issue, therefore, becomes that of timing. Without knowing the critical "when," the task of sketching future scenarios that may approximate reality is most difficult. Prognostication can easily get out of hand if one proceeds by developing elaborate "if—then, if not—then," tree structures, with each possibility and its consequences branching farther and farther and into unmanageable numbers of scenarios and variations thereon.

In order to avoid such "tree-climbing," this study will posit a set of basic assumptions—including timing—with the understanding that should any of these major assumptions not hold, serious adjustments would have to be made in the conclusions. This study's basic assumptions regarding the future Palestinian state are the following:

1. That a Palestinian state, largely or completely demilitarized, will be established in the framework of some sort of transitional arrangement and within the context of a comprehensive regional peace settlement that will include Jordan, Syria, and Lebanon.

2. That such a state will come into existence in the near term (five to ten years).

3. That the borders of the Palestinian state will be roughly the current borders of the West Bank and the Gaza Strip, with its capital in East Jerusalem and with the presumption that some sort of a land corridor will allow for easy travel between the two areas, although sovereignty over such a corridor would likely not be ceded by Israel.

4. That the state may opt for a loose form of confederation with the Hashemite Kingdom of Jordan.

Given the many variables and uncertainties involved, rather than predicting a series of certain outcomes, this study will highlight the major political challenges that a Palestinian state will confront. The following issue areas will be considered: formal state structure, leadership consolidation, political parties, absorption and integration, class divisions, civil society, the military, and regional ties. The underlying questions presented in each section concern the factors pushing for or militating against the development of a participatory system, as well as the pressures leading toward greater or lesser regime or state stability.

1. Formal Structure: The Road to Provisional Government and State

Although independence was declared on November 15, 1988, the formal structures of a Palestinian *provisional government*—still one step removed from the state structures that will actually direct the state after its effective establishment—have yet to be fully elaborated. Furthermore, only in practice can the constitutional provisions that are drafted be fully tested. Nevertheless, a sense of the direction in which the new state may move may be inferred from the political documents that have been published to date, as well as from articles and interviews about the content of discussions held since the nineteenth session of the PNC on the issue of the provisional government.

If one turns first to the Declaration of Independence, the section relevant to government structure reads as follows:

> The State of Palestine is the state of Palestinians wherever they may be. The state is for them to enjoy in it their collective national and cultural identity, theirs to pursue in it a complete equality of rights. In it will be safeguarded their political and religious convictions and their human dignity by means of a *parliamentary democratic* system of governance, itself based on freedom of expression and the freedom to join *parties*. The rights of minorities will duly be respected by the majority, as minorities must abide by decisions of the majority. Governance will be based on principles of social justice, equality and nondiscrimination in public rights on grounds of race, religion, color, or sex, under the aegis of a *constitution* which ensures the role of law and an independent judiciary . . . .The State of Palestine is an *Arab state*.[2] [emphasis added]

From this document, the following may be ascertained: that there is a commitment to a parliamentary democracy (on the European, as opposed to a US presidential model), that the state (unlike Israel) will be governed by a written constitution, that political parties will function, and the Arab character of the state will be emphasized. It is also worth noting that while freedom of religion is guaranteed, and there is no mention of Islam *per se* in the document, nevertheless, the text of the declaration starts with *Bism Allah al-Rahman al-Rahim* and ends with *Sadaqa Allah al-'Azim,* the traditional Islamic formulae for beginning and concluding a text.

The future shape of regional relations was hinted at in the political statement subsequently released by the nineteenth PNC. It "affirm[ed] its [the PNC's] previous resolutions concerning the distinctive relationship between the Jordanian and Palestinian peoples," and affirm[ed] that the future relationship between the two states of Palestine and Jordan should be "on a confederal basis as a result of the free and voluntary choice of the two fraternal peoples in order to strengthen the historical bonds and the vital interests they hold in common."[3] Salah Khalaf later clarified this position by stating that the decision to confederate was the prerogative of a sovereign state, thereby implying that Palestinian independence and sovereignty would be a prerequisite for entering into such a relationship with Jordan.[4]

Shortly after the nineteenth PNC, and in keeping with its decision that a draft constitution for the provisional government be submitted within six months, discussion began in earnest among the various Palestinian factions regarding the shape of the provisional government. Given Egypt's long history of advocating the establishment of a Palestinian provisional government or government-in-exile as well as the state of Egypt's relations with the PLO, it was natural that Egypt be drawn into the process in a support role. In mid-December 1988, Egyptian officials—among them top political advisor Usama al-Baz and Foreign Ministry official 'Umar Musa—met with three PLO representatives, including PLO Political Committee head Nabil Sha'th.[5] Consultations with non-government officials such as Lutfi al-Khuli, Nabil al-'Arabi, and other members of the Egyptian lawyers' union also were held.[6] Indeed, it was in Cairo that the PLO committee responsible for shaping the provisional government began its task of determining how to turn the liberation organization into a government.[7]

Nabil Sha'th, a long-time resident of Cairo, has stated that the new government will not be one of technocrats nor of a party (presumably a single party). All major factions are to be represented, as will be Palestinians from inside and outside the occupied territories. Sha'th indicated that cabinet portfolios would not necessarily be held by the most powerful men within the organization: Khalaf, Qaddoumi, and Hani al-Hasan would likely remain behind the scenes. He suggested that the PLO would not vanish, but might become an umbrella of parties, and indicated that most of the PLO's current departments (with the exception of the Military Department) are likely to be transformed into ministries e.g., Political (Foreign Affairs), Justice, Social Affairs, Education, and so on.[8]

Other indications of the direction the state may move came from Jamal Surani, Secretary of the PLO Executive Committee and head of the committee in charge of studying the legal aspects of forming a Palestinian government. According to Surani, the constitution of the new state will be based on the Declaration of Independence, but will further specify the various state institutions: the government, parliament, state council (*majlis siyadah*), and the judiciary. General rights of citizens will be spelled out and laws governing parliamentary government will be set down. He did not indicate how many ministries there would be, or how many there would be for the occupied territories, but said that the structure would be such that the government's work would not be disrupted if Israel were to prevent Palestinians living under occupation from participating in the government.[9]

Surani also stated that the structures of such a government will take into account the dispersion of the Palestinians, and will represent the Palestinian people both geographically *and* politically: all the major diaspora communities will be represented, as well as all political trends, from extreme right to extreme left. Given the sensitivity of the issue of elections, Surani indicated that government representatives, at least in the early stage, would be appointed. After the effective establishment of the state, however, all Palestinians, including those outside, will be accorded the right to vote for representatives (much like US citizens' right to vote by absentee ballot). He also stated that the constitution would not necessarily address the issue of the borders of the state, since Israel has not declared its borders: borders will be determined in the course of an international Middle East peace conference.[10]

After the flurry of activity and statements regarding the provisional government, meetings were held on January 14-17, 1989 in Tunis to work out the details. While all factions agreed upon the need to establish such a government, some reports noted differences among them over the question of timing.[11] Other reports indicated additional points of concern. Some argued that the government should be composed of the Palestinian academics and technocrats most acceptable to the US and the Western European countries, but others insisted that the government should maintain the structure of the PLO Executive Committee. The Democratic Front for the Liberation of Palestine (DFLP), Popular Front for the Liberation of Palestine (PFLP), and the Palestinian Communist Party (PCP) were most keen on this last point, in order to safeguard their representation. There is concern on the part of the PFLP and DFLP that the imperative to please outside parties through the naming of certain individuals to the proposed provisional government may effectively freeze the PFLP and DFLP out of the proportional representation they deserve. A further point of concern is that while some factions believe representatives from the occupied territories should be a part of the government, others fear this would expose them to arrest or deportation by the Israelis.[12]

Fatah's position on many of the issues appeared deliberately ambiguous. Moreover, it was reported that Yasser Arafat had not demonstrated any enthusiasm for the immediate formation of a provisional government, and he could be "expected to fight any suggestion which might curb his authority . . . . he is believed to favor a US-style presidency where the president appoints the government, rather than the European system [contrary to the provision of the Declaration of Independence]."[13] Indeed, on April 8, 1989, after heated debates that included severe criticisms of some of Arafat's statements since the nineteenth PNC as well as his "unilateral" leadership style and his violation of his commitment to collective decision-making, the PLO chairman was unanimously designated the first president of the Palestinian state by the PLO Central Council.[14] It remains to the Central Council to determine the length of the new president's term.[15]

The election of Arafat as president of the new state, however, is not as important as the way in which the draft constitution will deal with several of the issues Sha'th, Surani and others raised: What will be the relationship between the PLO, the PNC, the PLO executive and the new government? What will be the relationship between Fatah, as majority faction or party, and the new government? What will be the relationship between Fatah and the other factions or parties? And how will the transition from current structures to the new state structures be accomplished? It appears from the available statements that, at least initially, many of the standing PLO structures will be borrowed or adapted by the new government to serve functions similar to those they currently have. Likewise, it would seem that the various factions that now fall under the PLO's umbrella will be converted into political parties which, at least in theory, will compete on an equal basis. (Political party competition is further discussed below.)

One factor that should work to the benefit of the PLO and the Palestinians in the process of transforming the organization into a set of governmental structures is the fact that it long ago began the process of conversion from a revolutionary organization to a bureaucracy (unlike, for example, the situation in Algeria with the FLN just prior to independence).[16] In its early days, the 1967-70 period in Jordan, as well as in the pre-1976 period in Lebanon, the Palestinian movement most closely resembled one engaged in a "people's war": its fighters were mostly irregulars, the camps were the primary recruitment centers, weaponry was of the light kind appropriate for small-scale operations, and there was only minimal infrastructure. Because of the conflict between the government and the resistance that erupted in Jordan in 1970 and the subsequent armed assault on the resistance, it never had the opportunity to become more fully institutionalized and, hence, bureaucratized in Jordan.

This opportunity did not come until the concentration of the movement in Lebanon, where as a result of the civil war and the disintegration of the state, the Palestinians found themselves with the necessary opening to expand the PLO's political role and organize its services (which, as a result of government repression, had been impossible in the pre-1969 period). Consequently, the PLO increasingly assumed the trappings of a para-state. The offices of the various PLO departments grew, as did those of the various armed factions. In addition, however, other offices developed for women, students and workers, as did services in the fields of health care, education, employment and the like.[17]

Thus, the PLO has already gone a long way along the spectrum from "people's war" to government bureaucracy. A Palestinian state, therefore, would not have to pass through this difficult stage in the institutionalization of the "revolution." However, it must be stressed that the Lebanon experience also had its dark side, which must be borne in mind by the current leadership, the leadership of the future state, and those who attempt to speculate regarding the nature of the future state. Ranging from minor acts of thuggery and corruption to more serious crimes and infringements upon the rights of the populace, both Palestinians and Lebanese, the *tajawuzat* (excesses) of the Lebanon period both marked and marred the first Palestinian experience with semi-independent or autonomous political status.[18] While some of these activities are doubtless attributable to the prevailing political climate in Lebanon at the time, of which the PLO and the Palestinians were a part but not the sole nor the primary shapers, the history of such activities cannot be ignored.

Nevertheless, if one looks beyond the Palestinian experience in Lebanon to experiences elsewhere relevant to the state-building process, one finds that the Palestinian communities count among their numbers thousands of experienced managers and bureaucrats, many of whom have been instrumental in building and shaping the bureaucracies of the states of the Gulf in particular. A dearth of similar expertise was a critical factor that shaped the course of the Algerian state and economy after independence.[19] While it is true that not all these Palestinians may be expected to return to a Palestinian state, their skill and expertise are certainly commodities that could be drawn upon by those responsible for building such a state.

Palestinian sources indicate that a draft constitution is under preparation. The delay in the original scheduled release of the document has been attributed by high-ranking Palestinians involved in the process to unrealistic estimates of how long the process of drafting a document dealing with such a wide range and complexity of topics would take.[20] No firm answers to questions regarding the structure of the government will be possible until the constitution is released and approved. Likewise, no firm answers regarding the way the draft structures will operate in practice can be determined before the actual establishment of the state on the ground.

2. The Leadership: Inside vs. Outside

There seems little doubt among observers that if the state does emerge in the near term, the top leadership positions will be filled by the current, well-known leadership of the PLO. It is these men—unfortunately, on the highest levels there are no women to mention—who have led the liberation movement over the last twenty years. They are well-schooled in diplomacy and are known to the entire Palestinian community as well as to Arab leaders and other states.

However, if, as it appears will be the case, the Palestinian state is established on the heels of the success of or the pressures generated by the *intifada*, the hand of the West Bank-Gaza leadership in shaping the new state will also be extremely strong. Not only will they enjoy the momentum of having ultimately forced the issue of Israeli withdrawal (after twenty years of failure of the politics of the leadership outside), they will also be the effective local leadership, the elements that have formed and kept operating the Unified National Command of the Uprising. By the time of the establishment of the state, they will have enjoyed several years of experience, and the simple fact of being in place may well invest them with increased power and legitimacy to lobby for much of their vision of what such a state should look like. Alternatively, one may imagine a situation after independence in which the traditional West Bank and Gaza landowning/merchant elite families may reemerge to fill leadership positions.[21] Such a possibility is dependent in large part, it would seem, upon the degree of participation of these families (in their various branches) in the uprising in order to continue to command some legitimacy in the community, as well as the degree to which their economic power can be maintained despite the severe difficulties posed by the *intifada*.

3. Political Parties

Since the 1950s Palestinians have been involved in, and in some cases have been in the vanguard of, political organizing in the Arab world, whether on a pan-Arab, Palestinian national, or Islamic basis. Following the establishment of the PLO in 1964, and perhaps even more so after the assumption of the reins of authority of the organization by the commando factions in 1969, there has been an ongoing process of political competition and jockeying for power position among the factions. The vast majority of this competition has taken place within the framework of the PLO and its various sub-organizations and institutions. Only on rare occasions, the most notable and serious being the split in the PLO that followed the 1983 revolt in Fatah, have differences led to the withdrawal or ouster of factions from the PLO.

The experience over the last twenty-five years of trying to establish, develop, and hold together an organization and a people scattered across a region comprising widely varying regimes and buffeted by changing regional conditions has taught the seasoned leadership the need for pragmatism and compromise. Indeed, until the nineteenth session of the PNC, consensus was the rule of the day in Palestinian politics. The experiences of the ongoing *intifada* have further reinforced the understanding of the need for and the value of flexibility and coalition-building.[22]

It is true that there have been examples of Palestinian factions engaging in political assassination; however, unlike other liberation movements, the PLO has never engaged in an internal purge. Indeed, given the generally authoritarian climate that prevails in the countries in which the PLO is most active or has the largest presence, and given the constraints that this has placed on the PLO's own freedom of action and decision-making, the kind of diversity of opinion found in the movement should give a degree of hope for the future.

Assuming that the current PLO factions are likely to be converted into political parties with the effective establishment of the state, it is worth considering here what they may look like and what the nature of their interaction may be.

Fatah has traditionally attracted the widest support, in part because of its nonideological or simple Palestinian nationalist orientation, in part because as a result of that orientation it has generally been more tolerated by Arab regimes, and in part as a result of both factors, because it has received more contributions and has, therefore, been able to establish a wider network of patronage and services than have the other factions. However, in Palestine itself, the community has expressed greater political diversity. There the Democratic Front, the Popular Front, the Palestinian Communist Party and the Islamist trend have substantial organized backing. One indicator of the importance of these groups is the fact that the Unified National Command of the Uprising includes a representative of each, with the exception of Hamas (the Islamic Resistance Movement, *Harakat al-Muqawama al-Islamiya*). While the internal politics of all of these factions—whether of the right, left, or center—have often fallen short of democracy in action, the jockeying and bargaining among factions that has characterized the past in the PNC and other Palestinian institutions have become a tradition that may be expected to continue in the future state and that may serve as a buffer against countervailing pressures pushing the state toward authoritarianism.

Because of its size and importance, the post-independence shape of Fatah deserves special attention. Although by far the largest and wealthiest of the factions, Fatah's traditional Palestinian nationalist, nonideological, noninterventionist political platform is likely to lose much of its appeal after the establishment of a state. For in the wake of such a development, each of the factions turned political parties will have to detail programs to address the pressing economic, social, and political problems of the post-independence period. While the factions of the left have tended to have more comprehensive programs, Fatah has never tried to articulate an economic or social vision for the Palestinians.

It may be, if sufficient money continues to fill its coffers (or the state's coffers for its distribution, if the leadership of the new state is dominated by Fatah), that Fatah will continue to maintain its preeminence. However, given the diverse trends that have traditionally fallen under its umbrella, it would not seem unreasonable to assume that in the post-independence period, some Fatah supporters will be drawn to other movements that have a more fully articulated political program. In a situation in which participation in one of the parties of the left would presumably not result in (significant) intimidation from the Palestinian regime, left-leaning members of Fatah may be coaxed away, just as some of the more religious elements may be drawn farther to the right. Fatah is likely to continue to command a majority allegiance, to develop into the "government party." In large part because of its long and critical role in the movement, the "center" (Fatah) will probably hold, but it is likely to be a center-right configuration, attracting the Palestinian merchant and business class, the Palestinian upper class—largely from the Gulf, Fatah's traditional base of financial support—as well as the generally nonideological or conservative members of the Palestinian lower classes—particularly from the refugee camps. As such, and given its political orientation, it is likely to attract a great deal of support from the Arab states (and perhaps indirectly from Israel, in view of the alternatives), as well as from whatever international funding agencies become involved in post-independence development projects.

Fatah will, however, continue to be challenged by the more ideological (and better mobilized) parties of the left to take action on economic and social issues. The fact that, at least initially, the "opposition parties"—the DFLP, the PFLP, and the PCP—are likely to be guaranteed a certain number of cabinet portfolios will assure them some role in setting the basic course or agenda for the new state, even if Fatah maintains its majority position through continued popular support or through subtle intimidation based on financial resources or outside support.

The future role of the Islamist trend in a Palestinian polity is more difficult to predict. Hamas, for example, does not enjoy a long history of struggle against Israel, as do the other factions; and it is well known that Israel has indirectly supported the Islamist trend in order to weaken the nationalist forces in the territories. Moreover, the growth in importance of the Islamic movement in Palestine should be seen, not in isolation, but as part of the increased appeal that such movements have enjoyed throughout the Arab and Islamic worlds since the late 1970s. Placed in such a context, a context that indicates that the recent Islamic resurgence in the region has peaked, it seems unlikely that an Islamic movement or party in the future state would command sufficient support effectively to challenge a coalition of secular nationalist parties for control of the state.

4. Absorption

It is by no means clear which and how many Palestinians will return to the West Bank-Gaza state; or whether there will be any provision for some Palestinians to return to their former villages or towns, now in Israel. To be legitimate in the eyes of its constituency, however, the state must make a passport and residency available to any Palestinian who seeks them, wherever he or she currently resides and whatever passport or travel document he or she may have. Several Palestinian spokesmen have made clear that this is a point on which there is no room for compromise.[23]

Indeed, the greatest challenge to the Palestinian state will likely be that of absorbing those Palestinians who want to return to the state to live. While it is impossible to know exactly who will come and from where, it is a fairly safe assumption that the majority of them will be stateless and generally from the lower, rather than the higher socioeconomic strata of Palestinian society. A substantial number will no doubt come from Lebanon, the majority of whose 300,000-400,000 Palestinians hold only Lebanese laissez-passers, have not been allowed to own property, and generally have not been permitted to work legally. They have also, since the late 1960s, been most often and brutally subjected to violence. The likelihood that these refugees will seek to settle in the Palestinian state is increased by the fact that a comprehensive Middle East peace settlement will have to take into account the Lebanese conundrum, something that will be somewhat simplified, though not solved, by the departure of the Palestinians from the country.

The 250,000 Palestinians of Syria are a second likely candidate community for return. They, too, hold mere travel papers, although in practice, throughout the years they have enjoyed all the rights and responsibilities of Syrian citizenship (with the exception of the franchise). As a result, in Syria there has been greater integration of the Palestinian community, as demonstrated by the statistic that some 70 percent of all registered Palestinian refugees in Syria have prospered sufficiently to move out of the UNRWA refugee camps.[24] Nevertheless, the open hostility that developed between the PLO and the Syrian regime, beginning in 1983 with the revolt in Fatah, combined with increasing economic difficulties in the country, has put the community in a far less comfortable position than it enjoyed in earlier times. While it is unlikely that all Palestinians in Syria would choose to return to Palestine to live, it is possible—the Syrian government permitting—that even those who stay might opt for a Palestinian passport, while maintaining their residence in the country.

In addition, there are Palestinians residing in the Gulf (as well as other areas around the world) who hold travel documents (whether

Lebanese, Syrian, Egyptian, Iraq, Kuwaiti, or other) who would certainly opt for Palestinian passports as a kind of security both for their current residence and in order to ensure themselves a country in which they may retire. The large Palestinian community in the Gulf that holds Jordanian passports is another story. Many of them are among the wealthiest of Palestinians, having resided in the Gulf area since the late 1940s or early 1950s. These people, too, may want the option of retiring to Palestine. As a result of the Jordanian disengagement measure of late summer 1988, those whose normal residence (that is, where they go for family visits) is the East Bank maintain their Jordanian passports and nationality, while those whose normal residence is the West Bank may keep their Jordanian passports, but are no longer considered Jordanian citizens. How many of those who remain Jordanians will want to return to a Palestinian state is unclear, but the option must remain open for them as for any other Palestinians.

A further point to be mentioned here is that there may be tacit or explicit agreements either as part of the final peace settlement or between the Palestinian state and various Arab host states regarding resettlement. It is not unlikely that some Gulf states' financial support for such a state may in part be conditional upon Palestine's acceptance of substantial numbers of Palestinian expatriates residing therein or in other Arab countries. (For example, Saudi Arabia might make conditional for the receipt of aid the absorption of x-number of Palestinians from Lebanon or Syria, just as some of the smaller Gulf states might stipulate that their aid be conditional upon the gradual, "scheduled" departure of some number of Palestinian expatriate workers.)

More important for the domestic politics of the future state are the problems and issues involved in the actual absorption of the returnees. The problems of the expansion of various types of infrastructure will require detailed, advance planning and careful, efficient implementation in order to enable the process to be completed as swiftly and with as little internal disruption and dislocation as possible. When Israel began receiving large numbers of immigrants in 1949, it had the advantage of being able to settle many in the actual homes or on the lands of Palestinians who had been driven out or intimidated into leaving. The Palestinian state will not be as fortunate. Aside from some housing in Jewish settlements in the occupied territories, which may accommodate some returnees depending upon how the issue of settlers is treated in the peace settlement, the state will be sorely in need of new housing. This problem will be further exacerbated by the fact that since 1967, orders of the military occupation have severely restricted the building of new housing and the repair or improvement of old. Consequently, the demand for additional housing will be voiced not only among the returnees, but also among the current residents.

But housing is only one of the infrastructural absorption problems. Others include a swift expansion of the educational system (which in terms of personnel should not be difficult, given the large number of Palestinian teachers working in the Arab world), the health care system, employment possibilities, and physical infrastructure such as roads, sewers, electricity, and the like.

Another serious, but less obvious, potential problem is that of integrating members of the various diaspora communities into the political and socioeconomic structure of the state. In some respects, the Palestinian state is likely to encounter fewer problems in this regard than did Israel. In the first place, the vast majority of Palestinians continue to be of a fairly similar cultural background. While some have migrated to Europe and North America, their numbers are small in comparison with those who have continued to live in the states bordering Israel or in the Gulf. Their language is Arabic, and their traditions are Arab/Islamic or Arab/Christian. While each community has had a somewhat different experience from the others, the transient nature of Palestinian society and the transnational nature of Palestinian families has meant that many Palestinians have lived in a number of these communities. Each community has suffered in its own way: whether physical assault, the repression of authoritarian regimes, or insecurity over travel and residence. While the community in Lebanon has suffered the most in terms of physical assault, and the communities in the West Bank and Gaza will be viewed as those who pushed the liberation movement to its conclusion through their sustained uprising, the contributions of other communities over the years, whether financial, material, or physical, are well known. The sending of substantial material resources from outside, or the influx of such resources along with some of the returnees, will certainly help ease tensions.

Moreover, although in the wake of the 1948 war many families and communities were torn asunder, the period since then has witnessed the reconstitution of many of these ties. Palestinians have often made Herculean efforts to preserve family ties and to maintain their sense of identity with the homeland.[25] This factor should also presage less trouble in integrating the various communities socially into a new state. Nor should the development of a unified political identity be problematic. The experiences of the Palestinians, particularly since the founding of the PLO, have created a strong sense of Palestinianism among Palestinians wherever they live.

Having said that, there is still reason to believe that political and economic integration will provide the state with its greatest challenges. A large proportion of the returnees are likely to be of extremely modest economic backgrounds, many of whom have come to rely over the years on UNRWA or the PLO for financial or material assistance. The state will have to make available tremendous resources immediately to help with their resettlement and integration.

The fact that many West Bankers and Gazans have family members living in the communities "outside" may mitigate tensions, but it would be unrealistic to expect that there will not arise friction between those Palestinians coming from outside and those who have resided in the West Bank and Gaza for the last forty years. The issue of West Bank and Gaza land use for infrastructural development, as well as the potential economic and social dislocation that may well result from even the most efficiently implemented absorption plans, will constitute the most likely sources of tension and potential conflict. After all, a basic premise of such an integration scheme is that the Palestinians inside will be expected to share their most precious physical resources (land and water) with a substantial influx of their countrymen from outside. Dissatisfaction with state absorption policies may fuel feelings of jealousy, or create the sense that the rights of West Bankers and Gazans are being sacrificed for the sake of the returnees or vice versa.

One thing that is certain is that the period of absorption will be critical for the future political and economic course of the new state. The state will almost certainly give the maintenance of political stability the highest priority, and frictions arising from integration problems are the most likely sources of dissatisfaction and instability in the early period. Even a leadership strongly committed to a participatory system may be tempted or forced to suspend certain rights during such a period if serious problems arise. Therefore, the need for carefully thought-out policies to handle the influx will be crucial, not only for the future economic development of the country but also for the chances to build and promote democracy.

A related question is that of possible political and economic tension or rivalry between the West Bank and Gaza after the establishment of the state. The proximity of the two as well as their ethnic uniformity mean that a Pakistan-East Pakistan situation is unlikely to develop, but sources of potential conflict do exist. Perhaps because of its larger size, perhaps for other reasons, the West Bank had, at least until the *intifada,* received the lion's share of attention from researchers studying the occupied territories or journalists reporting from them. It is no coincidence that the shorthand for a Palestinian state has often been a "West Bank state" (with Gaza either implied or forgotten). For reasons of land area alone, it will have to be in the West Bank that most returnees settle. (Indeed, a settlement may well witness the movement of some Gaza refugees to the West Bank for reasons of space and resources.) Hence the West Bank may receive a majority of development attention. On the other hand, much of the PLO bureaucracy in Tunis and elsewhere is highly staffed with people from Gaza or its camps[26] and they may be expected to push for greater attention to the Strip if it appears that it is being neglected.

5. Class Divisions

Perhaps more important for the politics of a future Palestinian state than the provenance of its citizens will be their socioeconomic background. From a largely agricultural society with a substantial urban sector, Palestinian society in the diaspora since 1948 has developed a strong middle and upper-middle class.[27] Members of these classes owe their financial success in part to the struggles and hard work of parents, siblings, or other relatives that enabled them to receive an education and then join the professional classes (whether in commerce or the liberal professions), in conjunction with the opportunities that the states of the Gulf offered to such a displaced professional class-in-waiting.

While members of the traditional notable families may often still hold positions of economic power or political influence in some of the communities, it is in fact a Palestinian bourgeoisie of the Gulf, Jordan, and Lebanon that has gradually emerged to play a leading role in rebuilding Palestinian society through its financial support of the PLO and related Palestinian institutions. On the other hand, it has been the refugee camp residents (some of whom were, however, able to achieve financial success outside the camps) who have been the human mainstay of the resistance movement. If it has been members of the new bourgeoisie, or in some cases the traditional leadership, who have often taken leadership roles, it has been the poorer Palestinians (primarily those of rural origin) who have filled the ranks of the resistance's military organizations.

Even in the diaspora, in the course of the national struggle, class or socioeconomic interests have at times surfaced to divide the community or to create antagonism or suspicion. This is particularly true between camp dweller and non-camp dweller. The gap has often led the wealthier or more successful Palestinians to misunderstand or to ignore the many serious problems of the camp dwellers or to deal with them simply through occasional yearly contributions to such organizations as the Palestine Red Crescent Society or the General Union of Palestinian Women.

What may such divisions or differences mean for the future politics of a Palestinian state? Beyond seeking to be part of a sovereign Palestinian state that offers a passport, political protection, and a framework for expression of national identity, the interests of various socioeconomic groups within the polity will certainly vary. The middle and upper classes will be concerned largely with securing assurances, through the establishment of appropriate economic structures, that their investments in such a state will be secure and productive and that their children will have access to appropriate high quality education and, later, employment opportunities. This latter concern has increased over the years as more and more Arab universities that in the past had opened their doors to Palestinian students have limited the number of places available to them.

The camp dwellers, on the other hand, will have related, but different concerns. Despite the large number of camp dwellers in Jordan, Lebanon, and Syria who took part in the armed struggle, their inferior economic position has meant that they do not wield great power. They have traditionally been exploited in the labor markets of the host countries, at times by fellow Palestinians. Their interests will be in access to decent housing, to increased or broadened employment opportunities, to state services that will take the place of those UNRWA has provided (health, education, and perhaps food support or subsidies), and also in the opportunity to receive a decent education.

One of the greatest challenges to the state will be to mobilize the tremendous human resources represented by these people and channel them into the kind of productive economic activity that will serve both their individual interests and the nascent country's drive for political and economic development. It should be noted in this context that the fact that camp dwellers and poorer village Palestinians have played a major role in the ongoing *intifada* may strengthen the political hand of this socioeconomic group (at least those from the occupied territories) in the early stages of formulation of state policy in such areas as health care, economic development projects, education, and women's issues.

6. The Military

It is not the purpose of this study to explore in depth the likely security arrangements between the State of Palestine and its neighbors. Rather, here, the implications for domestic politics of the likely absence of a standing army will be examined. In current discussions of a Palestinian state, a common theme is that such a state would have to be demilitarized; that Israel, with its myriad concerns about the security threat that it believes such a state may constitute, is certain to demand that there be no standing army. While objectively such a demand is not "fair," and Palestinian concerns about the need to protect the state against potential aggression from its neighbors are justified, it seems unlikely that this is a point on which Israel is likely to concede.

The fact that the defeat and dispersal of the Palestinians in 1982 led to the destruction and dismantling of much of the PLO military or factional forces in Lebanon (despite some subsequent rebuilding) and that the PLO does not command military forces in the territory of the proposed state means that the potentially destabilizing process of disarming soldiers to achieve demilitarization is not a problem the State of Palestine will have to face. The projected stipulation that the state will be demilitarized may be viewed as a positive opportunity to depart from the norm in the Third World, where in many countries the military has become a mainstay of the regimes and a subtle or not so subtle actor in the domestic political arena. As such the military has also often—directly or indirectly—forced the state to appropriate substantial percentages of state revenue to it or its projects. Demilitarization would enable the Palestinian state to escape such a possibility.

However, the Palestinian state would certainly have a police force, and the absence of a standing army might lead the state to develop such a force more fully. The absence of a military apparatus may also lead to the development of an extensive internal security bureaucracy (*mukhabarat*) as an extension of the existing security apparatus. Indeed, for reasons related to domestic politics (see below), both

Israel and Jordan may have a stake in encouraging such a development. It is therefore quite possible that the State of Palestine's *mukhabarat* could come to play a role similar to that of the military or the *mukhabarat* in other Arab states.

7. The Civil Society

A critical indicator of the chances for the development of a participatory political system in the future state is the degree to which its population may be able to hold state authority at bay; that is, the degree to which it may develop institutions that stand outside the state, or between itself and the state. The difficulties of living in the absence of a sovereign state, and the struggle in which Palestinians have been engaged over the last forty years to reassert their identity and then organize around it, have led most Palestinian associations to focus on the national cause. In turn, most of the institutions that emerged, whether initially overtly political or not, have generally been drawn into the framework of the national movement, either becoming members of the PLO or affiliating with its constituent organizations. The question then arises: after achieving the major goal of the national movement, independence, can and will these sectoral organizations be depoliticized and come to serve as some of the bases of Palestinian civil society? Or has the association been too long? And will the efforts directed by the state toward the imperatives of national development lead to the continued association of these organizations with the state?

It would seem, at least in the early stages of state building, that such a depoliticization is unlikely. In the first place, the state will be attempting to extend its authority and to harness and coordinate all possible resources for the tremendous tasks ahead, not seeking to relinquish control. Just as important, however, it would seem likely that there will be a re-emergence of the jockeying for power among the various Palestinian factions that has often been so debilitating in the past (although set aside to a large extent by the interfactional coordination of the Unified National Command of the Uprising or UNCU). This is likely to occur no matter what formula is worked out for official representation at the national level in the various official political bodies. And the popular organizations (the general unions of Palestinian students, workers, women, teachers, journalists, artists, doctors, engineers, and lawyers),[28] the potential bases of civil society, which have been the scene of a great deal of interfactional competition in the past, are likely to continue as such in the early years of the state. Indeed, if steps are not taken to separate these institutions from the state as early as possible, it is unlikely that, after the initial period of exigencies associated with state building is over, they will be able to extricate themselves from such ties.

As long as the Palestinian state does not develop into a single-party state, that is, as long as the DFLP, PFLP, PCP, and the Islamic trends as well as others are able to attract substantial constituencies, the continuing association of the popular organizations with the state is less grave and foreboding: these factions represent genuinely different approaches to many of the political and economic challenges of development from that represented by the majority party, Fatah. Fatah has long dominated many of the popular organizations, in part at least because host governments have often moved against or repressed the more leftist-oriented factions. What political configurations will emerge in the framework of an independent state is an open question. However, there are few grounds for believing that Fatah, which has striven to maintain its control over such institutions—often at the expense of organizational effectiveness and activity—would readily or easily relinquish control over them if a non-Fatah majority should pose a challenge.

The trade unions and women's organizations are particularly important in this regard. Outside the occupied territories, the General Union of Palestine Workers has often been a mere extension of Fatah. Inside, however, splits that have occurred along political lines have led the movement to be highly politicized and fractured: several federations of trade unions exist in the occupied territories, organized according to political faction.[29] Forging a monolithic Palestinian trade union movement after the establishment of the state would therefore seem to be more problematic. It is possible that, in the beginning, the various unions may continue to serve as vehicles for factional jockeying. However, with the occupation ended and the opportunity of working more openly and effectively for real trade union issues present, the factionalism of the past may well give way to mobilization according to issues of wages, work hours, and benefits, rather than political ties.

The same may also hold for the various women's committees and federations in the territories.[30] One may expect a more unified women's movement following independence, although women's branches of the political factions turned political parties will no doubt continue to function. As a result of living in diaspora conditions, Palestinian women have been subject to a wide range of personal status laws, those of whatever country they are resident in. Certainly one of the first challenges to Palestinian women will be to play a role in drafting personal status laws for the new state on the issues of marriage, divorce, property rights and the like.

However, neither the PLO as a whole nor its factions has ever made women's issues an important part of their agenda. This raises the question whether Palestinian women will face obstacles—even under the auspices of a sovereign state—in their attempts to consolidate and preserve any changes in women's status achieved during the course of the uprising. According to the constitution, women are guaranteed freedom and equality. However, practice often differs from theory and there should be no illusions as to the likelihood that the new state, whose structures will be dominated by men, will attempt to implement steps to demobilize women and turn back some of the gains they may have achieved in the course of the uprising. It is possible, however, that if the post-independence political parties demonstrate a general lack of attention to women's concerns women could well unite across factional lines. One thing which is certain is that Palestinian women are unlikely to relinquish the gains achieved in the realms of greater freedom of movement, economic responsibility, political participation, and the like without a fight against state structures attempting to restrict them.

Several other signs that may bode well for the carving out of a viable independent realm of civil society should be mentioned. The first is the high percentage of university graduates and of holders of Ph.D.s among the overall population. Such a group is likely to exercise a great deal of independent thinking and push for a large realm of freedom of expression. Related to the high level of literacy and education among the Palestinians is the Palestinian press. With experiences of relative press freedom in Lebanon, Kuwait and now Cyprus (which have included a plethora of political and intellectual publications), as well as the occupied territories (at least with regard to subjects not related to the occupation), and given the role of Palestinians in the media, particularly in the Gulf, there are likely to be strong pressures for freedom of expression. Likewise, the variety of opinion expressed in the publications of the various factions would seem to augur well for continued diversity of expression in a new state. The existence of various Palestinian human rights organizations, most prominent among them al-Haq/Law in the Service of Man

(Ramallah), also bodes well for the protection of citizens' rights vis-a-vis the state.

Another form of association that could well strengthen civil or, more accurately, communal, society against the state are the various family *diwans* and town- and village-related charitable societies that have developed, particularly outside Palestine.[31] These organizations have served to maintain ties across the diaspora as well as to provide a source of social and economic support to members in times of need. The strength of such organizations in the diaspora could bode well for their introduction into the Palestinian state. Indeed, family or village ties may, as they have in some other Arab states, serve as additional structures that could hold the state at bay or mitigate its potential strength (while not necessarily, however, serving to promote democracy).

Also important are the Palestinian universities: Bir Zeit, Bethlehem, Al-Najah, Gaza Islamic, Hebron, and Jerusalem, as well as several women's and vocational colleges and numerous research institutes.[32] For territories with a population of around 1.8 million, the development of six major universities in spite of, rather than thanks to, the occupation is quite significant. University development has depended upon the resources of the Palestinian communities inside and outside as well as the support received from various Arab states. These institutions have striven to promote quality education despite various regulations and the harassments of the occupation: refusal for permission to develop certain new faculties and to expand buildings; difficulties in receiving books, journals, and other equipment; detention of students and faculty; and, of course, the periodic closings.

However, given the chance to reopen in a post-independence situation, the universities have the potential to develop into productive centers of learning, research, and free expression and thought. Indeed, after the establishment of the state, these educational institutions are likely to expand and others like them to open.[33] Such additional facilities will be needed to accommodate not only the young Palestinians of the territories and those of families coming to live in the state, but also the Palestinians from other communities in the Arab world. These would include the Gulf in particular (where some universities place limits on the number of Palestinians who may enroll), Jordan (which does not have enough places in its universities), and perhaps also Israel, since Palestinians there may feel their children are more likely to internalize a strong positive sense of ethnic identity through university work in a Palestinian environment.

Palestinian universities may in fact eventually attract Arabs from throughout the Middle East, eventually establishing or to a certain extent replicating the kind of educational environment that once existed around the American University in Beirut. The Palestinians are also in a unique position to staff such institutions quickly, given the large number of Ph.D.s among the population. Such an expansion in education facilities is extremely important if the state plans to develop the high-tech, service-oriented economy that many Palestinians feel is the only option for the country, given its small size and scarce water resources, which militate against the promotion of large-scale agriculture or heavy industry.

8. Linkage Politics

The previous sections of this study have discussed the Palestinian state as if its future were solely in the hands of those who will live in it and lead it. However, by virtue of geography, economics, and demography, the state will be born with a variety of ties to its neighbors, primarily Israel and Jordan. What role are these neighbors likely to play in the future state?

It has already been stated that the state will likely be demilitarized and may join in some sort of confederal arrangement with Jordan (unless the US and Israel should drop their insistence that there be no purely independent Palestinian state). However, the purpose of this section is not to delve into the details of or the form a confederation with Jordan may take. Instead, the discussion will touch on some of the less obvious roles that Jordan, Palestine, and Israel may play in each others' politics.

Although the initial period following King Hussein's cutting of legal and administrative ties with the West Bank (*fakk al-irtibat*) was one of great uncertainty for Jordanians of Palestinian origin, in some ways, it has made the future clearer: those Palestinians who wish to retain their Jordanian citizenship are permitted to do so; likewise, those who prefer to opt for Palestinian citizenship in the event of the establishment of a Palestinian state will be permitted to do so. Presumably, however, there will be time constraints or limits placed by Jordan (as well as the Palestinian state) on making such a decision. However, all ties have not been severed: the West Bank currency continues to be the Jordanian dinar; some banks in the territories are branches of Jordanian banks; the Jordanian Ministry of *Awqaf* retains responsibility for Islamic endowments in the West Bank, and so on.

Nor is it likely that the strong ties between the two states based on family and clan connections that currently exist will fade in the near term following Palestinian independence. Certainly large numbers of Palestinians will remain Jordanian citizens, based on social, economic, and political considerations. Nonetheless, some, if not many, will continue to view themselves as ethnically Palestinian. Therefore, the natural interest that residents of neighboring states have in each other's politics will be even greater in the case of Jordan and the Palestinian state. Consequently, political developments in Palestine cannot but have repercussions in Jordan. Indeed, some concerns are already being expressed by Jordanians—Palestinian and East Bankers— regarding the nature of the ties between the two. Among some, the concern is how the new state may threaten their position: i.e., among Palestinians tacitly or overtly supportive of the regime, there is concern that their status may be undermined by the establishment of a Palestinian state. Among some East Bankers, there is concern about what the role of the Palestinians in the kingdom will be until the effective establishment of the state, and then, about what shape the new state will take and how its existence will affect the political system in the Hashemite Kingdom.[34]

Particularly important will be the form of government the new state establishes. Pressures in Jordan have been mounting in recent years for greater liberalization in the political system. The cutting of legal and administrative ties with the West Bank necessitated the drafting of a new electoral law and, after the price hike riots of April 1989, parliamentary elections were promised and held.

The fact that some of the young Jordanian demonstrators took to the streets to throw stones and that some Jordanians referred to the riots as their own *intifada* exemplifies the kind of influence that the Palestinian state and Jordan will have on each other in the future.[35] Therefore, if the Palestinian state is able to establish and maintain some degree of popular participation, there cannot but be further pressures in Jordan from broad sectors of society for increased democratization (depending, of course, upon what happens in the interim in the Jordanian political system). Palestinian influence on Jordan would be enhanced by the presumed continued presence (at least in the near term) of Jordanian branches of largely Palestinian parties, particularly the PFLP and the DFLP (working in conjunction with other Jordanian opposition groups). At the same time, however, there will undoubtedly be countervailing pressures exerted by Jordan, although the length of the occupation and the successes of the *intifada* seem finally to have broken the power of the traditional pro-Hashemite elite.[36] In the near term, Jordan is unlikely to have the kind of monetary reserves necessary to influence a Palestinian state or its people, depending upon the issue in question (particularly if it involves Palestinian political agitation for greater political liberalization), but Jordan could likely find support for "interference" of various forms from other Arab states.

The extent to which Jordanian pressures on the Palestinian state will be effective depends to a great extent on the nature of the political and economic arrangements established between the two in the final settlement. However, the kingdom will no doubt have forms of economic and political leverage: sea access and land access for Palestinian goods to the rest of the Arab world; the possibility of imposing tariffs and import or transit duties; and possible monetary assistance to groups friendlier or less hostile to Hashemite concerns, or groups likely to exert more politically conservative influences in the future state. Here one may imagine, for example, Jordanian support for particular candidates or a party in elections, as well as pressure on the Palestinian state to mute or suppress media criticism of Jordan. Moreover, if the final arrangements for the Palestinian state leave responsibility for external security with Jordan as opposed to a Palestinian military force, the threat of military intervention might always loom in the background.

On the other hand, the Palestinian state is not without leverage, particularly with Jordan, precisely because of the large Palestinian population there. The concerns regarding Palestinian loyalty may be exacerbated in the immediate wake of the establishment of the state, and thus for reasons of domestic "survival" lead Palestinians who remain in Jordan to become politically quiescent or to become even more Jordanian. In any case, this large constituency will continue to be powerful in Jordan politically, socially and economically. Therefore, interference from the Jordanian regime (which, it should be stressed, also includes large numbers of Palestinians) could have domestic costs if it were perceived by Jordanians sympathetic to the Palestinian state as meddling.

Nor should one understand the future scenario as one in which the Palestinian state alone is pushing for greater democracy and Jordan alone is attempting to block it. As mentioned above, Palestine will have a police force and, without doubt, its own *mukhabarat*. If the bounds of acceptable political action or discourse are determined by the two leaderships in the beginning, it is not unreasonable to assume that the Palestinian *mukhabarat* may well play a role itself in curbing perceived "democratic excesses" in the new state. The leadership of the Palestinian state will, like any other leadership, be concerned with protecting its position as well as the sovereignty of the new entity. It may, therefore, as a result of external pressures, feel forced to clamp down on some domestic freedoms to prevent greater threats from outside.

Also critical will be the relationship of other Arab states to the new Palestinian state, particularly Syria and the states of the Gulf: the states of the Gulf because of the economic assistance they will likely offer the new state, and because of the influence on Palestinian politics they may have as a result of the kind of official and unofficial contributions they can make to Palestinian political factions, parties, or projects. In particular, Saudi Arabia and the role it could play in supporting and encouraging the Islamist tendency or at least the center-right party discussed earlier should be mentioned. The future role of Syria is less clear, but even if the conflict with Israel is settled and the Golan Heights are returned, economic and political competition with Israel for influence in Lebanon, Palestine and Jordan will no doubt continue. One can imagine the desire of a Palestinian state to attract Syrian tourists and investment; however, assuming the continued leadership of Arafat and Asad and given the bitter political struggles between the two since 1983 (which have left Syria virtually bereft of supporters in the territories), the appeal of the Syrian regime is likely to be limited. Moreover, Syria will not have at its disposal the forms of direct economic pressure (direct access to markets) that Jordan will have.

The future political relationship between Israel and the Palestinian state will be equally interesting. While there will be no military relationship, there may be cooperation between the intelligence services of the two countries to preempt any cross-border incidents, from whichever side they may be initiated. Such cooperation would be in the interest of the Palestinian state, which would not want to give Israel any pretext to reoccupy Palestinian land. Likewise, once having concluded an agreement that brings a comprehensive settlement, an Israeli government that appreciates the benefits of peace would be unlikely to risk jeopardizing such a settlement through, for example, the activities of zealots who might continue to push for Jewish sovereignty over parts of "Judea and Samaria."

It is also likely that the ultimate settlement will permit some of those Jews who have settled in the West Bank (and perhaps Gaza) the right to remain there (perhaps in exchange for some limited resettlement of Palestinians in Israel). Therefore, it is possible that the Palestinian state may have some Jewish citizens, just as Israel has Palestinian citizens, although certainly not in the same proportions. This factor, beyond the obvious security concerns, gives each state an interest in the domestic politics of the other. While it is unlikely that the Palestinian state will be able to do much to improve the third-class status of Palestinians in Israel (behind European and then Afro-Asian Jews), Israeli concerns for the status of Jews in Palestine may provide the Palestinian state some leverage in pushing for improving the status of Palestinians in Israel. The Palestinian leadership will certainly insist that the terms of the peace settlement guarantee that the status of the Palestinian citizens of Israel not in fact suffer as a result of the establishment of a Palestinian state.

Israel is also likely to be concerned with the potential influence of Palestinian political parties or factions on the Palestinian electorate in Israel. For, just as certain Palestinian factions have had branches or supporters in Jordan, there has recently been a similar trend in Israel.[37] The conclusion of a peace treaty is likely to be convulsive enough an event to lead to a great deal of questioning about the nature and future of the Jewish state, its purpose and mission. Since the state has become accustomed to living in a perceived or real state of war since 1948, concerns about the future and where the state should direct its energies will no doubt abound. The choice of what Yehoshafat Harkabi has called "a Zionism of quality, not a Zionism of acreage"[38] is likely to cause numerous dislocations in Israeli political discourse as well as practice. A lengthy, separate study is needed to examine or speculate on what changes or upheavals may occur in the Israeli political system as the result of a peace treaty. However, it seems clear that the results of these debates will have a direct impact on the Palestinian minority in Israel, and these developments will be of concern to the Palestinian state. This will certainly be the case in the early stages, and future developments will depend on the outcome of the debate (most eloquently discussed by Anton Shammas)[39] over whether this will be a Palestinian state, like most other states of the world, or whether it will be a state for the Palestinians, along the Israeli model of Israel as a state for the Jews, and thereby forever assert a claim to the allegiance of or even sovereignty over Palestinians wherever they may reside.

The economic ties that will certainly continue (if on new, more equal bases) between the two countries may also serve as two-way points of leverage between Israel and Palestine. Displeasure over policies could lead to strikes or work slowdowns by Palestinian workers in Israel, just as Israel could temporarily close its doors to such workers if a dispute arose.

In sum, the Israeli-Palestinian and the Palestinian-Jordanian borders are likely to be quite porous economically and politically in *both* directions. Each bilateral relationship has its points of strength and weakness, as well as implicit pressures that will both push toward and militate against intervention. In other words, there can be no illusions as to the effective independence that a state as small and as economically and geographically vulnerable as Palestine can sustain. If we look to another Middle Eastern example, Kuwait, we find a small state that has doggedly struggled to pursue an independent course in domestic as well as foreign affairs, but which is always aware of the presence of its powerful Iraqi, Saudi, and Iranian neighbors, all of whom have had a hand on occasion in pressuring Kuwait on matters of foreign and domestic policy, whether overtly or covertly. The case of Palestine may in some ways be comparable, although the state will not have the tremendous economic resources that have in part contributed to Kuwait's successes in steering an independent course.

9. Conclusions

As this study has attempted to demonstrate, the variables involved in calculating the domestic political configurations in a future Palestinian state are many. As a result, only the most general lines can be drawn with any certainty, and even they are subject to modification. On the critical question of whether meaningful participatory structures can be established and preserved in the new state, this study has attempted to show that in each critical area there are pressures militating in favor of as well as against authoritarianism.

On the side of the balance weighing against a participatory system are the need for stability through the early years of absorption and integration, the general climate in the region, the kinds of pressures likely to emanate from other regional actors, the less than democratic traditions operative among some of the current Palestinian leadership, and the negative aspects of the para-state experience in Lebanon. However, in assessing the potential of the future state, some, guided by their frustration with the failure of the PLO (prior to the *intifada*) to make progress toward a state as well as by their anger with the corruption that accompanied the Beirut era, have vilified the current leadership as hopelessly corrupt and authoritarian. On the other hand, the optimism generated by the gains of the *intifada* and support for its goals has led some to a substitution of hopes for reality. It is in fact quite easy for those who vilify the current leadership to be tempted at the same time to overromanticize the revolutionary nature of the *intifada* and its leadership.

Anger and frustration, hopes and dreams aside, there are reasons to believe that at least some degree of meaningful political participation can be achieved and sustained in a Palestinian state. The first is the tradition of political factions working together on the PLO executive, in the Central Council, in the PNC, and in the various diaspora community institutions. This 25-year tradition has been solidified by the experiences of the *intifada*. Other important elements in this equation are the high level of education among Palestinians, the number and influence of indigenous universities, and the tradition of a lively press. On the regional level, one should not overlook the popular pressures that have been brought to bear on standing regimes from Algeria to Jordan, forcing change or reform and suggesting that some opening up of the political systems in the area may be inevitable.

The question of democracy or authoritarianism will not be fully resolved prior to the actual establishment of the state on the ground, although the government structures detailed in the draft constitution will likely embody democratic principles, as indicated by the Declaration of Independence. It is only in practice, however, that the full extent of the workings of participatory principles and their institutional safeguards can be effectively tested. The state is certain to pass through a difficult period of adjustment in its early years, with substantial forces and pressures pushing in both directions. All that can be concluded is that, while authoritarian trends, traditions and structures in the region and in some sectors of the community and the traditional leadership are quite strong, the factors mentioned above combined with the continuation of the *intifada* give some grounds for hope that the state will be able to escape—if not completely, then partly—the authoritarianism that prevails in the area.

Notes

1. From "Qasidat Beirut," by Mahmoud Darwish, 1983. From the tape issued by the Palestine Democratic Committee (Lajnat Filastin al-Dimuqratiyyah).

2. For the text of the Declaration of Independence see "Documents and Source Material," *Journal of Palestine Studies*, 70 (Winter 1989), pp. 213-16.

3. For the text of the Political Communique of the nineteenth PNC, see *ibid.*, pp. 216-23.

4. Abou Iyad, "Pour la justice, pour la paix" (interview), *Revue d'Etudes Palestiniennes*, 30 (Winter 1989), p. 17.

5. *Christian Science Monitor*, December 27, 1988.

6. Discussion by the author with Abdel Monem Said Aly, senior researcher at the Al-Ahram Center for Political and Strategic Studies (Cairo), in Washington, March 10, 1989.

7. Jane Friedman, "Egypt aids PLO effort to set up a government," *Christian Science Monitor*, December 27, 1988.

8. *Ibid.*

9. *Al-Watan* (Kuwait), January 11, 1989, as translated in FBIS, January 13, 1989.

10. Interview with Jamal Surani, *Al-Yawm al-Sabi'* (Paris), January 30, 1989.

11. "Lam Nabhath Tashkil Hakuman . . . wa lam Nakhtalif," (We Did Not Discuss Forming a Government, and We Did Not Disagree), *Al-Yawm al-Sabi'*, January 30, 1989.

12. *Ibid.*; interview with Nayif Hawatmeh, *al-Anba'*, January 19, 1989, as translated in the Foreign Broadcast Information Service (FBIS) of February 7, 1989; interview with George Habash, *al-Safir*, January 23, 1989, as translated in FBIS of January 26, 1989; discussion by author with member of the Democratic Front in Washington, January 26, 1988.

13. Lamis Andoni, "The Provisional Government Debate," *Middle East International*, January 20, 1989.

14. Lamis Andoni, "'President Arafat' Under Fire," *Middle East International*, April 14, 1989.

15. "Al-Ijma' 'ala 'Arafat Ra'isan li-Dawlat Filastin," (Consensus On Arafat As President of State Of Palestine), *Al-Yawm al-Sabi'*, April 10, 1989, pp. 8-9.

16. For a discussion of the FLN and its transformation into a state leadership and bureaucracy, see William B. Quandt, *Revolution and Political Leadership in Algeria, 1954-1968* (Cambridge: MIT Press, 1969), chapters 9 and 10.

17. For a description of the PLO infrastructure in Lebanon on the eve of the Israeli invasion, see Cheryl Rubenberg, *The Palestine Liberation Organization: Its Institutional Infrastructure* (Belmont, MA: Institute of Arab Studies, 1983).

18. See Rex Brynen, "PLO Policy in Lebanon: Legacies and Lessons," *Journal of Palestine Studies*, 70 (Winter 1989), pp. 61-63; and Rashid Khalidi, *Under Siege: PLO Decisionmaking During the 1982 War* (New York: Columbia University Press, 1986), pp. 29-33.

19. See David and Marina Ottaway, *Algeria: The Politics of a Socialist Revolution* (Berkeley: University of California Press, 1970), chapter 3.

20. From an off-the-record discussion by the author with a PLO official, April 18, 1989.

21. I am grateful to Dr. Salim Tamari of Birzeit University for pointing out to me the possibility of the reemergence of the West Bank and Gaza elite as a political force in the post-independence period.

22. From several discussions by the author with Palestinian academics, intellectuals, and political organizers, spring 1989.

23. Remarks by Faisal al-Husseini at the Brookings Institution, March 14, 1989.

24. See Laurie A. Brand, "The Palestinians in Syria: The Politics and Economics of Integration," *The Middle East Journal*, Vol. 42, no. 4 (Autumn 1988), p. 624.

25. See, for example, Shafeeq N. Ghabra, *Palestinians in Kuwait: The Family and the Politics of Survival* (Boulder: Westview, 1987).

26. From a discussion by the author with a knowledgeable Palestinian source.

27. For a discussion of changes in class structure among Palestinians, see Pamela Ann Smith, *Palestine and the Palestinians, 1876-1983* (New York: St. Martin's, 1984).

28. For detailed descriptions and analyses of these general unions and their roles in the diaspora, see Laurie A. Brand, *Palestinians in the Arab World: Institution Building and the Search for State* (New York: Columbia University Press, 1988).

29. For the most detailed analysis of the trade union movement in the occupied territories, see Joost R. Hiltermann, "Before the Uprising: The Organization and Mobilization of Palestinian Workers and Women in the Israeli-Occupied West Bank and Gaza Strip," (unpublished Ph.D. dissertation, Department of Sociology, University of California, Santa Cruz, 1988), chapter 3.

30. The best source on the women's movement in the occupied territories is Hiltermann, *ibid.,* chapter 4. For the post-1948 history of the Palestinian women's movement in Egypt, Kuwait, and Jordan, see Brand, *Palestinians in the Arab World, op. cit.*

31. See Ghabra, *op. cit.*, pp. 105-110; 137-152.

32. For a description of the history and an evaluation of the standards and effectiveness of Palestinian universities, see Antony Thrall Sullivan, *Palestinian Universities Under Occupation* (Cairo: American University in Cairo Press, 1988).

33. For an assessment of the need for Palestinian universities, see Janet L. Abu-Lughod, "Palestinian Open University Feasibility Study, Part II, Annex I, Demographic Characteristics of the Palestinian Population: Relevance for Planning Palestinian Open University," (unpublished paper), (UNESCO, Paris, June 30, 1980).

34. From discussions by the author with Jordanians during a March 1989 visit to the Hashemite Kingdom.

35. See Alan Cowell, "Jordan's Revolt is Against Austerity," *New York Times*, April 21, 1989; "Jordan Riots Blamed on Extremism, Hunger," *Christian Science Monitor*, April 21, 1989; Patrick Tyler, "Security Forces Halt Riots in Jordan," *Washington Post*, April 23, 1989.

36. For an analysis of the decline of the traditional West Bank urban elite, see Emile Sahliyeh, *In Search of Leadership: West Bank Politics Since 1967* (Washington, D.C.: Brookings Institution, 1988).

37. Nadim Rouhana, "The Political Transformation of the Arabs in Israel: From Acquiescence to Challenge," *Journal of Palestine Studies*, 71 (Spring 1989), pp. 48-49.

38. Yehoshafat Harkabi, "Choosing Between Bad and Worse" (interview), *Journal of Palestine Studies*, 63 (Spring 1987), p. 47.

39. Anton Shammas, "The Morning After," *New York Review of Books*, September 29, 1988.

APPENDIX

SELECTED STATISTICS ON THE PALESTINIAN POPULATION

Compiled by Samer Khalidi*

*Researcher, Center for Contemporary Arab Studies, Summer 1989.

TABLE 1

Total Palestinian Population, 1946-89
(Estimates)

1946	1,364,300
1969/70	2,923,000
1982	4,739,158
1989	5,900,000

Sources: For 1946, the Report of the United Nations Special Committee on Palestine. Population statistics from the report can be found in Walid Khalidi (ed.), *From Haven To Conquest* (Beirut: Institute for Palestine Studies, 1971), p. 696. The 1969-70 statistics are reported in Nabeel Shaath, "High Level Palestinian Manpower," *Journal of Palestine Studies,* Vol. I, No. 2 (Winter 1972), p. 81. The 1982 statistics are from the *Palestinian Statistical Abstract for 1983,* as quoted by Laurie Brand, *Palestinians in the Arab World: Institution Building and the Search for State* (New York: Columbia University Press, 1988), p. 9. The 1989 statistics are estimates based on current population growth rates.

TABLE 2

Place of Residence of Palestinian Arabs, 1969/70 and 1984
(Estimates)

Place of Residence	1969/70	1984
West Bank	670,000	919,000
Gaza Strip	364,000	509,900
Jordan (East Bank)	900,000	1,297,550
Israel	340,000	602,700
Lebanon	240,000	492,240
Syria	155,000	245,288
Kuwait	140,000	336,530
Saudi Arabia	20,000	171,146
Other Gulf states	15,000	67,802
Egypt	33,000	37,668
Iraq	14,000	22,712
Libya	5,000	21,568
Other Arab states		56,218
United States	7,000	114,402
Rest of world	20,000	151,649
TOTAL	2,923,000	5,046,373

Sources: Shaath, *op. cit.;* the 1984 edition of the *Palestinian Statistical Abstract,* published by the Palestinian Central Bureau of Statistics, Damascus, p. 42.

TABLE 3

Age Distribution of Population of West Bank
(except East Jerusalem) and Gaza Strip, 1986-87
(Percentages)

	Age Group in Years						
	0-4	5-19	20-35	35-54	55-64	65 +	Total %
West Bank	18.9	38.8	23.9	10.2	4.5	3.7	100
Gaza Strip	19.8	39.3	23.4	10.8	3.9	2.8	100
Comparisons:							
East Jerusalem plus non-Jewish population of Israel*	15.1	39.7	24.3	14.3	3.5	3.1	100
Israeli Jews	10.4	27.9	22.6	21.1	7.9	10.1	100

*The non-Jewish population of Israel is almost entirely Arab.
Source: Israel, Central Bureau of Statistics, *Statistical Abstract of Israel, 1988*, Tables II/9 and XXVII/2.

TABLE 4

Time When Palestinian Arab Population May Equal Jewish Population in the Combined Area of the West Bank, Gaza Strip and Israel

[Estimates refer to a range of years; e.g., if both population groups have relatively high natural growth rates, their numbers would be equal some time between the years 2019 and 2023. This table is based solely on natural growth rates, and excludes the effects of immigration and emigration, which are unpredictable.]

		If Jewish Population Growth is Relatively		
		Low	Medium	High
If Arab	High	2010-2014	2014-2018	2019-2023
Population Growth is	Medium	2020-2029	2029-2038	2038-2046
Relatively	Low	2060-2070	2070-2080	2080-2090

Source: The estimates in this table have been calculated on the basis of population estimation techniques used by the Israel Central Bureau of Statistics. The table incorporates corrections of an official Israeli undercount of the population of the occupied territories. These corrections have been derived from the work of the West Bank Data Project directed by Meron Benvenisti. It is important to note that the high, medium and low growth rates for each population group are high, medium and low in the context of that group's recent patterns of demographic growth (i.e., a relatively "high" Jewish rate is still less high in absolute terms than a "high" Arab rate, because the recent Jewish growth rate has been much lower than the recent Arab growth rate).

CONTRIBUTORS

Islah Abdul Jawwad is a professor in the Cultural Studies Department of Bir Zeit University on the West Bank. She is currently engaged in research into the development of Palestinian women's organizations which examines their social significance and political impact.

As'ad Abdul-Rahman is a professor in the Department of Political Science at Amman University. From 1974 to 1984, he taught in the Department of Political Science at Kuwait University, where he was editor of the University's *Journal of the Social Sciences*. Dr. Abdul-Rahman has been a member of the Palestine National Council and the Central Council of the PLO since 1977.

George T. Abed is Director General of the Welfare Association, based in Geneva, Switzerland. He received his Ph.D. in economics from the University of California at Berkeley. He served in the Middle Eastern Department of the International Monetary Fund for ten years, and was Division Chief for five.

Ziad Abu-Amr is a professor in the Department of Political Science and Chairman of the Philosophy and Cultural Studies Program at Bir Zeit University. He received his Ph.D. from Georgetown University. He is the author of books in Arabic on political movements in the Gaza Strip and on the Islamic Movement in the West Bank and Gaza, English versions of which are being prepared.

Hanan Mikhail Ashrawi, currently the head of the English Department and Dean of the Faculty of Arts at Bir Zeit University, earned her Ph.D. in English Medieval Literature and Comparative Literature from the University of Virginia. Dr. Ashrawi has published studies on Palestinian poetry and fiction and has written widely on Palestinian culture.

Igor Petrovich Belyayev received his education in Middle Eastern Studies from the Moscow Institute of Oriental Studies, culminating with a doctorate in 1954. Dr. Belyayev then worked as a correspondent for *Pravda* in the Middle East and Africa, serving as the head of the Afro-Asian section and member of the editorial board from 1964-70. He is now a senior political analyst and columnist for the *Literary Gazette* in Moscow.

Laurie Brand is an Assistant Professor of International Relations in the University of Southern California. She received her Ph.D. from Columbia University. The author of a recently published book on *Palestinians in the*

Arab World: Institution Building and the Search for State, she was formerly the assistant editor of the *Journal of Palestine Studies.*

Yehoshafat Harkabi is the Hexter Professor of International Relations and Middle Eastern Studies at the Hebrew University of Jerusalem. In addition to several academic positions, Dr. Harkabi served as Deputy Chief of IDF Intelligence from 1950-1959 and headed strategic research at Israel's Ministry of Defense from 1963-1968. His most recent book is entitled *Israel's Fateful Hour.*

Joost R. Hiltermann earned a doctorate in sociology from the University of California at Santa Cruz and an M.A. in International Relations from the Johns Hopkins School for Advanced International Studies. He has worked as Research Coordinator at Al-Haq, the Palestinian affiliate of the International Commission of Jurists, and is currently a Visiting Researcher at Georgetown University.

Michael C. Hudson, Professor of International Relations and Government and Seif Ghobash Professor of Arab Studies at Georgetown University, received a Ph.D. in Political Science from Yale University. He is a member of the editorial board of the *Journal of Arab Affairs,* and served as President of the Middle East Studies Association from 1986 to 1987.

Riad al-Khouri is an Oxford-educated economist and consultant who is the Director of Associated Middle East Consultants (Beirut) and of Middle East Business Associates (Amman).

Hisham Sharabi earned an M.A. in Philosophy and a Ph.D. in the History of Culture at the University of Chicago. He is Omar al-Mukhtar Professor of Arab Culture at Georgetown University and Editor of the *Journal of Palestine Studies.* His most recent books include *The Next Arab Decade* (editor and contributor) and *Neopatriarchy: A Theory of Distorted Change in Arab Society.*

Salim Tamari, a professor in the Department of Sociology and Anthropology at Bir Zeit University, has been editor of the *Bir Zeit Research Review* since 1985. A contributing editor to *MERIP Reports,* he has also served as Editor of the quarterly journal of Palestinian ethnography, *Heritage and Society,* and written extensively on Palestinian society.

Valerie Yorke is a London-based analyst, writer and broadcaster on Middle East issues. Her publications include *Domestic Politics and Regional Security: Jordan, Syria and Israel; European Interests and Gulf Oil* (with Louis Turner); *Peace in the Middle East: Superpowers and Security Guarantees* (with David Astor); and a number of studies on Palestinian self-determination and Israeli security.

INDEX

ABC News 105, 106
Abram, Morris 108, 110
Abu Nidal ix
Abu Sharif, Bassam ix
Aden/Algiers accords 140
Algeria xii-xiv, 232, 233, 255
Algiers ix, 4, 13, 22, 48, 55, 119, 122, 123, 160, 161, 201
Amman Accord (1985) 7, 20
Amman Summit (1987) ix, 141
American Jewish Committee 104, 110
American Jewish Congress 100, 104, 108, 110
American University of Beirut 249
Anglo-American Commission of Inquiry 200
Arab League 172, 178, 183
al-Arabi, Nabil 230
Arafat, Yasser ix, 4, 6-8, 13, 14, 22, 46, 88, 90, 99, 105, 110, 120, 124, 125, 140, 143, 144, 160, 161, 180, 227, 232, 252
Arens, Moshe 99, 125
al-Asad, Hafiz 252
Associated Press 105

Baghdad Summit 145
Bahrain 99
Baker, James 93, 94, 96, 99, 101, 102, 112, 113
Ba'th Party 64
Begin, Menachem 109
Beirut viii, 227, 255
Beit Safafa 173
Beit Sahur 29, 71
Bekaa 140
Bellow, Saul 109
Benvenisti, Meron 210
Bernstein, Leonard 109
Bethlehem 27, 31, 38, 71, 248
Bireh 35, 71
Bir Zeit 248
B'nai B'rith 100, 111
Bookbinder, Hyman 108
Breira 109
Brickner, Balfour 108
British Mandate 47, 200
Bush, George xi, xv, 88, 92-96, 98, 99, 101, 102, 110-12, 161

Camp David vii, 11, 12, 21, 88, 89, 133
Carter, Jimmy 88, 161, 199
Chicago Tribune 104
Christian Science Monitor 103
Cohen, Steven M. 111
Commentary 108
Committee of Palestinian Women 67
Cyprus 189, 247

Darwish, Mahmoud 227
Declaration of Independence (Palestinian) 4, 37, 7, 13, 19, 119, 122, 132, 133, 170, 178, 186, 229, 230, 255
Democratic Front for the Liberation of Palestine 7, 8, 55, 231, 236, 237, 246, 250
Dole, Robert 99, 101
Dukakis, Michael 95, 97

Eagleburger, Lawrence 96
Eastern Europe xiv, 101, 192
Egypt
    Camp David Agreement 11, 12, 88, 89, 133
    and Israel 15, 20, 170
    and Israeli-Palestinian dialogue 101
    and Palestinians 139, 143, 170, 210, 230
    and US 98, 99
    and US-PLO negotiations 7
European Community (EC) 123, 148, 188

Fatah 4, 6-8, 38, 65, 74, 140, 185, 232, 235-38, 246
Federation of Palestinian Women's Committees 60
Fez 172
Foley, Thomas 101
Freij, Elias 13, 14
Funkenstein, Amos 158

Gaza Islamic University 248
Gaza Strip (see also *intifada,* Palestinian people, and West Bank)
    economic conditions 49, 147-49, 207-209, 220, 221
    and *intifada* 24, 69
    Islamic movement 8, 10, 11, 74
    political organization in 8, 16, 31, 37, 47, 57, 59

political repression in 17, 57, 58, 70
social conditions 45, 46, 52
General Federation of Trade Unions 48, 52-56
General Union of Palestine Workers 246
General Union of Palestinian Women 64-66, 243
Geyelin, Philip 103
Geyer, Georgie Anne 103
Gharaybih, Yusuf 142
Gilboa, Eytan 104, 105
Gillon, Philip 30
Golan Heights 167, 180, 184, 189, 202, 252
Gorbachev, Mikhail vii, xiv, 3

Haaretz 159,
Haass, Richard N. 96
Habbash, George 5
Habib, Philip 91
Hadashot 155
Haifa 135, 159, 160
Haig, Alexander 91
Hamas (Islamic Resistance Movement) xiii, 9-11, 15, 74, 88, 236, 237,
Hamilton, Lee 101
al-Haq/Law in the Service of Man 29, 247
Harkabi, Yehoshafat 159, 253
Harsch, Joseph C. 103
al-Hasan, Hani 230
Hebrew University of Jerusalem 133
Hebron 27, 29, 33, 38, 139, 160, 248
Helms, Jesse 94, 100
Hertzberg, Arthur 108
Higgins, William 101, 106
High Court 29
Higher Arab Committee (1930s) 26
Hizballah xiv, 94
Hussein, King 3, 10, 90, 141-44, 143, 144, 146, 165, 184, 249

International Monetary Fund (IMF) 146
Intifada (see also Gaza Strip, Israel, Palestine Liberation Organization, Unified National Command of the Uprising, West Bank)
boycotts 25, 35-39, 72
demonstrations 50, 69, 72, 73
and Islamic movement 8-10, 15
and Israel ix-xii, 5, 6, 12, 15, 16, 23, 25, 28-30, 53, 59, 121, 123, 127
leaflets 8, 14, 19-21, 34, 35, 38, 50, 51, 55, 69, 70
merchants 24-40

and Palestinian national consciousness 3, 20, 60, 74, 77, 79
and PLO vii, 4, 5, 8, 9, 12-17, 31, 142
popular committees 31, 55-57, 60, 70, 71, 81
and Soviet Union 124-26
strikes 25, 28, 29, 31-35, 39, 51, 53, 54
and US vii, 11, 13, 22, 87, 88, 102-12
women 60, 63-75, 81
Iran xiii, xiv, 88, 89, 91, 92, 99, 101, 254
Iran-Iraq war xii, xiv, 92
Iraq xii-xiv, 183, 184, 185, 189, 239, 254
Islamic Jihad 11, 31
Islamic Resistance Movement, see Hamas
Israel
and Arab countries 11, 128, 134, 167, 168, 170, 172, 174, 183
deportations by 158
elections proposal xi, 11, 12, 14, 93, 101, 129, 130, 161
and *intifada* ix-xi, 5, 6, 12, 15, 16, 23, 25, 28-30, 53, 59, 121, 123, 127
and PLO 4, 6, 7, 12, 14, 22, 128, 140, 155
policies in the occupied territories 26, 28, 29, 45, 47, 65, 66, 121, 208, 209, 210, 212
political trends in 130-32, 136, 158, 159, 165
relations with proposed Palestinian state 19-21, 119, 120, 135, 202, 252, 253
repression in occupied territories xii, xiv, 15, 17, 57, 58, 70, 79, 80
security concerns 131, 132, 165, 167, 170, 171, 179, 183, 184, 191, 192
settlements in West Bank 33, 53, 100, 121, 175, 206, 220, 239
and Soviet Union xiv, 124-26, 136, 157, 180, 186
and United States xv, 91, 93-95, 98, 101, 112, 113
and US Jewish community 87, 108-11, 135
and Western Europe 123

Jackson, Jesse 95-97
Jaffa 135, 159, 160
Jenin 38
Jericho 27
Jerusalem xvi, 31, 32, 35, 71, 93, 96, 102, 120, 169, 171, 178, 180, 182, 202, 203, 228, 248
Jerusalem Arabic Press 29
Jerusalem Post 32, 108

Jewish Agency 220
Jewish Defense League 108
Jewish Peace Lobby 111
Jibril, Ahmad 8
Jordan
    economy xii, 144-46, 246
    and *intifada* 142, 143, 147-49
    Palestinian population in 139, 140, 203,
        239, 242, 243, 249, 250
    and peace settlement role 10, 89, 90, 184,
        187-90, 200
    political parties xiii, 64
    and proposed Palestinian state 6, 19-21,
        119, 180, 183, 184, 212, 213, 228-30,
        251, 254
    relations with West Bank 27, 36, 47, 52,
        55, 140, 143, 147-49, 165, 210, 239,
        249-52
Jordan River 119, 129, 132, 168, 169, 175,
    184, 187, 188, 189, 190

Kach x
Kahane, Meir x
Kahn, Alfred E. 199
Karak 139
Kelly, John 97
Khaddouri Agricultural College 209
Khalaf, Salah (Abu Iyad) 4, 12, 93, 100,
    102, 160, 230
Khan Yunis 29
Khayat, S. 210
Khomeini, Ayatollah Ruhollah 88
al-Khuli, Lutfi 230
King-Crane Commission 4
Kirkpatrick, Jeane 103, 156
Kissinger, Henry 89, 96, 156, 161
Kuwait xii, 92, 99, 220, 239, 247, 254

Latrun 173
Leahy, Patrick 98
Lebanon viii, ix, xii, xiv, 5, 11, 12, 54, 89,
    91, 95, 98, 100, 101, 106, 109, 140,
    141, 179, 180, 184, 203, 228, 232,
    233, 238-40, 243, 244, 247, 252, 254
Lebowitz, Yeshayahu 159
Lerner, Michael 108, 110
Lewis, Anthony 103
Levine, Mel 99, 110
Libya xiii, xiv, 89, 91
Likud xviii, 129
Litfa 173
Los Angeles Times 104

al-Madhoun, Ribi' 36
Mahanbeh, Dr. Nayef 29

McGrory, Mary 103
Mitchell, George 99
Morocco xiv
Moughrabi, Fouad 103, 104
Musa, Umar 230
Muslim Brotherhood 10, 11

Nablus 27, 30, 31, 35, 37, 38, 139
al-Najah University 209, 248
National Salvation Front 141
Nazareth 139
Neturei Karta 155
New York Times 103, 105
Nicaragua 92
Nielson, Howard 98
Ni'meh 73

Obeid, Abdallah 106
Obey, David 98
Occupied Territories (see Gaza Strip, *intifada*,
    Palestinian people, West Bank)
Odeh, Nasim 29
Oman 99

Palestine Exploration Fund 200
Palestine Liberation Organization (PLO)
    divergent trends in 5-9, 14, 15, 21
    and Egypt 143, 230
    and *intifada* vii-ix, 4, 5, 8, 9, 12-17, 31,
        142
    and Islamic movement 9-11, 237
    and Jordan 19, 20, 139-41, 143, 144,
        228-30
    leadership of 13, 16-18
    military activities of 4, 5, 13, 242-44
    and peace settlement xviii, 11, 12, 14,
        22, 28, 128-30
    policy toward Israel 4, 89, 90, 128, 130,
        132, 155
    and Soviet Union 3, 4, 119, 124, 125,
        157
    and Syria 11
    talks with US xi, xviii, 7, 11-13, 18, 21,
        22, 90, 93, 97, 99, 100, 161, 227
PLO Central Council 232, 255,
PLO Executive Committee 7, 8, 230, 231
PLO Political Committee 230,
Palestine National Council 4-6, 8, 9, 12,
    13, 18, 19, 22, 48, 55, 119, 122-24,
    132, 133, 140, 155, 160, 172, 201,
    227, 229, 230, 235, 236, 255
Palestine National Front 47, 57, 66
Palestinian Communist Party 55, 231, 236,
    237, 246

Palestinian labor movement
  history and characteristics 47-49, 52, 53
  and *intifada* 50, 51, 55, 56
  and Palestinian nationalism 49, 50
Palestinian National Guidance Committee 57
Palestinian people (see also Gaza Strip,
    intifada, West Bank)
  bourgeoisie 30, 31, 237, 242
  culture 77, 78, 80-82, 162
  education 162, 163, 209, 215, 216, 248,
    249, 255
  in the Gulf 241, 242
  Islamic movement 8-10, 15
  in Jordan 139, 140, 203, 239, 241, 242,
    243, 249, 250
  and PLO 6, 10, 17, 18, 156, 235
  refugees 129, 132, 133, 138, 173-75, 202,
    203, 214, 215, 237, 238
  society 156, 163, 242
Palestinian state, prospective
  borders 171-73, 202
  economic base 163, 199-226
  PLO role in 231, 232, 236, 237
  political structure 163, 229-31, 234, 246
  population 173-75, 202, 203, 204, 214,
    215, 228, 238, 239
  relations with Israel 19-21, 135, 202, 252,
    253
  relations with Jordan 19, 20, 22, 119, 229,
    230
  resources 204-207
  security guarantees 165-98
Palestinian women's movement
  history 47-51
  and *intifada* 60, 69-73, 81
  and Palestinian nationalism 63, 68, 74,
    75
  and PLO 65, 66
  and resistance to Israeli occupation 64-68
  women writers 67
Peace-keeping forces, international
  administration and supervision of forces
    192, 193
  likely role in guaranteeing peace settlement
    187-192
Peace Now x, 108
Pelletreau, Robert 90, 93, 97
Peres, Shimon x, 144
Persian Gulf 26, 89, 92, 99, 149, 233,
    237-40, 242, 247, 248
Pickering, Thomas 94, 97
Podhoretz, Norman 108, 110
Pollard, Jonathan 109

Popular Front for the Liberation of Palestine
    ix, 5-8, 21, 55, 142, 231, 236, 237,
    246, 250
Popular Front for the Liberation of Palestine—
    General Command 8

Qaddoumi, Farouq 230
Qadhafi, Mu'ammar 91, 92
Qalqilya 34, 35, 173
Qutob, Khaled 149

Rabat Conference 46
Rabin, Yitzhak 30, 161
Ramallah 26, 27, 30, 31, 32, 35, 37, 38,
    51, 71, 160
Reagan, Ronald viii, 88-92, 94, 96, 99, 100,
    156
Rifai, Zaid 145
Ross, Dennis 93, 96

Sabra-Chatila massacre 109
Safire, William 103
Said, Edward 112
Salt 139
Saudi Arabia xii, xiii, 10, 11, 99, 145, 146,
    149, 239, 252, 254
Sawt al-Bilad 159
Schindler, Alexander 108
Scowcroft, Brent 96
Segal, Jerome 111
Shafiq, Yusif Abdallah 29
Shamir, Yitzhak x, xi, 12, 93, 94, 98-102,
    108, 109, 110, 111, 113, 129, 133,
    155, 161
Shammas, Anton 159, 253
Sharon, Ariel xi, 31, 91, 123
Sha'th, Nabil viii, ix, 230
Shevardnadze, Edward, 125
Shin Bet 28
Shomron, Dan 30
Shultz, George 90, 110, 112, 156
Sinai 184, 189
Soviet Jews xiv, xv, 101, 102
Soviet Union
  and Arab countries 157
  and Islamic resurgence xii, xiii
  and Israel xiv, 125
  and proposed Palestinian state 124, 178,
    186
  role in peace settlement 3, 4, 126, 166,
    167, 172, 190, 194-96
  and US 125, 136
Squadron, Howard 110
Suleiman, Michael 107

Sununu, John 96
Surani, Jamal 230, 231
Syria ix, xiii, xiv, 7-9, 11, 91, 140, 141,
    167, 172, 174, 179, 180, 183, 185,
    186, 203, 228, 238, 239, 243, 252

Tehiya Party x
Tel Aviv 93, 94, 122, 173
Tikkun 108, 110
Tivnan, Edward 109
Tulkarm 27, 38, 173
Tunis 231, 242
Tunisia xiii

Unified National Command of the Uprising
    (UNCU) 5, 8, 14-17, 19, 21, 22, 25,
    28, 31-35, 37-39, 50, 51, 55, 57, 59,
    69, 73, 234, 236, 245
UNIFIL 192
United Arab Emirates xii
United Jewish Appeal 108,
United Nations 4-8, 21, 22, 46, 89, 90, 93,
    94, 97, 103, 122, 123, 128, 133, 156,
    170, 172-74, 178, 180, 182, 186, 191-94
United Nations Disaster Relief Organization
    178, 179, 182
United Nations Relief and Works Agency
    (UNRWA) 175, 238, 241, 243
United States
    and Arab countries xiv, 91, 92, 98, 99
    Congress 90, 95, 97-100, 112, 113, 161,
        169
    Democratic Party 95-100
    and Islamic resurgence xii, xiii
    and Israel xv, 91, 93-95, 98, 101, 112,
        113
    and Israel lobby 87, 90, 93, 96, 99, 100,
        102, 107, 108
    Jewish community 87, 90, 95, 98, 100,
        102, 107-11, 112, 113, 135, 161

National Security Council 92, 96
news media 102-107
    and occupied territories 100
    and peace process 19, 88, 89, 94, 101,
        102
    and peace settlement guarantees 166, 167,
        172, 190, 194-96
    and PLO xi, xviii, 7, 11-13, 18, 21, 22,
        90, 93, 97, 99, 100, 161, 227
    public opinion 87, 99, 102-107, 112
    Republican Party 91, 100
    State Department 88, 93, 96, 100, 107,
        110, 112, 113

Waldegrave, William 138
Wall Street Journal 102
Warren, Charles 200
Washington Institute for Near East Policy 96
Washington Post 100, 103, 105, 106
al-Wazir, Khalil (Abu Jihad) ix
Weizmann, Chaim 200, 204
West Bank (see also *intifada*)
    chambers of commerce 27, 40
    economic conditions 26-28, 47, 49, 51-53,
        72, 147-49, 207- 209, 212, 221
    Islamic movement 8-11, 74
    political organization in 8, 16, 31, 37,
        47, 54, 55, 57, 59, 65, 66, 71, 236
    political repression in 15, 17, 29, 30, 57,
        58, 70, 79, 80
    social conditions 45, 46, 50, 56
Western Europe 123, 192, 231
Wieseltier, Leon 110
Will, George 103
World Bank 221
World Zionist Organization 219

Yedioth Ahronoth 161
Yemen, North xiii
Yemen, South xiii